The Bourne(s) Families of Ireland

THE BOURNE(S) FAMILIES OF IRELAND

THE
BOURNE(S) FAMILIES
of
IRELAND
by
Mary A. Strange

The genealogical material contained in this
book was collected by the author and

ELIZABETH BACON FITZGERALD

Arms:- Per chevron azure and argent in chief two mullets pierced or, and in base a bugle horn sable, garnished of the third and stringed gules.

Crest:- On a wreath of the colours, a garb between two doves respecting each other all proper.

Granted 15 October 1901 by Sir Arthur E. Vicars, Ulster King of Arms, to George Smith Bournes of the Rossport family. Illustration prepared by the Genealogical Office, Dublin Castle, Dublin.

VINCIT · QUI · PATITUR

❖ Bournes ❖

Foreword

Many family histories or genealogies are finally written because a family legend, passed down through the years from one generation to another, eventually caught and held someone's interest. Our family legend, especially as it pertained to Hannah Maria Bournes (née Maxwell), so captured the interest of Elizabeth B. Fitzgerald and the author that we were inspired to begin a further search for the records of our great grandmother and her family. Fortunately, many of these records were found and, equally important, we began to see that our legend was largely based on fact.

The information collected by Elizabeth B. Fitzgerald on the background of our Irish kin was, of course, molded and shaped by different generations as they re-told the story. Certain sections were embellished, others were unfortunately forgotten, but the largest portion of the legend was amazingly accurate. No actual records were known to have been kept by our family during their years in Ireland, or, if they were, none has survived. A Bible belonging to Hannah Maria's youngest daughter was our only written evidence and it is concerned primarily with the vital statistics of our parents and grandparents generations.

The legend told by Ellen Bournes, second oldest daughter of Hannah Maria, was the most important source of information that we had. Its value became more apparent as we searched the repositories in Ireland and in this country. Since this legend formed the basis of our search, we felt it might be of interest to paraphrase the story for others to see

The earliest members of the Bournes family to come to Ireland were four brothers who were said to have received grants of land for faithful service during the Cromwellian period The names of these brothers are not known but their lands, or estates, were inherited by descendants One estate was at Castleconnor, Co. Sligo and the owner's name was thought to be either James or Robert Bournes Another estate was that of Matthew Bournes of Ballinakill,[1] he was a physician and had at least two daughters, Eleanor and Jane

Our grandmother was Cecelia Bournes who married Malachi Maxwell, an Episcopal clergyman The Bournes came from the area of Ireland that is on the northwestern coast [2] Here they had a leasehold of salmon fisheries until 1848 when the lease expired. The daughter of Reverend Maxwell and his wife, Cecelia Bournes, was Hannah Maria Maxwell, born in Ballina 1809 The Reverend died soon after her birth and the widow and only child went to live with his brother, a bachelor and a clergyman also

Hannah Maria Maxwell married her cousin, William Bournes, about 1830 or 1833 They met while he was a student at Trinity College in Dublin and following their marriage returned to the leasehold to live William Bournes was the son of John and Ellen Bournes and one of nine children The other children's names were John, Thomas, Matthew, Margaret, Jane, Alicia, Eliza and Mary Anne One of William Bournes' brothers, John Bournes, owned an estate at Castlebar and was a solicitor. This same brother had a son who practiced law in Dublin Another brother was a doctor and the three brothers were joint heirs to the Rosserieke estate [3] Mary Anne married Captain Green who became head of the Rosserieke

---

[1] There are several "Ballinakills" in Ireland and as no county was given by Ellen Bournes, we have been unable to verify this It is interesting that there is a Ballinakill in Queen's Co See the Bourne family of Terenure

[2] We assume that Ellen is referring to her grandmother's family

[3] Rosserieke is the ancient spelling for Rosserk, a townland near Ballina, Co Mayo

estate but later sold his interest to Colonel Arthur Gore. The names of Green, Rutledge, Foster and Lloyd are all family names [4]

As our search progressed we discovered that Ireland had been well populated with Bournes families in all four provinces Although the Bournes of Connaught were of greatest interest to us, we decided to include in this book, the other families whose records we were gradually collecting in our search While it is possible to show that there may be some relationship between the various Bournes families of Connaught and elsewhere, it is disappointing not to be able to prove the connection Numerous records, many from previously unpublished sources, will be found in the Appendix. Some of these records we have been unable to fit into the matrix of our account of the several families, but it is our hope that they may assist others.

We had also hoped to find the origin of the Connaught Bournes family Certain evidence which is given in the chapter devoted to the history of Ireland and the history of the barony of Erris, leads one to believe that they came from England Other evidence indicates they may have originated in Scotland (see the Rossport Bournes family). Still further evidence indicates that there were Bournes among the Huguenots who sought refuge in Ireland from religious persecution In this connection, it is interesting to note that there was a Huguenot settlement at Killala, Co Mayo in the late eighteenth century

It should be mentioned that there are various spellings of this name in the official and unofficial records. The original name was Bourne, but clerical errors and the phonetic spelling of the seventeenth through the nineteenth centuries created many variants To name a few, we found Born, Bourn, Bourns, Bournes, Boarnes, Bowens, Burns and occasionally Byrne We have attempted to use caution with these variants

[4] Green, Rutledge and Lloyd were proven subsequently to be "family names", Foster was not The name Fawcett (Faussett), however, was found among the many Bournes family records Is it not likely that Foster and Fawcett were confused in the re-telling of the family legend?

and did not assume we had a "Bourne" unless we found
sufficient evidence or proof Individual families adopted the
spelling that they preferred, e g the Rossport family adhered
to Bournes, Dublin and Cork families retained the original
spelling of Bourne, while other groups wavered between
Bourn, Bourns and Bournes

Today many descendants of the Bourne families in Ireland
and the United States have chosen Burns as their preferred
spelling In order to make the genealogy and history of the
family simpler for the reader, the name in this text will be
spelled as Bournes,[5] unless actual records are cited or quoted
In doing this we apologize to those who have adopted one of
the other spellings

In the interest of clarity, we have also endeavored to
achieve a comfortable balance between the phraseology used in
Irish and American genealogies The chapters, included in
Parts One and Three, are devoted to the Bourne(s) families of
western Ireland, as well as those who resided elsewhere in this
country The families are classified according to the geo-
graphical areas, or lands, on which they lived and the individual pedigrees begin with the first known generation,
designated by a Roman Numeral I A chart pedigree, found in
the Appendix, shows the established relationships between the
Connaught Bournes families, as well as the relationships based
solely on conjecture

Vital statistics are given, as found, even though in some
cases the results may be rather startling One example is that
of our own great grandmother, Hannah Maria Bournes, née
Maxwell, who left the British Isles at 44 years of age According to the ship's manifest, she was 40 years old but by the time
she was located in an American census enumeration seven
years later, she was recorded as being only 35! She had, therefore, become progressively "younger" after sailing

Our concern with the story of Hannah Maria and her seven

[5] With the exception of the Cork and Dublin Bourne families

daughters (see Part Two) has given the distaff side of this particular family a greater prominence than is usually found in genealogies. For this, we offer no apology After all, Hannah Maria was the one who stimulated our interest in Irish genealogical research!

In conclusion, we wish to say that although we regret that we have been unable to trace each family group to the present day, we have indeed tried Many descendants have been approached, and the material that was received is presented as sent to us. Others unfortunately, did not reply to letters seeking information. Therefore, incomplete as this family history is, we hope it will be enjoyed by the many descendants of the Bourne(s) of Ireland, as well as other readers

Elizabeth B Fitzgerald
Mary A Strange

Table of Contents

TABLE OF CONTENTS (Cont)

Acknowledgements

First, a word about Elizabeth Bacon Fitzgerald, whose name appears on the subtitle page. Mrs. Fitzgerald is a first cousin of the author Some years ago, the two of us began a systematic and comprehensive search for records pertaining to our mutual Irish ancestors Fortunately, Mrs Fitzgerald had collected family memoranda over a period of twenty years, so we had a foundation, more solid than we originally suspected, on which to build. As anyone who has seriously engaged in genealogical research might have anticipated, the project gradually expanded far beyond our direct ancestors and into parts of the country that were only remotely associated with our original base This kind of proliferation inevitably multiplies the opportunity for errors and, to the extent that these may be present, the burden is entirely on the shoulders of the author

The material from family sources and public repositories, that appears within the pages of this book has been provided by literally scores of persons. My cousin and I extend our sincere thanks and appreciation to all of them.

Basil O'Connell, K M. of Newtown, Pennsylvania, an eminent genealogist and authority on Irish records, assisted us from our first efforts to the conclusion of this work His counsel and infectious spirit cleared many hurdles Although his contributions to this endeavor are numerous, one is of such importance that it should be cited. He acquainted us with the invaluable source material to be found in old newspapers and personally spent many hours on our behalf at the British Museum Newspaper Library, Colindale, London, England

John Patrick Bournes of Stonefield, Co Mayo wholeheartedly joined us in our research, and we are especially grateful for his assistance He did much of the fieldwork in Erris and surrounding areas, enabled us to become well acquainted with this barony and offered valuable suggestions regarding little known sources Through him we were able to find the key to many family relationships and much of the text of the Connaught Bournes is the result of his advice and guidance

We deeply appreciated the privilege of studying the old deeds at the Land Commission, Dublin Mr Thomas J O'Sullivan, Keeper of the Records, personally showed the author many of the original documents His interest in the project and his permission to use the material found in this book are gratefully acknowledged

We are greatly indebted to Dr. J H Delargy, Honorary Director of the Irish Folklore Commission, Dublin. for his kindness in allowing us to study the Erris manuscript, written by the late Michael Corduff This manuscript, consisting of seven volumes, is concerned with seanchas (folktales) of Erris, a barony in Co. Mayo Several folktales involve, or refer to, the various Bournes families of that area and have been used to provide human interest and local color in the text of the Connaught Bournes The authority to publish some of this material is sincerely appreciated

As much of the actual research in the repositories of Ireland, England and in the United States was done by others on our behalf. we wish to acknowledge with gratitude the unusually perceptive work of Dr Patrick Smythe-Wood, Ballycastle, Northern Ireland, who, in addition to research, contributed material from his personal records Credit should also be given to Eric McAuliffe, Dublin, Michael Leader, London; Mrs Gertrude Soderberg, Washington, D C.; Mrs Jennie Weeks, Salt Lake City, Utah and Mrs Alice M Runyon, North Tairytown, New York for their assistance

We wish to acknowledge the help provided by the following individuals, societies and repositories, as well as their permission to publish material· Dr. Richard Hayes, former Director of the National Library, Dublin, Mr P Henchy, present Director of the National Library, Mr Gerard Slevin, Chief Herald, Genealogical Office (Office of Arms), Dublin Castle, Dublin, Miss Margaret Griffiths, Assistant Deputy Keeper of the Records, Public Record Office, Dublin, Mr Kermit Darwin, Deputy Keeper of the Records, Public Record Office, Belfast, Northern Ireland, Mr P O'Keon, Assistant Registrar, Registry of Deeds, Dublin; Mr Breandán Mac Giolla Choille, Keeper of the State Papers, State Paper Office, Dublin Castle, Dublin, Royal Society of Antiquaries of Ireland, Dublin; Representative Body of the Church of Ireland, St Stephen's Green, Dublin and the Irish Genealogical Research Society, London

Material concerned with the Higgins family of Co Mayo was obtained from letters deposited at the National Library of Australia, Canberra, Australia and indexed as The Higgins Papers (MS 1057). These were brought to our attention by Miss Aileen Palmer of Victoria, Australia and her sister, Miss Helen Palmer of Sydney, Australia, both descendants of Anne Bournes Higgins We appreciate their generous and courteous assistance and their permission to publish segments of this material, as well as extracts from their mother's book, "Henry Bournes Higgins, A Memoir"

Mr. Harold L. White, National Librarian, National Library of Australia, was equally helpful and his kindness in allowing us to publish the family photographs from the Palmer Collection is duly acknowledged

Many persons contributed their family records while others

XIX

shared their knowledge and, more importantly, gave of themselves To the following persons in Ireland and elsewhere, we extend our appreciation John Patrick Bournes and Thomas Bournes of Stonefield, Co Mayo, Reverend J Ashton and Mr Nial McCormick of Killala, Co Mayo, Mr and Mrs Tod Ryan of Newtownwhite, Co Mayo, Archdeacon W J. Ewart, Easkey, Co Sligo, Father Terence Cunningham, St Patrick's College, Maynooth, Co Kildare; Dr J C Simms, Trinity College, Dublin, Mr Leo Corduff, Dublin; Miss Rosemary ffolliott, Dublin, Misses Aileen and Helen Palmer, Victoria and Sydney, Australia, Mrs Archibald McLean, Tacoma, Washington, Mrs A B Munn, Montclair, New Jersey, Mrs Ned Lentz, Nashville, Tennessee; Mrs John Collins, Los Angeles, California, Mr Maurice Moore, lately deceased, Santa Barbara, California, Mr Howard K Larimer, Neenah, Wisconsin, Dr Gareth W Dunleavy, Milwaukee, Wisconsin; Mr Paul G Sotirin, Librarian, Local History, Milwaukee Public Library, Milwaukee, Wisconsin and Miss Laetitia Kennedy-Skipton, Shakespearean Folger Library, Washington, D C

Finally, the author wishes to acknowledge the many contributions, not the least being the continual encouragement, given by her husband, John G Strange.

Glossary

TERMS

Appurtenance .	That which belongs to something else
Assignment	Transfer of title or interest by writing
Bar	The nullifying of a claim or action, the process of bringing this about
Caution	Word introduced by Anglo-Norman settlers in Ireland, signifies a quarter from quarteron, a French word Medieval land measurement, varying in amounts from 60 to 100 acres
Conveyance .	Instrument which transfers title to property or the right to hold it from one or more persons to one or other people by deed, mortgage, trust, lease, assignment, marriage settlement etc
Covenant	An undertaking or promise of legal validity, an agreement
Defeasance	The annulment of a contract or deed
Defalcation	Reduction, abatement
Demesne	Possession of real estate as one's own Formerly the land belonging to a Lord and not rented or let but kept in his hands
Demise	Act of the grantor was called a demise
Distram	To coerce or punish by levying a distress
Encumbered	A claim or lien attached to property, as a mortgage
Equity	Resort to general principles of fairness and justice whenever existing law is inadequate, an equitable right or claim
Grantee	A person to whom a grant is made
Grantor	A person who makes a grant
Hereditament .	Any property that is inheritable
Indenture	Written contract or agreement

Inpersonam	Against the person In law designating an action, or judgement against a person as distinguished from one against property
Jointure	In law an arrangement by which a husband settles property on his wife for her use after death, or the property thus settled, widow's portion
Lease ..	Tenure by lease If transferred to another, a fee was paid to the landlord
Lease, Release	Avoided the statue of enrolments which then required conveyances to be recorded by taking advantage of the rule that a tenant in possession could take a release (renewal) without notorization being required Thus a tenant who held a leasehold by his ancestors for a lengthy period claimed the right to it by "lease and release" (This method is no longer in use, once was common)
Lessee	A person to whom a lease is given, a tenant
Lessor	A person who gives a lease, a landlord
Licentiate	University degree intermediate between that of bachelor and doctor
Lively of Seizen	Method by which the ceremonial conveyance of land was formerly made
Mears	Boundary
Mesne	Intermediate, middle of
Messuages	Dwelling house with outhouses and adjacent land
Moiety	Half, or a part
Oise	Otherwise
Pensioner	One who pays for his living in the university commons
Quaisi	As if, in a sense or manner, seemingly
Reversion	Right of the lessor, or grantor, to have possession of the land again at the end of the term, or sooner, in case of forfeiture was called a reversion
Seise	To take possession of
Sizar	Student who receives from the University an allowance towards his college expenses
Socius Comitatus	Fellow commoner who paid double fees, (i e of a Pensioner) and who enjoyed certain privileges, including that of finishing the college course in three years instead of four
Tail	Limited in a specific manner as to inheritance, as, fee tail
Tenement	Land, buildings, etc held of another by tenure
Tenure	A holding, as of property, the length of time something is held, the right to hold property
Term	Right of the grantee was called a term

ABBREVIATIONS

b . ..	born
bp	baptised
bur	buried
circa, ca	about
d .	died
d s p	(decessit sine prole) died without issue
G O	Genealogical Office
H E I C S	Honorable East India Company
I G R S	Irish Genealogical Research Society
J P .	Justice of the Peace
Lic	Licence, Licentiate
L M. .	Licentiate in Midwifery
L R C P I	Licentiate Royal College of Physicians in Ireland
L R C S I	Licentiate Royal College of Surgeons in Ireland
M R C P I.	Member Royal College of Physicians in Ireland
M R C S I	Member Royal College of Surgeons in Ireland
mar arts	marriage articles
mar setts	marriage settlement
m	married
M Ch .	Master in Chicanery
M D	Doctor of Medicine
M L A .	Member of the Legislative Assembly, i e a member of the State or Provincial Parliament
M L B	Marriage Licence Bond
M P .	Member of Parliament
M O . .	medical officer
n d . .	no date
N Z C S .	New Zealand Civil Service
O B E	Order of the British Empire
P R O	Public Record Office
Pro	proved
R A S C . .	Royal Army Service Corps
R I C...... .	Royal Irish Constabulary
R M C .	Royal Military College
R S A I	Royal Society of Antiquaries of Ireland
S C .	Socius Comitatus Fellow commoner
S F T C D	Senior Fellow Trinity College, Dublin
sic .	when placed in brackets following a word or expression means that such a word or expression is exactly as shown in the record
T C D	Trinity College, Dublin

Part One
The Bournes Families

I. Historical Background

As one follows the threads of families through several generations, he is increasingly conscious of the interplay between local, regional and national history It is said that the novelist Hilaire Belloc was fascinated by the twists and turns of country roads and highways Most of us, if we think at all about these bends, probably attribute them to the whims of some ancient or not so ancient surveyor In many cases, however, there is a story or human drama associated with the contours Sometimes this story is intensely personal. Other times, it is a kind of foot print of a much larger event in the course of social or economic affairs. And so it is with the "twists and turns" that are encountered in genealogy.

Thus, the history of the locale and times in which our predecessors have lived, can be important for at least two reasons. First, it adds color and understanding to the rather sterile dates and lineages that we may assemble, and second, it often provides the clue we may need for searching records or picking up the "scent" in another part of the country or even, perhaps, in another country across the sea

As we worked our way through the records of the various Bournes families of Ireland, it seemed that it might be of some assistance for the reader to know a little of the history of the times in which these people lived An understanding of the background of Ireland, as we have indicated, was im-

portant to us in our research and should be equally important
for those who read the Bournes story

While we will not attempt any scholarly presentation, nor
could we do so, we would like to give in capsule form some of
the highlights of Ireland's past. Following this capsule account, will be a more detailed presentation of the history of
the barony of Erris Erris is one of eight baronies in County
Mayo within the Province of Connaught and is very important
to the story of the Bournes families of western Ireland These
particular families are, of course, of great personal interest
to us and the reason why this book was written

It should be noted that Ireland's history is exceedingly
complicated, for throughout the centuries, religious, social and
political differences have prevailed The country was frequently torn by strife and discord and beset by wars. Irish
land exchanged hands may times from the period of the
Normans and during the reigns of the Tudors and early
Stuarts Not until the Cromwellian era was an enduring basis
for land ownership established and this continued up to the
end of the nineteenth century

The very early history of Christian Ireland, from the
Gaelic Celts, through the repeated invasions of marauding
bands of Norwegians and Danish invaders, to the era of Brian
Boru, King of Ireland in the year 1000 A.D , is fascinating and
highly recommended reading For our immediate purposes,
however, Ireland's history begins in the twelfth century, when
the English Normans, seeking new land for themselves and
more men for their armies, invaded Ireland This period saw
the beginning of the feudal system in Ireland with its manors,
abbeys, castles and fortresses

As time passed, the descendants of the Anglo-Norman
settlers gradually melded their original concepts and loyalties
with those of their adopted land Subsequent rulers of England
were fearful that this "Irish" orientation might threaten the
supremacy of the mother country, and various restrictive
steps were taken to preserve the English character of the Pale,

a limited area around Dublin Elsewhere, the settlers became
more and more identified with the original Irish.

The Reformation (early sixteenth century) added the bitter-
ness of religious differences between the Irish people and their
overlords, and reprisals were made against any insurgent
Irish or Anglo-Irish who did not follow the dictates of the
Crown The most common type of reprisal seemed to be the
sweeping confiscations of Irish land by the Crown and the
subsequent planting of English colonies

Rebellion against the English quickly spread throughout
Ireland and for years the Irish people, led by their Gaelic
chieftains, fought against the domination of their powerful
neighbor By the conclusion of Queen Elizabeth's reign in
1603 Hugh O'Neill and Hugh O'Donnell, the most powerful
of the Ulster[1] chieftains, were defeated and independent
Gaelic Ireland came to an end.

The Irish were now subdued and the way was cleared for
James I, who ascended the throne in 1603, to send English and
Scottish settlers into Ulster, thus marking the beginning of the
Great Plantation in this area. The colonization of Ulster and
of other parts of Ireland continued into the reign of Charles I
(1625-1649), and it is not surprising that the Irish, chafing
under this prolonged domination, eventually rallied against
the erosion of their land holdings

A general uprising, enhanced by religious and political
grievances, commenced throughout Ireland in 1641 and in
February of 1642 the English Parliament retaliated by passing the Adventurers Act This legislation had the double-edged
purpose of punishing the rebellious Irish and, at the same
time, underwriting the financing of English armies to suppress
the uprising. Land held by those who opposed the English
government was declared "forfeited " Part of this property

[1] The Province of Ulster was then comprised of nine counties, i e Antrim, Armagh,
Cavan, Donegal, Down, Fermanagh, Londonderry, Monaghan and Tyrone In 1920,
the Government of Ireland Act established separate parliaments and governments for
Northern and Southern Ireland Six of the Ulster counties became "Northern Ireland"
and are still united with England Cavan, Donegal and Monaghan were attached to
Southern Ireland and are now a part of the Republic of Ireland

was offered to the English soldiers as a reward for their campaigning and the rest was to be sold to subscribers (or Adventurers) as a means of enhancing the national treasury

Shortly after the passage of the Adventurers Act, the long-standing estrangement between Charles I and Parliament finally led to the outbreak of the English Civil War in August 1642 The turmoil caused by this conflagration added further confusion to the Irish picture Many Catholics within Ireland declared themselves on the side of Charles I, and the confrontations between those who were pro-Charles and the other Irish (and their allies) who were pro-Parliament are known in Irish history as "The Confederate War " The Adventurers Act was more or less disregarded during this period of instability.

After Charles I was deposed in 1649, the English Commonwealth government was established and Oliver Cromwell was declared Lord Lieutenant and General by the Parliament of England Secure in their own domain, Cromwell and Parliament again focused their attention on Ireland An army, led by Cromwell, invaded Ireland and inflicted the massacres which deepened the wounds between the English and Irish The Adventurers Act of 1642 was recalled and used as a basis for further legislation, which culminated in the Act of Satisfaction in 1653 The latter was passed for the satisfaction of the Adventurers and soldiers and repeated the provisions of the earlier act in that land was given to Cromwell's invading soldiers in lieu of payment for their services and to the Adventurers in proportion to what they had subscribed

The Province of Connaught played an unhappy role in this phase of Ireland's history Following Cromwell's victory, the English Parliament began to clear the Irish from their lands in the three provinces of Munster, Ulster and Leinster.[2] Connaught, as well as the County of Clare,[3] was set aside for

[2] These Irish included the native Irish as well as the Anglo-Irish, descendants of the former Norman settlers

[3] Clare is within the Province of Munster which adjoins the Province of Connaught.

the transplanters and the "Cromwellian scheme provided for the allotment to Irish Catholics of land in proportion to their original estates and to the degree of guilt imputed to them for their share in the Confederate War."[4] The historical events of this period are noteworthy, especially as a prelude to the history of Erris

Although the Province of Connaught was, and still is, composed of five counties[5] not all of them were to be finally assigned to the displaced Irish as the "claims of Cromwell's army were so heavy that the Irish area was cut down."[6] County Sligo was set aside for the soldiers, as was the barony of Tirawley in County Mayo. Galway, Roscommon and certain baronies of Mayo and Clare were reserved, however, for the Irish but Leitrim was eventually taken by the soldiers

Transplanters from Down and Antrim, both counties in the Province of Ulster, were to be settled in the baronies of Clanmorris, Carra and Kilmaine in County Mayo Irish from the other Ulster counties were to be sent to the baronies of Murrisk, Burrishoole, Erris and Costello, all in County Mayo. Although Mayo was not originally intended for the transplanting of Irish from the Provinces of Leinster and Munster, a number from these areas were eventually sent to this county.[7]

The English who were residing in Connaught and Clare at this time could receive, if they wished, land in one of the other provinces equivalent to their former holdings However, the native Irish and Anglo-Irish residing in this western province had no such opportunity and they suffered by this "invasion" of transplantors as much as the transplanted Irish did themselves Connaught's land was not sufficiently fertile or productive to accommodate such a population explosion. Much of Connaught is bog and mountain land and it is fre-

[4] J G Simms, "Mayo Landowners in the Seventeenth Century," *The Journal of The Royal Society of Antiquaries of Ireland*, Vol 95 (1965), p 241

[5] Connaught includes the five counties of Mayo, Sligo, Galway, Roscommon and Leitrim

[6] Simms, op cit , p 241

[7] *Ibid*, p 242

quently said that the expression "to Hell or Connaught" was coined during this period of settlement.[8]

Oliver Cromwell died on the 3rd of September 1658 and the Protectorate which had been established in the latter years of his reign soon fell apart After several months of striving between the army and Parliament, a compromise was finally reached whereby the monarchy was restored, and Charles II (1660-1685) was recalled to the throne

This was a time for some measure of rejoicing in Ireland as the Catholics had generally supported the Stuart dynasty, and they anticipated religious toleration and the recovery of their former estates In his effort to resolve the land question, Charles was confronted with a most difficult problem His sympathies lay with the Catholics and he encouraged them to believe that they would recover their property On the other hand, he had promised the Commonwealth Army that he would retain the Cromwellian land settlements The Act of Settlement (1662) tried to resolve these conflicting obligations by a compensating mechanism which was thoroughly unworkable and in 1665 an interpretive piece of legislature, called the Act of Explanation was passed When the dust finally settled, most of Ireland remained in the hands of English and Protestant landholders The Catholics retained a little more than twenty percent of the country, in comparison with the approximately sixty percent they had owned in 1641 [9]

The death of Charles II and the ascent of James II (1685-1688) to the throne of England brought no lasting solution to the problems of either England or Ireland James II was not successful in attempting to resolve the grievances of Religion and Land in Ireland and the three Kingdoms of Ireland, Scotland and England divided in the continuing turmoil James found it necessary to flee to Ireland for sanctuary, and, while

[8] Others claim that the expression is connected with the rise of the Orange Society 1795

[9] J G Simms, "The Restoration and the Jacobite War (1660-1691)," *The Course of Irish History*, ed T. W Moody and F X Martin (1967)

the Catholic Irish rallied to his support, thousands of Irish Protestants fled to England.

In February of 1689, the Parliament of England conveyed the Crown to William III and Mary The new Protestant rulers were determined to rid Ireland of the Catholic·Stuart, King James II, and return this country once more to England's domination. The Williamite War began, resulting in the crushing defeat of James II at the Battle of the Boyne in July of 1690 The usual confiscations of land continued during this period, as the Protestants first surrendered their land to James II and later recovered this same property following William III's victory

William ruled until 1702,[10] when Queen Anne (1702-1714) came to the throne During these two reigns, the English Settlement, as conceived by the Cromwellians, finally came into being. "A considerable part of the county was colonized by new English settlers, who were brought over as tenants by the new landowners and given land on which they built their houses and laid out their farms. The title of most of the owners of land in Ireland is ultimately derived from grants made under the Acts of Settlement and Explanation"[11]

The reign of Queen Anne and the ensuing Hanoverian regimes during the eighteenth century were difficult years for the Irish Catholic The Penal Laws were imposed depriving them of practically all their rights as citizens There was no immediate sign of rebellion, but toward the conclusion of this century the smoldering hatred of the Irish Catholic for their oppressors flared French forces landing at Killala, Co. Mayo, in August of 1798 as part of the Napoleonic War created an opportunity for the Irish to strike back. From the county farmhouses, men and boys joined the invading soldiers but the strategy of the French was ill conceived and the effort unsuccessful. The Irish who did not join this rebellion were dubbed

---

[10] Queen Mary died in 1699

[11] Liam Price, "The Place-Names of the Books of Survey and Distribution and Other Records of the Cromwellian Settlement," *The Journal of the Royal Society of Antiquaries of Ireland*, Vol 81 (1951), p 92

the "Suffering Loyalists"[12] and subsequently were allowed claims to compensate them for their losses during the engagement.

The following century is best known for one of the greatest tragedies that ever befell a country This was the era of the Great Famine which began in 1845 and lasted three years. Although the time span was comparatively short, the Famine had a profound effect on Ireland's economy. The country's population prior to this event was over eight million. Close to a million were wiped out by starvation and disease, and more than a million and a half emigrated to America and other countries The decline in population persisted during the balance of the nineteenth century, and by 1900 the census was barely one-half the number before the Famine As one writer has observed, "the habit of going away was formed "[13]

Ireland's history in recent years is known, in at least a general way, to anyone whose curiosity may have led him to read this book It might be said that the intensive strivings, the turbulence and finally the violence that is now recorded as the "Anglo-Irish War" (1919-1921) were the inevitable results of economic and political events of the preceding decades The emergence of the Republic of Ireland and the northeastern sector that is known as Northern Ireland are facts that still play upon our emotions From the more pedestrian standpoint of the genealogist, one of the tragedies of this period was the loss of great volumes of critical records and vital statistics

Modern Ireland is a viable nation, growing in its industrialization and playing a responsible part in world affairs. Following its progress and treasuring its rich history and legends are literally millions of "alumni," the descendants of the thousands of families that emigrated in the past two centuries, and more, to America, Australia, New Zealand, and other parts of the globe We are proud to be a part of this great heritage

[12] See Appendix, p 293

[13] Roger Chauviré, *A Short History of Ireland* (New York Devin-Adair, 1956), p 120

II. Erris

The barony of Erris is situated in the northwest part of
Co Mayo in the Province of Connaught. It is bound on the
West and North by the Atlantic Ocean and Blacksod Bay and
on the South and East by the baronies of Burrishoole and
Tirawley. Erris was divided at one time into two parishes,
Kilmore and Kilcommon. Kilmore Parish was confined to
what was then called "Within the Mullet," a peninsula
separated from Kilcommon Parish by a strip of land and the
bays of Blacksod and Broadhaven The Mullet, though a
greater distance than Kilcommon Parish from the market
towns of the eighteenth century, became the early residence
of English settlers in this barony Kilcommon Parish, or "the
Mountains," as this area was once known, was the mainland
of the barony which includes the lands that are so important
to this story.[1] It should be remembered that not until the mid-
eighteen hundreds were roads built making Erris more acces-
sible to overland travel Previous to this period, a trip to
Erris was mostly made via boat, the alternate being a tedious
and hazardous excursion by land.

In the course of the Norman Settlement, a Barret family
acquired extensive lands in Tirawley and Erris and they still
held most of this latter barony during the reign of Queen

---

[1] Today Kilmore is still within the Mullet peninsula but Kilcommon is divided into
three parishes Kilcommon in the northern part, Kiltane to the South and Belmullet in
the West

Elizabeth (1558-1603) [2] On the 10th of March 1605, the
Barrets received a confirmation of their estates by James I
and sometime before the conclusion of his reign, a large portion
of these estates was purchased by a Munster lawyer, Dermot
(or Darby) Cormick who came to Mayo from the "lands of
Feale, near Abbeyfeale" in Co Limerick [3]

By 1641, we find Michael Cormick, a descendant of Dermot,
as the owner of Mongeneboe, a townland in Kilcommon Erris.
Other landholders in this parish then were Erevane Mc Phillip
who held Lecarrowneglogh and Lecarrow mcteige and John
Oge Barret and Edmund Bourke who held Rosduagh [4] These
particular townlands will be mentioned in some detail later

Apparently the Cormick and other families in this area
forfeited the greater part of their land, because during the
reign of Charles II (1660-1685) a grant is found of the whole
half-barony of Erris, consisting of approximately 95,000 acres,
to Sir James Shaen and held in trust for him by Sir Thomas
Vyner (or Viner) and others in satisfaction of £8000 This same
grant included the lands of the Parish of Dunfeeny in the
barony of Tirawley, Co. Mayo and the lands of the Parish of
Termonroe in the barony of Ballintober, Co Roscommon.[5]

In an old quit-rent receipt for the properties in Erris and
the Parishes of Dunfeeny and Termonroe (the receipt says
Doonfeney and Tarmonbarry), dated 1687 and signed by
John Price, Receiver-General, are the ancient names of the
townlands later leased to members of the Bournes family
Lecarrowneyglogh (Stonefield); Lecarrowmactoige (Carrowteige), Rosdowagh (Rossport) and Mungonboy (Muingnabo

[2] J G Simms, "Mayo Landowners in the Seventeenth Century," *The Journal of the
Royal Society of Antiquaries of Ireland*, Vol 95, (1965), p 240

[3] John O'Donovan, *Letters Containing Information Relative to the Antiquities of
County Mayo, Collected During the Ordnance Survey in 1838*, Vol I, pp 197-198

[4] Robert C Simington, *Books of Survey and Distribution* (Dublin 1956), Vol II,
p 203

[5] Thomas Johnson Westropp, "The Promontory Forts and Early Remains of the
Coasts of County Mayo," *The Journal of the Royal Society of Antiquaries of Ireland*
Vol 62, (1912), p 198 According to Dr Simms' article "Mayo Landowners in the
Seventeenth Century," previously cited, Charles II gave the Parish of Kilmore Erris to
Sir Robert Viner, a London Goldsmith, to whom the King owed money Viner subse-
quently disposed of it to Sir James Shaen

or Menoboe) are all listed but Portacloy, if included on this
receipt, is not decipherable [6] The reader may notice in these
two records of land, the one of 1641 and the quit-rent receipt
of 1687, that the spelling varies considerably Names of townlands, as well as surnames, were spelled phonetically resulting
in a kind of whimsy which is one of the largest impediments
to accurate research [7]

Sir James Shaen was the son of Sir Francis Shaen "who
had been connected with Mayo from the reign of Queen
Elizabeth and before whom the first preserved Elizabethan
Inquisition on County Mayo was taken in 1587 "[8] Sir James
Shaen was appointed Lessor Collector of Ireland in 1660,
Surveyor-General in 1667 and in 1692 was one of the Farmers
of the Revenue He married 28 July 1656, Lady Frances
Fitzgerald, daughter of George, 16th Earl of Kildare When
he died 12 December 1695, he left an only son, Sir Arthur
Shaen, Baronet of Kilmore, Co. Roscommon [9]

Sir Arthur Shaen took a continuing interest in the Erris
estates inherited from his father and did a great deal to improve them He brought a Protestant colony to the Mullet
and gave them allotments of land for their residences in the
level peninsula with certain baurs, or grazing lands, in Kilcommon Parish (the Mountains) and leases of lives renewable
forever at very nominal rents [10] A clergyman of the Established
Church, Reverend John Tollett accompanied the colonists In
1708, Reverend Tollett's name appears as the vicar of the
Parish of Kilcommon-Erris,[11] thereby shedding some light on

---

[6] Patrick Knight, *Erris in the Irish Highlands* (Dublin, 1836), pp 66-70 Portacloy
cannot be identified either in the Erris townlands of 1641

[7] The author has been told that the correct Irish spelling of Stonefield, Carrowteige,
Rossport, Menoboe and Portacloy is Ceathrú ná gClogh, Ceathrú Thaidhg, Ros Dumhach, Muing na Bó and Port a' Chlóidh

[8] Westropp, op cit , p 193

[9] John Burke and John Bernard Burke, *Genealogical and Heraldic History of the
Extinct and Dormant Baronetcies of England, Ireland and Scotland* (London, facsimile
ed , 1964), p 164

[10] Knight, op cit , p 63

[11] Canon J Leslie, "Biographical Succession of the Diocese of Killala and Achonry,"
Church of Ireland Representative Body, Dublin (John Tollett v of Kilcommon Erris
1708-1718)

the approximate time of the colonists arrival in this barony. Sir Arthur Shaen apparently did not give any of the original inhabitants comparable leases, with the exception of members of the Cormick family [12]

According to accounts of this colony, the settlers evicted the early inhabitants, built their own homes, made enclosed vegetable gardens and improved the farms [13] This eviction, or "clearing out" as it was called, provoked a violent reaction by the displaced persons Their reaction is described in a petition from several of the colonists to Sir Henry Bingham, Governor of Connaught and gives us some conception of the conditions during that period [14]

"The humble petition of the subscribers in behalf of themselves and other, the Protestant inhabitants in the Half-barony of Erris, most humbly offered to the Honourable Sir Henry Bingham, SHEWETH, That your Petitioners (her Majestie's most loyal subjects) however, since their coming into the country, met with several discouragements by the wicked combinations of those that are no friends to the Protestant interest For, not to mention the many depredations committed by privateers, (which though the laws in that case do redress, yet have been a great uneasiness, and the trouble and expense in recovering the same has been so little) the Papists have since taken the measures as might escape your Petitioners, and now effectually ruined us; and that is by the most secret artifices of stealing our cattle to the number of 75 within the space of nine months, besides sheep without number, not to mention the plundering of our gardens, stealing our corn, both out of the field and haggard etc. The natives had carried off all so privately, and the plot so well laid, that it was by mere accident that the late discoveries have been made; and they are since closely confined to your Honour, which service has laid your Petitioners under the greatest obligations

[12] Knight, op cit , p 63
[13] *Ibid*
[14] O'Donovan, op cit , pp 199-200

imaginable. And your Petitioners most humbly beg that your Honour will be pleased not to bail them for such reasons as the bearer will make known to your Honour, and which would be too tedious here to insert. We humbly beg your Honour's pardon for this trouble, which our great grievances, however, forced us to, and do entirely throw ourselves on your Honour's protection and doubting but Sir Arthur Shaen will make a grateful acknowledgement of all your Honour's good offices and services, as do your Honour's Petitioners, and will ever pray for your Honour's health and prosperity "

The petition was then signed by the following colonists. Thomas Higganbotham, James Maxwell, John Denistoun, Will Linney, Clement Langford, Josiah Tollett,[15] George Houston, Peter Houston, Phill Parker, Henry Gamble, Sam Calwell and Sam Lon

After several years of discord the English and the natives gradually learned to live together and hostility died out "The English had to allow the natives to share the soil . marriages took place, and the strangers were absorbed into the life, language, and religion of the majority, head-rents and renewal fines were unpaid, and at last only two of the English families remained Protestant in 1836 "[16]

As noted above, Sir Arthur Shaen took a continuing interest in his western Ireland estates. He resided in Erris at Shanahee (Shanaghy), in The Mullet peninsula, "until he saw the whole colony settled, each individual his own division of land, and probably prospering under his own immediate protection and superintendence "[17] He was High Sheriff of Co. Mayo in 1708,[18] had "Shaen's Cut dug between the bays of Belmullet, and built smelting works beside a little stream north from that village "[19] He married first, Jane, daughter of Sir Samuel

---

[15] Leslie, op cit In 1724 a Josiah Tollet was the vicar of Kilcommon Erris He was born about 1676/77 at Marthell, Cheshire, England the son of James Tollet Josiah entered T.C.D. as Sizar 20 March 1696/97 and had a son, Josiah, born in Co Mayo

[16] Westropp, op cit , p 194

[17] Knight, op cit , p 66

[18] P R O Belfast #D O.D 302, High Sheriffs of Mayo

[19] Westropp, op cit., p. 194

Hele, Baronet of Fleet, Co Devon but by her had no issue.
He married secondly, Susanna, daughter of Morgan Magan,
Esq of Togherstown, Co Westmeath and by her had three
daughters, two who survived him when he died 24 June 1725 [20]
The eldest daughter, Frances Shaen married 1 June 1738, John
Bingham of Newport, Co Mayo, a descendant of Sir Henry
Bingham, former Governor of Connaught The youngest
daughter, Susanna, married twice, first in 1739 to James
Wynne of Hazelbrook, Co Sligo, who died in 1748 without
issue She married secondly, 23 February 1750, Henry Boyle
Carter of Castle Martin, Co. Kildare and great grandson of
Thomas Carter, distinguished in the service of King William [21]
Susanna Shaen Carter survived her husband and died at her
residence, North Saint George St , Dublin, October 1807, at a
very advanced age. [22]

Subsequent chapters will show the importance of the Shaen
colony in relation to the Bournes story Though the name of
Bournes is not included in the list of colonists who signed the
petition, it is possible that at least one member of this family
had been in Erris that early.

The names of Sir Arthur Shaen's descendants are equally
important and for this reason have been given in some detail.
After his death in 1725, the names of these descendants appear
in many leases and other transactions As he only had daughters, the Shaen name therefore disappears, but one finds
Bingham and Carter as later representatives of the former
Shaen estates

---

[20] Susanna Magan Shaen married Robert Dillon of Clonbrock following the death of
her husband and subsequently became the grandmother of the first Lord Clonbrock
[21] Burke, op cit , p 164
[22] *Dublin Evening Post,* issue of 20 Oct 1807

III. Castleconnor

Castleconnor Parish, in the barony of Tireragh and county of Sligo, extends along the northern shore of the Bay of Killala and the River Moy. Its name is derived from an ancient castle called Casileu mic Connor, or Dun mic Connor, meaning the castle or dun of the son of Connor [1] The ruins of this castle may still be seen near the north bank of the Moy, not far from the town of Ballina. The present parish church of Castleconnor is only a stone's throw from the ruins of the old Killanley Church and its adjoining graveyard, once used by the Bournes family who resided in the area.

Prior to the rebellion of 1641, the townlands of this parish were held by David Dowd, Edmond Kernane, John Nolan, Edward Browne, William Linch, and Roger McEdmund.[2] When the census of Ireland was taken, ca 1659, John Nicholson was listed as the owner, or "Titulado," of the townland of Castleconnor This ownership was subsequently confirmed by Charles II in 1667, but in this instance the same land was described as the western part of Slewmaneskerry.[3] The remaining townlands of Castleconnor Parish were confirmed to Robert Morgan, Lord Collooney, Lewis Wingfield, Thomas Wood and Fitzgerald Alymer [4]

[1] T O'Rorke, *The History of Sligo, Town and County,* (Dublin, n d) Vol II, p 419
[2] Royal Irish Academy of Ireland
[3] Reports of the Irish Records Commissioners 1821-1825, p 162
[4] Royal Irish Academy of Ireland.

It has been difficult to establish with any precision the first appearance of the Bournes family in Connaught There is evidence of a Thomas Burne(sic) who resided in 1665 at Stewnamesky in the Parish of Castleconnor,[5] and roughly thirteen years later, on 21 November 1678, we find a James Burne(sic) of Castleconnor among the parties in an Exchequer Bill [6] Finally, a list of Protestants attainted for treason by James II in 1689 includes the name of "Thomas Burne of Castle-cannure, tanner .   of County Sligoe."[7]

We have abundant proof that a "Thomas Bourne of Castleconnor" received a grant of land in 1707 and there is good reason to believe that this Thomas was not the first of his family at Castleconnor As we have noted in the Foreword, Irish surnames are rather frequently confused by different phonetic versions and in such incidences one often has to look for other common threads, or clues, the most reliable being the townlands on which they resided Castleconnor is a relatively restricted area and there is, therefore, a very strong implication that the names Thomas and James "Burne" were phonetic versions of the "Bourne" family which appears in Castleconnor a generation or so later This assumption is perhaps fortified by the commonality of their christian names.

Our family tradition says that four brothers came to Ireland during the Cromwellian period and received grants of land for faithful service Descendants of these men inherited these lands, one such estate being Castleconnor It is tempting to relate this tradition to the documentation we have developed in respect to Thomas and James Burne. Could they have been two of the "four brothers" and is it possible that the other brothers settled elsewhere in Ireland?[8]

[5] Edward McLysaght, ed Seventeenth Century Hearth Money Rolls of Co Sligo The townland of Stewnamesky is undoubtedly the same as the Stewmaneskerry confirmed in 1667 to John Nicholson by Charles II

[6] Rev William Ball Wright and Helen Crofton, Crofton Memoirs (York, 1911), p 288 James Burne of Castleconnor appears with Philip Ormsby, Francis King, Edward Nicholson and Adam O'Hara opposing Henry Crofton of Mohill, Henry Crofton of Longford House and Rose O'Hara

[7] Archbishop William King, The State of the Protestants of Ireland under the Late King James' Government (Dublin, 1730), p 217

[8] For example, we found a John Bourne of Burren and Clooncallabeg, Co Cork who received a grant of land during the reign of Charles II See Part Three.

Unfortunately we can neither prove nor disprove this conjecture All that we can say is that in view of the history of
this period and subsequent land records our tradition is plausible In setting forth the family pedigree which follows, we have
taken the liberty of assuming that a Thomas Bourne(s) was
the earliest representative of the Castleconnor family

Land records thus become increasingly important as one
attempts research among Ireland's eighteenth century sources.
They are, in most instances, the only available means to trace
a family In order to understand these records it is necessary
to examine briefly the manner in which land was conveyed.
Conveyance was accomplished by various legal "instruments"
such as leases, renewals (releases), marriage settlements, or
assignments to name but a few

Although there are several types of leases, the one that has
predominated in this research is known as the "lease for three
lives " In the next few pages an early lease for three lives[9] is
cited because it provides an interesting example of the importance of this kind of record, genealogically as well as
historically One notices that Sir Arthur Shaen, Baronet of
Kilmore, Co Roscommon was the grantor, or lessor, Thomas
Bourne(sic),[10] Gentleman of Castleconnor, Co Sligo was the
grantee, or lessee. Within the phraseology of the document one
learns also that Thomas Bourne may hold the lands of
"Rosduagh and Muingnabo"[11] for the term of his life and the
lives of his brothers, William and George Bourne providing,
of course, that certain terms and covenants are upheld

The failure (death) of any of the lives mentioned created
the necessity of renewing the lease A fee had to be paid by the
remaining "lives" within a stated period for the inconvenience
to Sir Arthur Shaen, or later to his descendants, in renewing
the lease Thus a renewal was actually a mechanism, which, in

[9] Land Commission, Dublin

[10] In the very early leases the name was spelled "Bourne" but to simplify reading the
account of the Connaught families, the name will be "Bournes " This latter spelling, as
mentioned previously, was used by most of the western Ireland families

[11] Muingnabo is frequently found in leases as Meneboe

effect, enabled a family to hold land for an indefinite period.
To a present day researcher, a renewal was a unique document
for it contained the history of the land and thereby fragments
of the family's history

In addition to the grant made to Thomas Bourne, Sir
Arthur Shaen executed two other leases on the same day, 10
June 1707, to early members of the Stonefield, Carrowteige
and Portacloy families Inasmuch as the recitals embodied in
these leases are identical, the wording of the lease cited here
may be regarded as representative of all three instruments,
except, of course, for specific descriptions of the land granted
and the names of the grantees

THIS INDENTURE made the *tenth* day of *June* Anno Domini, One
thousand seven hundred and *seven* BETWEEN Sir ARTHUR SHAEN
of Kilmore, in the Barony of Athlone and County of Roscommon,
Baronet, of the one part and *Thomas Bourne of Castleconnor in the
County of Sligo, Gentleman* of the other part, WITNESSETH that the
said Sir Arthur Shaen for and in consideration of the yearly rents,
covenants, conditions and agreements herein after mentioned which
on the part and behalf of the said *Thomas Bourne* his heirs and assigns
are or ought to be done and performed HATH demised, granted,
leased, set and to farm let, AND by these presents doth demise grant,
lease, set and to farm, let unto the said *Thomas Bourne* ALL *that
cartion of land called Rossdaugh containing by estimation one and
thirty acres of profitable land and five hundred and ninety six acres of
unprofitable or Mountain land such as cattle might graze upon being part
of the same land and also all that cartion of land called Menebo containing
by estimation two and twenty acres of profitable land and one thousand
three hundred and ninety five acres of unprofitable or Mountain land
such as cattle might graze upon being part and parcel of the same by
means and bounds and now divided and lately surveyed* containing by
estimation *fifty three* acres of profitable land and *one thousand nine
hundred and ninety one* acres of unprofitable land such as cattle might
graze upon situate, lying and being in the Half-Barony of Erris in the
County of Mayo, Except and always reserved out of this Demise and
Lease unto the said Sir Arthur Shaen, his heirs and assigns the liberty
of hunting, hawking, fishing and fowling during the said Lease and
all mines and minerals, also the liberty of searching for mines and
minerals and carrying away the same at his will and pleasure and also
excepting and reserving all averyes of hawks, and all woods, timber
and underwoods now being and growing or hereafter to be growing
on the said Demised Premises TO HAVE AND TO HOLD all and
singular the said Demised Premises with the appurtenances unto the
said *Thomas Bourne* his heirs and assigns from the *five and twentieth*
day of *March last past* for and during the natural lives of the said

Thomas Bourne William Bourne brother of the said Thomas Bourne and George Bourne another brother of the said Thomas Bourne and the survivor or survivors of them and for and during the natural Life and Lives of such other persons as by virtue of these presents shall from time to time successively and for ever be added during this Demise YIELDING AND PAYING therefore yearly and every year during the said term for lives hereby granted unto the said Sir Arthur Shaen, his heirs or assigns the rent or sum of *nine* pounds sterling (and yearly *nine* shillings as Receivers Fees) of good and lawful money of England the same to be paid on the two usual Feast-Days or Days of Payment in the year, viz the five and twentieth day of March and the nine and twentieth day of September, yearly by even and equal portions the first payment thereof to begin and be made upon the nine and twentieth day of September next ensuing hereof, without any deduction for taxes or charges whatsoever imposed or to be imposed by authority of Parliament or otherwise howsoever (Crown-Rent only excepted) PROVIDED always that if it shall happen the said Yearly-Rent or any part thereof shall be behind or unpaid in part or in all by the space of one and twenty days next after any of the said Feast-days or Days of Payment at upon which the same ought to be paid as aforesaid, that then it shall and may be lawful to and for the said Sir Arthur Shaen, his heirs or assigns into the said Demised Premises or any part thereof to enter and distrain and the distress or distresses so taken to dispose of according to law and if no sufficient distress or distresses can be found on the said Demised Premises it shall and may be lawful to and for the said Sir Arthur Shaen his heirs or assigns into the said Demised Premises or any part thereof in the name of the whole to re-enter and the same to have again repossess and re-enjoy as in his and their first and former Estate any thing herein contained to the contrary notwithstanding AND the said Sir Arthur Shaen doth hereby for himself his heirs, executors and administrators covenant, promise and agree to and with the said *Thomas Bourne* his heirs and assigns by these presents or upon the death or failure of the aforesaid lives or life of the said *Thomas Bourne, William Bourne and George Bourne* or any of them which shall survive the said *Thomas Bourne* his heirs or assigns paying or causing to be paid unto the said Sir Arthur Shaen his heirs or assigns the full and just sum of (unreadable) pounds sterling over and above the Yearly Rent hereby reserved within Six Months after the failure of such life or lives and upon nomination of the life of such other person by the said *Thomas Bourne* his heirs or assigns his or their request to be put and inserted in the place and stead of the person so happening first to die as aforesaid that then he the said Sir Arthur Shaen his heirs or assigns shall and will within Six Months from the death of such person so happening first to die as aforesaid add and insert to the time and term of this Lease the life of such person so nominated in the place and stead of the person so happening first to die as aforesaid which life so added and inserted is to be endorsed on this Lease or to be written in a label or parchment to be affixed to this Lease for that purpose and in like manner from time to time successively for ever upon the failure of every other

several life in this Lease now nominated or hereafter to be successively
nominated as aforesaid and upon like payment of the entire sum of
(unreadable) over and above the Yearly-Rent hereby reserved within
Six Months next after the failure of every such Life and upon the like
nomination of any other Life successively in lieu of every several Life
so failing as aforesaid, that then he the said Sir Arthur Shaen his heirs
or assigns successively shall and will within six months next after the
failure of every such other several Life nominated as aforesaid, add
and insert to the term and time of this Lease from time to time for
ever the several Life or Lives of such person or persons to be nominated, in the place and stead of the Life or Lives of the several person
or persons successively happening to die as aforesaid which several
lives to be added and inserted successively are to be endorsed on this
Lease or written in a Deed, Label or Parchment to be affixed hereunto
as aforesaid AND the said *Thomas Bourne* doth hereby for himself his
heirs or assigns, covenant, promise and agree to and with the said Sir
Arthur Shaen his heirs and assigns that he the said *Thomas Bourne*
his heirs or assigns from time to time and at all times hereafter upon
the failure of every Life of the several person or persons herein before
mentioned for whose Life this present Lease is made or hereafter shall
be renewed as aforesaid shall and will for every life that shall fail
satisfy and pay unto the said Sir Arthur Shaen his heirs or assigns the
full and entire sum of *nine* pounds over and above the Yearly-
Rent hereby reserved within six months next after the failure of every
such Life every such payment made without any deduction or defalca-
tion whatsoever PROVIDED always that if it shall happen upon the
failure of any Life herein before mentioned or hereafter to be nominated as aforesaid the said *Thomas Bourne* his heirs or assigns shall
or do not pay unto the said Arthur Shaen his heirs or assigns for
every Life so failing as aforesaid the said sum of *nine* pounds sterling
over and above the Yearly-Rent herein before reserved within six
months next after the failure of every such life and also shall not
within the said space of six months after such failure nominate the
Life of some other person in lieu thereof to be added to the term and
time of this Lease as aforesaid that then it shall and may be lawful to
and for the said Sir Arthur Shaen his heirs or assigns forever thereafter to deny and refuse the said *Thomas Bourne* his heirs or assigns to
add insert, nominate or put in any other Life or Lives the term or
time of this Lease, other than the Life or Lives which then shall be in
being and (unreadable) in such case also the Demised Premises from
and after the determination of the Lives which then shall be in being
shall be and remain to the said Sir Arthur Shaen his heirs and assigns
at the (unreadable) the said Sir Arthur Shaen his heirs and assigns
AND the said *Thomas Bourne* doth hereby for himself his heirs and
assigns covenant, promise and agree to and with the said Sir Arthur
Shaen his heirs and assigns in manner following (that is to say) that he
the said *Thomas Bourne* doth hereby for himself his heirs and assigns
covenant promise granted well and truly pay said Sir Arthur Shaen
his heirs and assigns the said reserved Yearly-Rent at the days and
times herein before limited and appointed for payment thereof clear of

all taxes (Crown-Rent excepted) AND also the said *Thomas Bourne* his heirs or assigns shall during the said term and time maintain and keep all the houses now built, or to be built or (unreadable) premises in good and tenantable repair and at any expiration of the said term shall so leave and yield up the same and the possession thereof together with the hedges, ditches, bounds and (unreadable) and such other improvements as shall be on the said Demised Premises unto the said Sir Arthur Shaen his heirs or assigns AND it is further agreed upon by and between the said parties to these presents that *Thomas Bourne* his heirs and assigns and his and their tenants shall do suit and service to the Court and Courts of the Manor of Shaen AND also the said *Thomas Bourne* his heirs or assigns shall yearly and every year until the said Demised Premises shall be drained, cut make and drain at least *fifty* perches of drain on the said Demised Premises which said drain (unreadable) yearly shall be at the least six foot broad and six foot deep or as much draining as will answer the same or in case of neglect or refusal shall for every such neglect or refusal forfeit and pay to the said Sir Arthur Shaen his heirs or assigns yearly *twenty* shillings sterling AND also the said *Thomas Bourne* his heirs or assigns shall yearly cut his turf in the bog in straight lines down to the fall of water in order for the better draining of the same and not in holes and in case of neglect or refusal so to do shall pay for every such neglect or refusal yearly *ten* shillings sterling AND the said Sir Arthur Shaen doth hereby for himself his heirs and assigns covenant, promise and agree to and with the said *Thomas Bourne* his heirs and assigns that he the said *Thomas Bourne* his heirs and assigns paying the said Yearly-Rent and observing all other the covenants and agreements herein before mentioned shall quietly and peaceably hold and enjoy the said Demised Premises without any disturbance let or hindrance of the said Sir Arthur Shaen his heirs or assigns or any person lawfully claiming under him AND the said Sir Arthur Shaen hath and by these presents doth give and grant unto *Elias Bourne* full power and authority to give livery and seisin of the said Demised Premises or any part thereof in the name of the whole unto the said *Thomas Bourne* to enure unto the said *Thomas Bourne* his heirs and assigns according to the true intent and meaning of these presents IN WITNESS whereof the parties first above named to these present Indentures, have interchangeably set their Hands and Seals the day and year as above written

(signed)   ART SHAEN

The lease dated 10 June 1707 was signed and sealed in the presence of three witnesses. Two of the signatures are still discernible, namely "Jane Bourne" and "Anthony Barry."

There are several handwritten paragraphs, or memoranda, on the reverse side of this ancient document. Though time has faded some of the writing most of it is quite easily read. The first paragraph states "Memorandum livery and seizin of all and singular the lands within mentioned were given and delivered by the within named Elias Bourne unto the within named Thomas Bourne this___ ___day of____Anno Domini 1707 according to the tenor of the within written Indenture in the presence of us " The signatures of the three witnesses are not decipherable

Another memorandum was signed "Art Shaen" and reads as follows "Memorandum on sealing hereof it is agreed that the within named Thomas Bourne shall have liberty of taking sea weed for manuring the lands within written from off the shore on the lands of Kilgalligan "[12]

A careful study of the lease of 1707, as well as the memoranda given above, discloses that the name of Elias Bourne(sic) is important to a full understanding of this conveyance. Elias, who in the lease was given "full power and authority to give livery and seizin . . . in the name of the whole . . ," is revealed hereby as the original occupier[13] of the lands of Rosduagh and Muingnabo He, in effect, as is shown in the memoranda, turns over these lands to Thomas Bourne(sic)

Thomas Bourne, as subsequent records show, was actually the son of Elias and most likely the eldest of the three brothers As it was customary to name the eldest son after his grandfather, it may also follow that he was named after Thomas Burne (or Bournes) of Castleconnor, tanner

It is quite natural to speculate further, for if Elias was the "occupier" in 1707, or before, might he not have been one of the members of Shaen's early colony? We do not know the answer but again it is tempting to relate the history of the barony of Erris with the above record in respect to Elias Bourne

---

[12] Kilgalligan is on the northwestern coast of Erris, adjacent to the lands of Stonefield and within a few miles of Rosduagh and Muingnabo

[13] Occupier need not be literally interpreted In this instance, Elias Bournes may have used these lands for the grazing of sheep and cattle, not as a residence

The Bournes of Castleconnor

I Thomas Burne, recorded as residing in the Parish of Castleconnor, Co Sligo in 1665, probably was the progenitor of the Connaught Bournes families It is chronologically possible that he was the same Thomas, tanner of Castleconnor, attainted for treason by King James II in 1689

II. Elias Bournes of Castleconnor was possibly the son of Thomas He had issue.

   i   Thomas Bournes q v

   ii   William Bournes (see Carrowteige and Portacloy family)

   iii   George Bournes (see Rosspoit family)

III Thomas Bournes of Castleconnor, the eldest son and heir, demised all his interest in the lands of Rosduagh 21 November 1727 to his brother George Bournes of Knockaskeehaun, Co Mayo.[14] Thomas Bournes' Will was dated 3 May 1764 and proved 8 September 1764.[15] He had issue of at least one son

   i   Elias Bournes q v

IV Elias Bournes of Castleconnor was probably the eldest son He was a witness to a marriage settlement dated 19 July 1752, which is mentioned in some detail in the account of the Carrowteige and Portacloy family In a renewal of lease made the 22nd of January 1757, Elias Bournes nominated his eldest son, Thomas, to replace George Bournes of Knockaskeehaun, one of the original lives, now deceased [16] On the 9th of December 1761, Charles Atkinson of Rehins, Co. Mayo demised to Elias and to his heirs the lands of Tawnynaboll in the barony

[14] Registry of deeds #65 165 44882 Knockaskeehaun is in the Parish of Kilfian and barony of Tirawley, Co Mayo

[15] Sir William Betham, *Armagh Wills Index* P R O , Belfast This particular copy of the Armagh Wills Index also includes the Index to the Wills of the Diocese of Killala and Achonry

[16] Registry of Deeds #180 604 123282

of Tirawley, Co Mayo [17] As these lands are subsequently found in the possession of the Bournes family of Ardglass, Co Roscommon, they will be referred to in the chapter devoted to this family Elias Bournes died before 2 September 1777 and left issue

    i   Thomas Bournes q v

    ii Robert Bournes (see Hatley Manor family)

    iii David Bournes, named as the second brother of Thomas Bournes in a renewal of lease dated 2 Sept 1777 (see Ardglass family)

    iv John Bournes (see Stonefield family)

    v   Matthew Bournes (see Stonefield family)

    vi William Bournes, named as the youngest brother of Thomas Bournes in the same renewal of lease, 2 Sept 1777 He married Mary O'Brien who was born ca 1758 and who died 28 Feb 1800, aged 42 She was buried in Killanley Cemetery [18]

V. Thomas Bournes of Castleconnor, called Thomas "the elder," was named in a renewal of lease dated 2 September 1777, as the eldest son and heir of Elias Bournes, deceased, and the grandson of Thomas Bournes, one of the original lives named in 1707 [19] He married Eleanor Rutledge, born ca. 1737 and who died in 1784, aged 47 [20] Thomas Bournes died ca. 1817 [21] and was buried with his wife in Killanley Cemetery [22] They had issue

    i. Thomas Bournes q v

    ii James Bournes, called the second son of Thomas Bournes "the elder," was born ca 1778 [23] and resided at Farrangarode in the Parish of Castleconnor In a renewal of lease dated 14 Dec 1792, he was named as a "life" to the Rosduagh and Muingnabo lease in place of William Bournes, one of the original lives of 1707, now deceased [24] He resided at Castleconnor, in the parish of this same

[17] Registry of Deeds #251 128 162789

[18] Killanley Cemetery gravestone inscription

[19] Registry of Deeds #466 11 295267

[20] Killanley Cemetery gravestone inscription

[21] P R O Dublin Will Index

[22] Killanley Cemetery gravestone inscription

[23] Land Commission, Dublin, Registry of Deeds #461 525 296529 In a renewal of 1792, he was said to be "about 14 years of age"

[24] Registry of Deeds, #461 525 296529

name, by 1834 and in 1853 was of Knockroe House, Castlecon-
noi [25] On 19 Jan 1859, he was said to be the last "surviving life
to the last renewal of lease made in 1792   "[26] James Bournes
married 18 May 1806, Mary Anne Bournes of Ballina in the
Parish of Kilmoremoy [27] Her death was recorded in the register
of this same parish, buried 14 Jan 1862, aged 68 They had issue,
all born in the Parish of Castleconnor

(1) Thomas Bournes born ca 1810, was of Knockroe House,
Castleconnor He married Elizabeth Kilroy and died intestate
15 May 1845, aged 35,[28] buried in Killanley Cemetery [29]
They had issue

a James Bournes, born 29 Dec 1844, baptised 8 April 1845
in the Parish of Castleconnor.

(2) John Bournes who married 7 Oct 1846 in the Parish of Castleconnor, Church of Killanley, Catherine, daughter of Alexander Lowrie, Esq of Castleconnor The ceremony was witnessed
by Alexander Lowrie and Charles Lowrie [30]

(3) Eleanor Bournes, baptised 16 May 1810

(4) Marianne Bournes, baptised 23 Sept 1812

(5) James Bournes, baptised 23 Sept 1820, was residing at
Castleconnor in 1853 [31]

VI Thomas Bournes, the eldest son and heir, was born ca.
1776[32] and called Thomas "the younger" of Castleconnor He
may possibly have been the Thomas Bournes(sic) who matriculated at Trinity College, Dublin as a Pensioner 7 July 1792
and received his B A in 1797 [33]

He married first in 1801, Hester, daughter of the late John
O'Brien, Esq of Drumrahan, Co Leitrim by Alice, daughter

[25] State Paper Office, Dublin Castle, #W 10/1853

[26] Land Commission, Dublin Indenture dated 19 Jan 1859 between Thomas Shaen
Carter, of the first part, and Fergus Farrell, of the second part

[27] The M L B of the Diocese of Killala and Achonry shows "James Bourns and
Marianne Burns, 1806"

[28] P R O Belfast, #T 1021/25-31

[29] Killanley Cemetery gravestone inscription

[30] Custom House register

[31] State Paper Office, Dublin Castle, Dublin #W 10/1853 James Bournes Sr., his
father, was of Knockroe House, Castleconnor, Co Sligo this same year

[32] Land Commission, Dublin Thomas was said to be "about sixteen years of age"
in a renewal of lease made in 1792

[33] Burtchaell and Sadleir, *Alumni Dublinenses, A Register of the Students, Graduates,
Professors and Provosts of Trinity College in the University of Dublin, 1593-1860*

of Robert Whitelaw, Esq.[34] The marriage settlement dated 12 October 1801 was made by Thomas Bournes "the elder" and Thomas Bournes "the younger," Esquires of Castleconnor of the first part, Hester O'Brien of the second part; William Stack and John Crofton, Esquires and Executors of the last Will and Testament of John O'Brien of Drumrahan, deceased (Will dated 28 March 1792, proved 24 Nov 1792) of the third part, James Jackson Caddell Farrell of Springfield, Co Leitrim and Robert Bournes of the Town of Carrick, Surgeon of the fourth part, Edward Carleton of the City of Dublin, Esq and David Bournes of Ardglass, Co Roscommon of the fifth part.[35]

Hester O'Brien, born ca. 1780, was buried 29 November 1807, aged 27, in the Killanley Cemetery.[36] By this marriage two daughters were born

Thomas Bournes married secondly, 7 November 1823 at the Church of Hollymount, Co. Mayo, Elizabeth, third daughter of David Rutledge of Togher, Co Mayo, Esq[37] and by her had one son Thomas Bournes died 9 December 1829 at Castleconnor[38] and was buried in Killanley Cemetery His widow, Elizabeth Rutledge Bournes, married for a second time 15 January 1836, in the Rathfarnham Church, Co. Dublin, Henry Gardiner M D of Ballina, Co Mayo[39]

By Hester O'Brien, Thomas Bournes had issue

   i   Eleanor Anne Bournes q v

   ii   Alicia Bournes, baptised 18 May 1806 in the Parish of Castleconnor, married (marriage articles) 1 Dec 1826, James Peter, son of David Rutledge of Togher They had issue of one daughter,

[34] Sir Arthur Vicars, ed *Index to the Prerogative Wills of Ireland, 1536-1810* (Dublin, 1897), Genealogical Office, Dublin Castle pedigree Registry of Deeds #876 120 581620 Robert Whitelaw, Esq may be the "Robert Whitelaw" who was High Sheriff of Drummeen and Grange, Co Leitrim whose wife, it has been suggested, was possibly the daughter of George Crofton M P of Lisdorne, Co Roscommon (*Irish Genealogist*, Vol I, no 10, Oct 1941)

[35] Registry of Deeds #848 204 567704, #839 383 563383

[36] Register of the Parish of Kilmoremoy The Killanley Cemetery gravestone inscription "departed this life 28 Nov 1808, aged 30 "

[37] *Ballina Impartial*, issue of 17 Nov 1823

[38] *Mayo Constitution*, issue of 17 Dec 1829

[39] *Western Star*, issue of 22 Jan 1836

Belinda Rutledge [40] She married secondly (mar arts) 29 April
1828, Fergus, eldest son of James Jackson Caddell Farrell of
Gibralter House, Co Sligo by Anne O'Brien and grandson of
Fergus Farrell of Lackugh, Co Sligo [41] They had issue of at least
two daughters for in the *Mayo Constitution* (issue of 15 Oct
1839) an article states that "Anne Farrell, second daughter of
Fergus Farrell of Newport Pratt, Co Mayo, R I C , died 11 Oct
1839 " The Farrells resided at Newport Pratt and by 1859 were
of 12 Richmond Ave , Fairview, Dublin [42]

By Elizabeth Rutledge, Thomas Bournes had issue

iii Thomas David Bournes, born 18 Aug 1830, died shortly after
13 Dec 1834 at Castleconnor [43]

VII Eleanor Anne Bournes, the eldest daughter of Thomas
Bournes "the younger," was baptised 3 May 1802 in the Parish
of Castleconnor. She married 7 February 1824 at Moylough
Church, Co. Galway, George, son of David Rutledge of Togher,
Esq [44] George Rutledge at the time of his marriage was of
Broomville Lodge, Co Mayo and in 1837 was of Knockroe
House, Castleconnor [45] The only other record that can be
found referring to Eleanor Anne is one in which she was a
witness to the marriage 13 July 1825 of Maria, daughter of
David Rutledge of Togher, Esq , and John Fair of Fortville,
Co. Mayo, Esq., son of Robert Fair by Jane, daughter of
John (Robin) Fair of Lavally, Co Mayo [46] George Rutledge
died 6 November 1876, aged 74, at Togher House and was
buried in the Hollymount Cemetery. [47] They had issue

1 David Rutledge, called the eldest son in a deed dated 8 March
1834

[40] Registry of Deeds #876 120 581620

[41] *Ibid*

[42] Land Commission, Dublin Indenture dated 19 Jan 1859, op cit

[43] *Ballina Impartial*, issue of 23 Aug 1830, Registry of Deeds #1839 17 41

[44] *Ballina Impartial*, issue of 9 Feb 1824

[45] Samuel Lewis, *A Topographical Dictionary of Ireland* (London, 1837) Vol II,
p 291

[46] Register of the Parish of Kilmaine, From the records of Dr Patrick Smythe-Wood,
Ballycastle, Co Antrim

[47] Hollymount Cemetery gravestone inscription The inscription states that George
Rutledge was "late of Castleconnor "

ii   Thomas Rutledge, called the second son in a deed dated 8 March 1834

iii James Peter Rutledge, called the youngest son in a deed dated 8 March 1834 [48] He married 3 May 1856 at St Peter's Church, Dublin, Julia Mary, the youngest daughter of John Gray of Claremorris, Co Mayo At the time of his marriage, James Peter was of Beechgrove, Co Mayo and called "the eldest son of George Rutledge, Esq "[49]

iv   William Robert Rutledge, born ca. 1838, died Dec 1868 at Harold's Cross, Dublin, age 30 He was called the third surviving son of George Rutledge, Esq , late of Togher [50]

v   Hester Olivia Rutledge, the eldest daughter, was born ca 1832 and died 10 Dec 1839, aged 7 At the time of her death her father, George Rutledge, was of Togher [51]

---

[48] Registry of Deeds #1834 8 122.
[49] *Tirawley Herald*, issue of 8 May 1856.
[50] *Ballinrobe Chronicle*, issue of 5 Dec 1868
[51] *Mayo Constitution*, issue of 29 Dec 1839

IV. Rossport

The name of Rosduagh (Ros Dumhach)[1], or An Ros as it
was known in ancient records, means the peninsula of the
sandbank At one period there were extensive sandbanks at
the western end of this townland but time and the gradual dis-
integration by erosion, reduced the large sandy dunes to a
small tract [2] Located in the western part of Co Mayo, in the
barony of Erris and Parish of Kilcommon, this peninsula once
jutted out from the mainland into the channel of Sruwaddacon
(Sruth Fada Con), meaning in Irish, the Long Current of
the Hound.[3]

Rossport and the adjacent land of Muingnabo (Muing
na Bó) were granted to Thomas Bournes of Castleconnor, Co
Sligo on the 10th of June 1707 Twenty years later on the 21st
of November 1727, he demised his interest in Rossport to his
brother, George Bournes George Bournes in 1707 was of
Knockaskeehaun, a townland in the Parish of Kilfian, barony
of Tirawley, Co. Mayo. Later records show that he subsequently resided in Erris He was of Rossport when he dated
his Will, 27 July 1756, and he died sometime between this date

---

[1] Rossport is the translation of the Irish word, Ros Dumhach, Rosdaugh is the
Anglo-Irish version of the same place name Unless actual records are cited, Rossport
will be used

[2] Michael Corduff, "Notes on Erris," *Irish Folklore Commission*, Dublin, 1941,
Vol I, p 1

[3] Today Sruwaddacon would be termed an inlet

and 6 March 1759, when his Will was proved [4]

George Bournes was undoubtedly the earliest member of this branch of the Bournes family to reside in Erris Later owners presumably were absentee landlords of Rossport and they collected the rent and tithes from the tenants by periodically sending a representative to the area for that purpose.[5] Nineteenth century deeds refer to the lease made by Thomas Bournes of Castleconnor in 1727 when he granted Rossport to George Bournes, his brother This transaction is described as the original lease to Rossport which it indeed was insofar as the Rossport family were concerned

It is seemingly impossible to establish the relationship of the various members of the Bournes family who at one time or another had an interest in the lands of Rossport and Muingnabo Not until we come to George Bournes of Moyne are we able with any degree of accuracy to trace further descendants

The Bournes of Rossport

I George Bournes of Moyne, Co Mayo and later of Killala in this same county, was born ca. 1766 and possessed a life interest in the land of Rossport [6] He married (mar sett) 1 August 1789, Mary, born ca 1772, the daughter of Samuel Smith by Jane Ormsby [7] George Bournes died 4 November 1825, aged 58, and was buried in the Ardnaree Cemetery, Ballina [8] His wife died 12 November 1855, aged 83, at Rossport House, the home of Samuel Bournes, her son [9] She was buried in the Rossport Cemetery [10] They had issue [11]

[4] Sir William Betham's Index to Wills, Diocese of Killala and Achonry, op cit

[5] Corduff, op cit , p 12

[6] Registry of Deeds #1812 8 147

[7] Ibid, Nial McCormick of Killala, family records

[8] Ardnaree Cemetery gravestone inscription Register of the Parish of Kilmoremoy states that he was "of Erris," aged 59

[9] Tirawley Herald, issue of 22 Nov 1855

[10] Rossport Cemetery gravestone inscription

[11] Registry of Deeds #1812 8 147 George Bournes' sons were named in order of birth

1 William Bournes the eldest son, born ca 1796, was attached to
the North Mayo Regiment of Militia [12] He was the Parish Clerk
of Ardnaree and in 1816 married (M L B Killala and Achonry)
Sarah Whiteside, born ca 1795 William Bournes inherited a life
interest in the lands of Rossport from his father but by an Indenture of Conveyance, dated 13 Jan 1832, released his interest in
favor of his younger brother Samuel [13] He died at Ardnaree 19
April 1862, aged 66, and his wife died there also 28 Jan 1855,
aged 60 [14] They had issue, all born in the Parish of Kilmoremoy.

(1) William Bournes, born 12 Nov 1818, was baptised 15 Nov
1818 He married 27 Dec 1852 at Ballina, Jane Smith Bren-
nen, widow, and the daughter of Thomas Smith The marriage
was witnessed by John Bournes and Sarah Bournes William
Bournes was a member of the R I C and he died 27 Dec
1883, aged 65, in Ardnaree [15] His Will was dated 26 Dec
1883 and proved 31 Dec 1884 [16] His wife died 9 June 1882,
aged 70, at Ardnaree [17]

(2) Jane Bournes, born 6 March 1821, was baptised 7 March
1821

(3) John Bournes, born 11 Nov 1825, was baptised 14 Dec
1825 He married Jane, daughter of John Walker of Ballina,
16 March 1854 The marriage was witnessed by James Walker
and William Power [18] John Bournes was a printer and resided
in Ballina where he died 21 Oct 1912, aged 86 [19] They had
issue, all born in the Parish of Kilmoremoy

a Louisa Bournes, born 17 April 1855, was baptised 12 May
1855

b John Bournes born 25 April 1857, was baptised 16 May
1857

c Anne Bournes, born 9 July 1859, was baptised 7 Aug
1859

d Sarah Bournes, born 1 Nov 1861, was baptised 29 Dec
1861

e Mary Jane Bournes, born 3 Nov 1863, was baptised 13
Jan 1864

f Katherine Bournes, born 10 March 1866, was baptised 18
April 1866 She married 4 July 1888, John, son of Alex-

---

[12] *Tirawley Herald*, issue of 24 April 1862

[13] Registry of Deeds #880 87 583587 Henry Bournes, the second son of George of
Moyne, also released his interest in favor of Samuel Bournes

[14] *Tirawley Herald*, issues of 1 Feb 1855 and 24 April 1862

[15] Custom House Registers

[16] P R O Dublin Will Index

[17] Custom House Register

[18] *Ibid*

[19] P R O Dublin Will Index

ander Clinton of Newport, Co Mayo The marriage was witnessed by Thomas Green and John Bournes.[20]

g Arthur Robert Bournes, born 19 Jan 1876, was baptised 8 April 1876

(4) Eliza Bournes, born 4 June 1828 was baptised 15 June 1828

(5) Sarah Bournes, born 6 June 1832, was baptised 17 June 1832 She married in Ardnaree, 7 March 1859, Henry, son of Francis Kerr The marriage was witnessed by Robert White and William Bournes.[21]

II Henry Bournes, the second son,[22] was a merchant of Crossmolina, Co Mayo and a member of the Established Church of Ireland He was confirmed 29 Sept 1821 in the Parish of Crossmolina.[23] Shortly before 1840, he joined the Wesleyan Methodist Church and was listed as a Leader in 1841 and a Trustee by 1851.[24] Henry Bournes married in the Parish of Kilmoremoy, 27 Dec 1822, Frances, daughter of Andrew Watts of Ballinglen, Co Mayo by Anne_____ The marriage was witnessed by Richard Faussett M D [25] and Henry Edgar Prior to the marriage a settlement was made by "Henry Bourns of Crossmolina, Merchant of the first part, Fanny Watts of Castleglyn spinster, of the second part, Richard Faussett of Ardnaree, Medical Doctor and Thomas Bournes, Esq of Castleconnor, Trustees of the third part   " One of the witnesses to this settlement was Robert Davis Bournes of Killala, Surgeon [26] Frances and Henry Bournes had one daughter, Anne Bournes, who was born in 1825 Anne and her descendants will be treated separately at the conclusion of the Rossport chapter Henry Bournes' wife presumably died shortly after the birth of their daughter for on 14 May 1828, he married Elizabeth J Young of Castlebar at the Turlough Parish Church This marriage was witnessed by Henry Ayres and William Young [27] Henry Bournes died 4 Feb 1865 at Castlebar, aged 71,[28] leaving issue of the following children, all born in Crossmolina

---

[20] Register of the Parish of Burrishoule, Co Mayo

[21] Custom House Register

[22] Register of Deeds #880 87 583587 This deed suggests that Henry Bournes was the second son but his age at death, i e 71, would indicate he was born ca 1794, therefore making him the eldest son

[23] Register of the Parish of Crossmolina

[24] Methodist Registers, Lists of Classes and members of the Ballina Circuit, 1841-1851

[25] The surname of ' Faussett" is frequently found as Fawcett This family, closely related to the Bournes, made their home in the Parish of Ballysakeery at Ballinglen, or nearby

[26] Register of the Parish of Kilmoremoy, Registry of Deeds #1842 8 147 See Hatley Bournes family

[27] Register of the Parish of Turlough, Vol 4 (1822-1845)

[28] *Tirawley Herald*, issue of 9 Feb 1865

Henry Bournes, merchant, of Crossmolina, Co. Mayo. Artist unknown. Reproduced from the Palmer Collection, National Library of Australia, Canberra, Australia.

Rossport House, Rossport, Co. Mayo. Photograph taken 1965.

(1) Maria Bournes, born 17 March 1829, was baptised 19 April 1829 in the Parish of Crossmolina She married 29 Aug 1849 at the Wesleyan Chapel, Crossmolina, Robert Campbell, a Wesleyan minister and son of Rev John Campbell of Belmullet, Co Mayo The ceremony was performed by Rev J H Atkins and witnessed by "H Bournes and Robert Scott ' Following the ceremony the couple proceeded to the residence of John Fawcett, Esq of the Glen, Co Mayo [29] The Campbells moved frequently but in 1859 were in Crossmolina [30] They later moved to England and resided in Nottingham [31] Maria Bournes Campbell died prior to Aug 1867 when Robert Campbell married again His second wife's name is unknown [32] Robert and Maria Campbell had issue [33]

a   John (Jackie) Campbell

b   Kathleen Campbell

c   Lillie Campbell

(2) Henrietta Anne Bournes, born 12 July 1835, was baptised the same day in the Parish of Crossmolina

(3) Henrietta Bournes, born 20 July 1837, was baptised 20 Aug 1837 in the Wesleyan Methodist Church [34] She married 17 Dec 1867, James, son of Jacob Culbert of the Mall, Westport, Co Mayo Witnesses were Samuel D Bournes and Davis R Sand [35]

(4) George Claudius Bournes, born 28 July 1838, was baptised 19 Aug 1838 in the Wesleyan Methodist Church [36] In 1857 he emigrated to the United States and became a soldier in the Army serving six years before being discharged He married and resided in Oregon Letters written about 1866 indicate that he had a child, Annie Lincoln Bournes [37]

(5) William Fletcher Bournes, born 8 April 1840, was baptised 10 May 1840, in the Wesleyan Methodist Church [38] He joined the South Mayo Militia and eventually became a member of the 88th Foot in 1859 [39] In Dec of 1860, he sailed from Liverpool to New York and finally settled in California [40]

[29] Thawley Herald, issue of 30 Aug 1849, Custom House Register
[30] Higgins Papers, National Library of Australia, Canberra, Australia MS 1057.
[31] Ibid
[32] Ibid
[33] Ibid
[34] Ballina Circuit Baptisms 1836-1946
[35] Methodist Registers, Westport Marriages 1864-1897
[36] Ballina Circuit Baptisms, op cit
[37] Higgins Papers, op cit
[38] Ballina Circuit Baptisms, op cit
[39] Higgins Papers, op cit
[40] Ibid

(6) Edward Harding Young Bournes born 11 April 1841, was baptised 23 May 1841 in the Wesleyan Methodist Church.[41] He emigrated to Quebec via Londonderry in 1862 but returned to Ireland In Nov of 1865, he again emigrated, this time to Queensland, Australia [42]

(7) Samuel Davis Bournes, born 25 Aug 1842, was baptised 2 Oct 1842 in the Wesleyan Methodist Church [43] He was a volunteer in the South Mayo Militia and became a member of the 88th Foot [44] Samuel D Bournes was married to Anne_____ and died 23 July 1876, aged 33, in Castlebar.[45] They had issue

a Samueleta Davis Eliza Bournes, born 7 Jan 1877, was baptised 8 April 1877 [46]

(8) Henry Osborne Bournes, born 26 Nov 1844, was baptised 9 March 1845 [47] In 1859 he went to sea with Captain McNeely of Sligo [48]

iii Samuel Bournes q v

iv John Ormsby Bournes, born ca 1797, was possibly a son of George Bournes of Moyne He married 19 Dec 1824, Margaret, born ca 1804, daughter of Hugh O'Donel of Erris by Mary daughter of John Martin Rogers of Castlebar The witnesses to this marriage were Samuel Bournes and Benjamin Wilson [49] John O Bournes and his wife resided in the Parish of Kilmoremoy and he died there, 13 Sept 1837, aged 40, buried in the Ardnaree Cemetery [50] His widow spent the remainder of her life in Belmullet, Co Mayo where she died in 1890 They had no issue [51]

II Samuel Bournes of Killala, Co Mayo and later of Rossport, Erris, was the youngest son of George Bournes of Moyne He was born ca 1798 and married Maria, born ca. 1809, the

[41] Ballina Circuit Baptisms, op cit

[42] Higgins Papers, op cit

[43] Ballina Circuit Baptisms, op cit

[44] Higgins Papers, op cit

[45] Custom House Register

[46] Castlebar Baptisms, Wesleyan Methodist Church, 1829-1954

[47] Ballina Circuit Baptisms, op cit

[48] Higgins Papers, op cit

[49] Register of the Parish of Kilmoremoy Rosemary ffolliott's family records It is interesting that a Benjamin Wilson was a witness to this marriage The name "Wilson" is found in the Hatley Bournes family and it is also found in another connection with the Rossport family From the *Tirawley Herald*, issue of 3 Feb 1847 "On the 27th of Jan at Rossport House, Erris, seat of Samuel Bournes, Esq , died Miss Marie Wilson deeply and devotedly regretted ' It would appear that there was some relationship, other than friendship, between the Wilson and Bournes families

[50] Register of the Parish of Kilmoremoy, Ardnaree Cemetery gravestone inscription

[51] *Irish Times*, issue of 20 Jan 1967 (See Rosemary ffolliott's "Two Fairy Stories ")

youngest daughter of the late Andrew Watts of Ballinglen, Co. Mayo by Anne_____, 16 October 1827 at Ballycastle, Co Mayo [52] He was a landlord, Chairman of the Belmullet Union in 1854 and a Trustee of the Belmullet and Rossport Methodist Church, 1859 [53] Samuel Bournes died 30 April 1864, aged 66, and his wife died 14 January 1864, aged 55, at Rossport where they were buried [54] The administration of his estate was granted in 1864 to his eldest son, George Smith Bournes, then of Clara, King's Co [55] They had issue

  i George Smith Bournes q v

 ii Anna Maria Bournes was baptised 19 Sept 1830 in the Parish of Killala and was married 2 March 1852 at the Belmullet Church, Co Mayo, by the Rev Daniel Foley, to Rev Thomas William Baker, Wesleyan Missionary of Ennis and son of William Baker, Gent of Rossport The marriage was witnessed by "J W Faussett and George S Bourns "[56] Anna Maria died 15 March 1875 and was buried in the Rossport Cemetery [57]

 iii Andrew Watts Bournes was born ca 1835 and died unmarried 1 July 1865, aged 30, at Rossport He was buried in the Rossport Cemetery [58]

 iv William Henry Bournes, born ca 1838, was admitted licentiate 9 Dec 1855 to the Royal College of Surgeons and Physicians, Dublin; M D Queen's University, Belfast 1859; Member of the Royal College of Surgeons, England 1860, L M Coombe Lying-in-Hospital, Dublin 1860 and Medical Officer of the Ballycroy Dispensary, District of Newport Union 1861 [59] In 1861, he resided at Castlehill, Ballycroy, Ballina, Co Mayo and in 1862 was of Prospect House, Belmullet in this same county He continued to live there until his marriage 29 May 1867, when he was described as residing at Ballycastle, near Killala, Co Mayo. Dr Bournes married Elizabeth Anne, born ca 1842, eldest daughter of Thomas Burgess, Esq of 27 Royal Terrace, Kingstown, Co Dublin, in the Monkstown Church, Co Dublin The ceremony was performed by the Rev Allen Wilde and the attendants were Henry

[52] *Ballina Impartial*, issue of 22 Oct 1827

[53] Methodist Church Register List of Lessees and Trustees of Belmullet and Rossport Wesleyan Chapels, 9 May 1859

[54] Custom House Register, Rossport Cemetery gravestone inscription

[55] P R O Dublin Will Index

[56] *Tirawley Herald*, issue of 4 March 1852

[57] Rossport Cemetery gravestone inscription

[58] *Tirawley Herald*, issue of 6 July 1865, Rossport Cemetery gravestone inscription

[59] Medical Directory of 1861

and Mary Bournes, Dr Bournes' brother and sister [60] In 1871, he and his family resided at Killala [61] Dr Bournes died 16 Jan 1875, aged 37, and was buried in the Killala Cemetery [62] His wife died 26 April 1887, aged 45, at her parents' Kingstown home She was buried in Mt Jerome Cemetery, Dublin.[63] They had issue

(1) Samuel Burgess Bournes who died 26 May 1874, aged 5, at Killala [64]

(2) Nannie Maria Robinson Bournes who died 22 Feb 1870 at Ballycastle, in infancy [65]

(3) Thomas Henry Charles Wilson Bournes, born 17 Oct 1871, was baptised 29 Oct 1871 [66] He died 15 March 1887 at 15 Tivoli Terrace, Kingstown, Co Dublin, and was buried in Mt Jerome Cemetery [67]

(4) Maria Elizabeth Watts Bournes, born 15 April 1873, was baptised 12 Oct 1873 [68] She died 12 Jan 1874, in infancy at Killala [69]

(5) William Henry Bournes (birth date unknown) of Kelso Junction, Natal, South Africa was educated at Meath Hospital Dublin His degrees are given as L R C P I , L M , L R C S I and L M 1906 He was District Surgeon Ngotshe and Captain of the South African Medical Corps [70] Dr Bournes died, 16 June 1960 unmarried, at Umzinto, Natal, South Africa [71]

v   Henry Ormsby Bournes, born ca 1839, died 12 March 1873, aged 34, unmarried at Beechmont, Clara, King's Co He was an accountant [72]

vi   Mary Bournes who was living at Rossport, unmarried in 1876 [73]

When Samuel, youngest son of George Bournes of Moyne, acquired the land of Rossport in 1832 he began to make plans

[60] Higgins Papers, op cit According to the Custom House Register of Marriages they were married 5 June 1867 Other information from the *Tirauley Herald*, issue of 13 June 1867

[61] Medical Register 1862, date of registration 3 March 1860

[62] Memorial Inscription to Dr Bournes in the Rossport Cemetery

[63] Custom House Register, Mt Jerome Cemetery records

[64] Custom House Register

[65] *Ibid*

[66] Methodist Register, Ballina Circuit

[67] Mt Jerome Cemetery records

[68] Methodist Register, Ballina Circuit

[69] Custom House Register

[70] Medical Directory, 1952

[71] Master of the Supreme Court, Pietermaritzburg, South Africa

[72] Custom House Register

[73] Methodist Register, Visitation Lists of 1873 and 1876

to build a home there. The site for this home was chosen at
Gort na hAscaile (the Field of the Arm) where there was a
sufficiently deep harbour for large boats [74] Transportation to
western Mayo during this period was mostly by water for the
existing roads were such that travel by land was both slow
and hazardous

The Sean-Mháistir (the Old Master), as Samuel Bournes
was known locally, built Rossport House, called An Teach
Mór, or the "Big House," with the help of his tenants Tenants
at this time were obligated, in addition to paying rent, to
provide their landlord with twelve days free labor a year With
these *Dualgas* days, as they were called, and with additional
remunerative labor, the necessary work was completed. Beside
the home for his family, Samuel Bournes eventually erected
homes for relatives, built a police barrack, a Protestant church
and also cultivated previously unclaimed land and created
parks and gardens [75]

It is said in the Corduff manuscript that the Bournes
family moved to their new home shortly before 1847, or before
the famine years It is more likely that they actually came to
Erris at least ten years earlier, perhaps in the latter part of
the 1830's.[76] At that time there was no road nearer to Rossport
than Belderrig (Béal Deirg), about 18 miles away "The family
traveled by farm carts and horseback along the road to Belderrig, thence along the cliffs to Shraughattagle (Straith an
Seagail) on horseback and on foot, and put up for the night
in the house of Thomas Garvin   ."[77]

"The next morning the Rossport Tenantry met the Bournes
there as pre-arranged, taking with them to Shraughattagle any

[74] Michael Corduff, "Notes on Erris," *Irish Folklore Commission*, (1941), Vol I,
p 619

[75] *Ibid*, pp 12-17

[76] Mr Corduff tells an interesting story in Vol I, pp 18-19 about his own grandfather who assisted Samuel Bournes in the family's move to Erris by carrying George
Smith Bournes, the eldest son, on his back George Smith, as will subsequently be cited,
was baptised 10 Dec 1828 and in 1847 would have been about 19 years of age This
would seem to indicate that the event described by Mr Corduff took place some years
before 1847

[77] Corduff, op cit, p 17

available blankets, quilts and clothing to serve as covering for the younger members of the Bournes family in their trek across the mountains . to Rossport. They traveled via Muing na lee (Muing na Laogh) which is now a small townland near Porturlin (Port Urlainn) across the moors to where Gianny (Greannaigh) Chapel now stands and came on to the estuary at the 'Island' There was strand at the particular hour of their arrival [and] . . the tide was out Presumably, the time had been arranged to facilitate their passage across the strand from the Cornboy (Corán Buí) side to Rossport All the way from Shraughattagle, they had been escorted and assisted by the Rossport inhabitants The procession wended its way along the strand until it reached the mouth of the Fiodán, or as it is yet known Bun an Eddain (Bun an Fhiodáin) From here, there was an old pathway leading to an old road known as Bóthar Caonachain, Keenaghan's Road The procession meanwhile gradually swelled by the reinforcement of more numbers of men and women, old and young, as well as children. Along this old road they came as far as the present 'cross-roads' and finally reached the 'Big House,' a few hundred yards distant at Gort na hAscaile . "[78]

Accompanying Samuel Bournes were his wife, their six children, his mother-in-law, Anne Watts, his mother, Mary Bournes, and several domestic servants Relatives eventually came to reside also at Rossport.[79]

The scanchas[80] related in the Corduff manuscript give us some idea of Samuel Bournes' character. We find that he was

---

[78] Corduff, op cit, pp 17-18

[79] Corduff, op cit, p 20 "Mrs McOrmond, a sister of Anne Watts, came to live at Rossport and occupied a house built for her by the landlord on the hillside near the old R I C Barracks Her niece, Miss Mary Bournes, lived with her and the field attached to the house is locally known to the present day as 'Páirc Miss Mary' (Miss Mary's Park)"

[80] Scanchas means a friendly chat, reminiscence and story telling In penal times when the Irish were not allowed an education their only method of recording news and other events was by "registering" them on the brain These stories would pass from father to son It is known that some story-tellers could re-tell a story a number of times and not add or subtract as much as one word in doing so This was proven by making several recordings of the same story

a stern and exacting master but he was also a humane and thoughtful landlord

During the famine years of 1846 to 1848, there was a complete failure of the potato crop The potato blight first made its appearance in the summer of 1846 shortly before the crop was ready Consequently, there were scarcely any potatoes that year and as there were no seeds for future planting the situation was critical "Potatoes, fish and stirabout from home grown cereal were the exclusive articles of diet among the peasantry . . "[81] with the potato forming the principal part of their meals. Stirabout represented only a small fraction of their food and, in the absence of the staple diet, many died throughout the country It was therefore a great achievement that "in Rossport and adjacent localities no one died of direct starvation during these terrible years Of course people were hungry and had to resort to eating turnips, cabbages and even certain wild roots, called Buscorlawon."[82]

"At Rossport and other places along the seashore where there were estuaries and strands, the people made extensive use of shell fish, cockles, limpets, periwinkles, bonndals,[53] razor fish etc. etc Little fish caught under the stones and rocks of the sea shore, sand eels, flukes and numerous other kinds of inshore Crúsach[54] were also eaten In addition there was a daily ration of Indian Meal (Min Bhuí) stirabout supplied to every person at the 'Big House' boiler The boiler was a huge iron tank and was continually in operation for the feeding of the hungry With all the faults and harshness traditionally attributed to landlordism, it redounds to the memory and credit of the Bournes that they worked indefatigably to preserve the peoples' lives from the scourge of famine "[85]

[81] Corduff op cit , p 28

[82] Corduff, op cit , p 29

[83] Bonndal, a pear shaped shell about ten times larger than periwinkles, found buried to a depth of twelve inches in the strand

[84] Crusach includes periwinkles, limpets sloak and trípéad The latter two grow on the rocks under high water level and are a satiny type of seaweed

[85] Corduff, op cit , p 30

In minor illnesses or accidents, Samuel Bournes himself ministered to the afflicted, and it was said that in his youth he had studied to become a doctor When a serious case appeared, he sent for his son, Dr William Henry Bournes, then residing in Belmullet, who made no charge for his services "Though a stern taskmaster, Samuel Bournes was a charitable man and he did a good deal to uplift his tenants . Many instances of his charity and benevolence are traditionally recorded "[86]

During the famine years, Samuel Bournes, in addition to supplying stirabout to the people, "had hookers plying between Westport and Rossport carrying meal, as well as bread. He also had smaller craft of his own which used to make frequent runs to Belmullet, where he had a store "[87] Most of the transportation of that day was by sea and curraghs[88] were more numerous than they are now

The wife of Samuel Bournes was affectionately called Maisteras Ruadh (red haired mistress), and apparently she interceded on behalf of any tenant who was in difficulty with her husband, the Sean-Mháistir [89] Her charms and kindliness were extolled in an Ode composed by a local poet of Erris Much of the precise meaning and poetry is lost through translation, and the original version is given below for those who can read the Irish language [90]

An Máistreá Ruadh

Tá Máistreas Bournes gan gruaim,
Ar Thaoibh an Chnuic seo thuas,
Agus na h-areagáin go buan
　　dá breágadh

---

[86] Corduff, op cit , p 36

[87] *Ibid*

[88] Curraghs are a type of rowboat However, they are not planked or sheeted but have a strong gunwale with light ribs covered with calico The calico is given two coats of boiled tar and pitch so it will be watertight

[89] Corduff, op cit , p 372

[90] *Ibid* "Mistress Bournes is without a frown/On the hillside here above/And the organs playing her a constant lullaby/Her throat is whiter than/The wave's foam on the strand/And the windswept snow on the mountain top

Is gile a píobán agus a bráighe,
Ná cúbhai na tuinne ai thráigh,
Agus ná sneachta séidthe ai
bhan sléibhe

In 1855, when Mary Bournes, the mother of Samuel, died she was buried in Kilgalligan (Cill Challigan) Cemetery which is northwest of Rossport and was the burial place of the Bournes families of Carrowteige, Portacloy and Stonefield. While the Bournes were all Protestant, the cemetery was Catholic dedicated to St. Galligan Anne Watts and two domestics died about this same time and they also were interred at Kilgalligan. When Samuel Bournes built a Protestant church with a lofty belfry[91] at Rossport, he had his mother and mother-in-law reinterred there Mr Baker, a Protestant minister, then living at Rossport, officiated at the burial [92] The two domestics were presumably Catholic and for that reason were not re-buried at Rossport Cemetery.[93]

"On the night the burial at Rossport took place, the banshee was heard near the 'Big House' as well as other unearthly crying. The crying and wailing was believed to be the result of the separation of the bodies of the two ladies from those of the two servants who were so devoted to them in life."[94]

An interesting tale entitled "The Man with One Eye" is contained in the Corduff manuscripts It concerns the Bournes of Rossport and is set forth below [95]

"Some years before the famine a poor woman of Rossport was visited by a strange one-eyed man who warned her not to touch a certain tree which stood by a well on the site of a prehistoric cemetery She said, 'You will have a bite to eat,' and she proceeded to ladle some stirabout, which was cooking in a

---

[91] Samuel Bournes built a Wesleyan Methodist Chapel at Rossport The cornerstone, according to family letters, was laid in Oct 1850 by "Uncle McCormick" Higgins Papers, op cit

[92] Mr Baker was Thomas William Baker, a Methodist clergyman, who became Samuel Bournes' son-in-law in 1852

[93] Corduff, op cit , pp 20-21

[94] Ibid, p 21

[95] Corduff, op cit , Vol III, pp 233-240

pot beside the fire, into a vessel to give the old man On raising
herself from her stooping position over the pot and looking
towards the place where the old man was sitting, she saw that
he had disappeared.

"She looked out of the door but he was not to be seen
anywhere so she then called to the houses next door to make
inquiries, but nothing whatever was known about him there
The inhabitants of these houses had not seen the man at all
and the strange old man was never seen from that day 'till
this The unanimous conclusion of the people was that he was
not a living man at all but a spirit—the spirit of the old man,
who was, it was presumed, long dead.

"The woman then told the neighbors . . . the purpose of
his mission and they were glad and grateful that they had been
apprised in time They were all quite satisfied as to the truth
of the woman's story relative to punishments in the shape of
losses and accidents sustained by quite a number of people
who had been tampering with the forbidden tree. For instance,
one man got seriously ill and barely recovered, another broke
his arm, a child was badly burned, animals died or were
drowned etc., all under rather mysterious circumstances, now
ascertained to be the penalty for their thoughtlessness and
wantonness.

"After the visit of the mysterious stranger there was no
further damage done to the forbidden tree, and it was allowed
to flourish and grow until it became a fine and stately tree
It is said that sometimes people use to pray there, though
the spring never acquired the character of a holy well   The
belief was that it had spiritual associations and the fact that
it was situated in the vicinity of the 'stone circle' with its
supposedly subterranean passage to the sea and Crocán a'
Chollata,[96] or Chodhatia, a high mound of earth . . believed
to be an ancient burial ground, lent additional evidence and

---

[96] Crocán a' Chollata means literally mound or hillock of the sleep

colour in the traditional sanctity of Tobar na Craoibhe (well
of the tree).

"Time passed and so did the people and a new generation
sprung up Landlord Bournes and his family and relatives
came to live in Rossport and he built the 'Big House' quite
convenient to Tobar na Craoibhe He reclaimed the wild lands
and mountain adjoining, built walls and roads and carried out
a comprehensive scheme of reconstruction and reclamation on
his estate in the course of which he gave a good deal of employment to his tenantry during the days of the Great Famine one
hundred years ago   .

"In the course of his development works in the neighborhood of his residence, Tobar na Craoibhe came in for attention
under the scheme He decided to have it reconstructed with
walls around it, to have it deepened with stone steps leading
down to it, water pipes and other fittings inserted and so on.
The tree, he decided, was an obstruction and should go Workmen were loath to embark on the work and many of the local
people positively refused to tamper at all with the old well.
There was much comment about what was considered to be
the profanation of a spot of such cherished traditions, and of
Protestants and their faith The Bournes, who were Protestant, became the subject of much hostile criticism

"Many of the Rossport people risked the displeasure of
the landlord by refusing to work on the well and had angry
and bitter controversies with him in the course of which he
threatened their eviction and expulsion from Rossport It is
said of one man who was so threatened that on one occasion
he said to Mr Bournes, 'I will, please God, be living in Rossport when the worms will be eating your body in the ground
and there will be my descendants in Rossport in days to come,
when there will not be a trace of even one of your posterity
here Your 'Big House' and your 'preaching house' will be
yet a rookery for the crows, and so will all your other big
houses and buildings ' It appeared that the only comment
the landlord made to this abusive tirade was, 'Well! you may

be right None of us knows what the future has in store for us
Time in its passage is ever and always working and leaving
changes in its trail but I am not going to be deterred from
carrying out my projects through any uncanny fears of
superstitious evil I do not give in to such silly nonsense If
you and your kind were less addicted to superstition and
ghostly beliefs and carried out your work in a practical and
sensible manner, ye would be much better off '

"Mr Bournes did not inflict any punishment on the man
for his refusal to work and subsequent invective He was
allowed to carry on and live in Rossport unhindered by the
landlord who was a man of wisdom and foresight and took
little notice of occasional altercations with tenants and workmen on whom he looked more with compassion than disfavor.
He was very diplomatic and knew how to handle them and
get the best out of them No doubt the insubordinate conduct
at times was disturbing but he was diplomatic enough to over-
look the ideology and theories of a people who were so steeped
in tradition and an ancient culture

"Mr Bournes would not, of course, be dissuaded from
going on with the contemplated work on Tobar na Craoibhe . . .
And then it was said, an old woman of the village who use to
do odd chores at the 'Big House' went specially to the landlord
and implored him to desist from further development work on
the well and above all not to root up the tree, or that surely
wrath would fall on himself and his family and descendants,
because the project was nothing short of desecration 'Ah!' said
Mr Bournes, 'This is more of the superstition I have already
been warned of dire consequences on account of the work, but
I cannot allow the place to remain there as it stands—an eye-
sore in front of my hall door I may say, the well is of little or
no value as it stands and I need not tell you I am not afraid
the fairies or spirits will harm me for improvement of the
place, so I cannot possibly abandon the idea. The work must
go ahead ' 'Oh! very well then,' said the old woman, 'Some
day you will have reason to remember my warning.'

"And so the work was carried out, the tree was uprooted and a regular transformation of the scene was affected. It looked new and nice but the old glories and familiar old objects had disappeared to the regret of the old people Mr Bournes and his family were by now at the height of their prosperity and their interests flourished But within twelve months of the completion of the new 'Big House Well,' by which name it was then called, Mr Bournes' son, Andrew, contracted glanders from one of his father's horses and suffered for a long time until he died. This was the beginning of the flow of trouble that befell the Bournes family. One calamity on top of another followed Mrs Bournes, the landlord's wife, died a short time after and the old gentlemen himself, Mr Bournes, who was not much over sixty years of age   died suddenly out on the field and, be it noted, very convenient to Tobar na Craoibhe. The surviving members of the family went away one by one to England and the place was let to English gentlemen who individually made it their abode for a time Houses which were built for and occupied by ex-Army and Navy officers became vacant and fell into disrepair and final dilapidation. The church, or 'preaching house' as the natives called it, was deserted and fell into ruins The old Royal Irish Constabulary barracks, another of the Bournes' hereditaments, is now also a ruin The only edifice which has survived, though only in a decaying condition, is the old 'Big House' itself which now houses the local Civic Guards [97] One exception to all this decay and decadence is the Lodge, originally built for a Protestant clergyman, which now stands well preserved and flourishing.[98]

"Within a comparatively short number of years, all this ruin and devastation overtook the Bournes. It appears there are very few of the grandchildren of the old landlord, Samuel

[97] Today Rossport House is used as a secondary school, known as Coláiste Chomáin It was named after St. Coman for the old Kilcommon Church across the estuary from the school

[98] The Lodge eventually became the residence of Robert Buchanan, noted author and poet (Corduff, Vol V , p 47), and later the home of the Corduff family

Bournes, living today One of them, a son of William Bournes M D , living in South Africa visited Rossport a few years ago and inspected the little Protestant cemetery where lie the bones of his ancestors After all the glory and power of the Bournes in Rossport was comparatively short-lived, but it must be admitted that it was sufficiently long to enable the landlord to leave many useful works executed on the estate—works which endure to the present day.

"With all their faults, the Bournes of Rossport were good and charitable people who helped to preserve the natives from starvation during the Great Famine. May the Lord have mercy on their souls and so ends my tale of the ghostly one-eyed man of 'Tobar na Craoibhe ' "

III George Smith Bournes, the eldest son and heir to the land of Rossport, was baptised 10 December 1828 in the Parish of Killala He married 5 July 1855, at the Westport Church, Co Mayo, Elizabeth Hartley Isabella, eldest daughter of the late Charles P Wallace (who died 27 Oct 1854 at Belmullet),[99] Resident Magistrate of Lime Park, Co Galway and at one time of the 40th Regiment of Foot The marriage was witnessed by S McCormick and Horatio Wallace.[100] A memorial of indenture of marriage settlement was dated 5 July 1855 and made between "Samuel Bourns, Esq of Rossport House of the first part; George Smith Bourns, son of Samuel Bourns, of the second part, Anne Wallace of Westport, widow and relict of Charles P. Wallace, Esq , late of Balmullet, Stipendary Magistrate of the third part; Elizabeth Wallace daughter of Anne Wallace of the fourth part, William Wallace, Esq of Athlone, Co Roscommon and Henry William Faussett, Esq of Glen House, Co Mayo of the fifth part."[101]

George Smith Bournes was Clerk of the Union of Belmullet in 1853 and Chairman of the Fishery Conservators, Bangor

---

[99] *Tirawley Herald,* issue of 2 Nov 1854
[100] *Ibid,* issue of 12 July 1855, Custom House Register
[101] Registry of Deeds #1855 25 165

District in 1858 [102] He and his father were Trustees in 1859 of the Belmullet and Rossport Methodist Church [103] He resided at Rossport House until about 1865 when he was of Beechmont, Clara, King's Co [104] By 1881, he and his family had moved to England where he was a partner in the firm of Dolton, Bournes and Dolton, London timber importers They lived at Cambridge House, the Grove, Blackheath, Kent where he died 20 September 1910 His wife died there 19 August 1902.

George Smith Bournes had always been interested in his family's ancestry and, as a child, was attracted by a coat of arms which his father displayed in the living room of Rossport House He knew the family's tradition was of an early ancestor who received a grant of land, for valour, during the reign of William III Presumably he also knew the Bournes had the right to bear arms for when he applied for a confirmation, it was subsequently granted, 15 October 1901. This confirmation was made to him and to his descendants and the other descendants of his father, Samuel Bournes of Rossport House, by Sir Arthur E Vicars, Ulster King of Arms [105]

It is known that the arms of a family are often a clue to their early origin so with this in mind we asked the Genealogical Office, Dublin if their records might provide further information on the ancestry of the Rossport Bournes Unfortunately, they were unable to help, so correspondence was initiated with the College of Arms, London. Conceivably, a Bourne(sic) family of England might have had similar arms and thus a common origin.

On 17 March 1965 the following reply was received from J P Brook-Little, Bluemantle Pursuivant of Arms, College of Arms, London

"He [George Smith Bournes] was granted a version of a coat used by

---

[102] *Tirawley Herald*, issues of 20 Oct 1853 and 11 Sept 1858
[103] Methodist Register, List of Lessees and Trustees of Belmullet and Rossport, dated 9 May 1859
[104] In 1922 King's Co became known as Co Offaly
[105] Genealogical Office, Dublin M S no 111 See Frontispiece

certain families of Burn in Scotland The Scottish books of arms show that in about 1757, arms were matriculated by Burne of Coldoch, which may be blazoned Or a Crescent Gules between two Spur Rowels in chief and a hunting horn in base, Sable Again in 1757 Edward Burn of Lisburn, Portugal matriculated the following coat Or in chief two Spur Rowels Sable and in base a hunting horn of the second stringed and garnished Vert In the grant of George Smith Bournes the field was divided per chevron and the colors altered, but the basic pattern of two Spur Rowels in chief and a hunting horn in base was maintained .

"A great many Irish families came to Ireland from Scotland and no doubt there was a traditional Scottish descent in the Bournes family it would be very difficult to establish whether there was in fact such a descent or whether the family descended from one of the English families of Bourne There are several families of this name, bearing arms, but the arms they bear are in no way similar to the arms of Burn of Scotland Generally speaking they consist of rampant lions either in conjunction with a chevron or a bend "

While the result of this search was disappointing and inconclusive it was felt that in the interest of giving as complete an accounting as possible, this information should be included in our review

George Smith Bournes and Elizabeth H I Wallace Bournes had issue

   i Anna Maria Bournes, born 29 April 1856 at Rossport, was baptised 11 May 1856 by her uncle, Rev Thomas W Baker [106] She died 13 March 1860 at 49 Longwood Ave, Dublin, aged 4, and buried in Mt Jerome Cemetery, Dublin [107]

  ii Caroline Wallace Bournes, born ca 1859 at Rossport, died 6 March 1860 at 49 Longwood Ave, Dublin, aged 1 She was buried in Mt Jerome Cemetery Dublin [108]

 iii Anna Maria Caroline Wallace Bournes, born 5 Aug 1861 at Rossport, was baptised 10 Aug 1861 [109]

  iv Maria Louisa Bournes, born 3 April 1863 at Beechmont, King's Co died 24 Oct 1918 unmarried at St Peter's Vicarage, Ipswich, England She resided, prior to death, at 22 Landsdown Road, Kent [110]

---

[106] Higgins Papers, National Library of Australia, Canberra, Australia MS 1507
[107] *Tirawley Herald*, issues of 8 May 1856, 17 March 1860, Methodist Registers of Erris Baptisms 1851-1861, Mt Jerome Cemetery Records
[108] *Tirawley Herald*, issue of 10 March 1860, Mt Jerome Cemetery Records
[109] Methodist Registers of Erris Baptisms 1851-1861
[110] *Tirawley Herald*, issue of 11 April 1863, Somerset House, London

    v Emily Frances Edith Bournes was born probably at Beechmont, Clara, King's Co [111] She married the Rev Edwin Coupland Aspinall in 1892 He was Vicar of Whernstead, near Ipswich, born in 1862, son of Joseph Aspinall of Birkenhead, Co Cheshire by Helen Beresford Shirley, daughter of Captain Shirley, Newdick, H E I C S. They had issue [112]

        (1) George Shirley Coupland Aspinall, born 10 July 1895

        (2) Marjorie Marigold Aspinall, born 16 Oct 1896, married C A Bender and resides in Shaftesbury, Dorset, England

        (3) Elizabeth Beresford Aspinall, died in infancy

        (4) Frank Aspinall, died in infancy

        (5) Wallace Bournes Aspinall O B E , born 27 Jan 1900, was a Brigadier of Naivasha, Kenya, Africa He married, and died 27 July 1965 at Docklow House, Herefordshire, England [113]

        (6) Helen Beresford Aspinall, born 28 Jan 1902, married _____ Roscow

        (7) Harry Haworth Aspinall, born 11 Sept 1904

        (8) Nora Crena Aspinall, born 17 April 1906, married _____ Newson and resides in Richmond, Surrey, England

    vi Samuel George Bournes, born ca 1866, died 25 July 1871, aged 5, at Beechmont, Clara, King's Co He was buried in Mt Jerome Cemetery, Dublin [114]

    vii Henrietta Marian Bournes was born 3 April 1867 in Beechmont, Clara, King's Co She died 20 Aug 1930[115] unmarried at 22 Landsdown Road, Kent

    viii Georgina Elizabeth Bournes was probably born in Beechmont, King's Co 14 June 1869 [116] In 1942 she resided at 68 Belmont Park, Lewisham, London and died unmarried 6 Jan 1944 at the Vicarage, Dunmow, Essex, England [117]

    ix Charles Wallace Bournes, born ca 1870, died 31 July 1871 in Beechmont, King's Co , aged 1 year He was buried in Mt Jerome Cemetery, Dublin [118]

    x George Henry Bournes was born 4 July 1873 in Beechmont,

---

[111] A daughter named Emily is referred to in letters written by George Smith Bournes to Rev John Higgins during 1861-1865 Higgins Papers, cp cit

[112] Henry Oswald Aspinall, *The Aspinwall and Aspinall Families*, (1923), pp 166-177.

[113] *London Daily Telegraph*, issue of 28 July 1965

[114] Custom House Register Mt Jerome Cemetery records

[115] Custom House Register, Somerset House, London

[116] Custom House Register, The christian name of the daughter born to the Bournes is not given in the Register However, a baby called Georgina, is referred to in letters written by George Smith Bournes about this time Higgins Papers, op cit

[117] Somerset House, London

[118] Custom House Register, Mt Jerome Cemetery records

King's Co [119] He was educated at the Blackheath Proprietory, Pensioner, Corpus Christi, 1893, B A Cantab 1898 ordained Deacon by the Bishop of Marlborough 1899; curate of St Philip's Bethnal Green 1899-1900, curate Oakham Rutland 1900 [120] During World War 1, he was attached to the Royal Engineers [121] and died 31 March 1921 at Solingen, Germany at which time he was with the 3rd Battalion of Royal Scots He was unmarried [122]

xi Elizabeth Ada Wallace Bournes who married _____Kerr and had issue of five children [123]

xii Daughter who married L T Molesworth She died in 1933 at the Vicarage, Dunmow, England and left issue [124]

(1) Elizabeth Wallace Molesworth married 3 Dec 1918, the Rev Edward Noel Mellish at St Paul's Deptford Rev Mellish, born 24 Dec 1880 at Oakleigh Park Barnet, North London, was the son of Edward and Mary Mellish He was educated at Saffron Walden Grammer School, served as a trooper in the South-African War, with Baden-Powell's Police from Dec 1900 to the end of the war, ordained in 1912, becoming curate of St Paul's Deptford, served in European War as the Acting Army Chaplain, May 1915 to Feb 1919 and was awarded the Victorian Cross 20 April 1916 He became vicar of St Mark's Church, Lewisham [125] They had issue

(2) Daughter

Anne Bournes

III Anne Bournes, only child of Henry Bournes by his first wife, Frances Watts, was born in February 1825 at her father's home in Crossmolina, Co Mayo [126] She spent much of her childhood, and later as a young girl, "staying with her uncle, Samuel Bournes, who had married her mother's sister Her uncle's house at Rossport faced the Greyhound River and the

[119] Custom House Register

[120] Crockford (1901) Venn's Alumni Cantabriensis

[121] *Ibid* This record states that he fell during active service in 1919

[122] Land Commission, Dublin, Probate of Will Further information obtained from the Army Records Center, London says that "Corporal G H Bournes, Royal Fusiliers attached to the Intelligence Corps died 31 March 1921 and was buried at Cologne, Southern Cemetery " It is believed that his complete service record was destroyed during World War II

[123] Stonefield Bournes family records

[124] *Ibid*, Somerset House, London, Will of Georgina E Bournes.

[125] Sir O'Moore Creagh and E M Humphries, ed , *The V C. and D S O*, Vol I, pp 207-208

[126] Register of the Parish of Crossmolina

Atlantic,[127] and Anne Bournes used to walk for miles along
that wild coast .   "[128]

When Anne went to a Dublin boarding-school, she traveled
from Connaught on a horse-drawn barge via the Royal Canal
"She received a sound education, especially in music and a
rather rhetorical French What she used to call her 'pro-
nunciation, enunciation and punctuation' had been well
guarded from her earliest days by her mother's mother, 'Mama
Watts,' a great purist, who used to read family prayers with
memorable dignity When Anne returned home from boarding-
school it was to a place, where. owing to her step-mother's
character and unfriendliness, studies and music had to be
given up . ."[129]

In her early twenties, Anne was courted by a young Methodist clergyman, John Higgins It is quite likely that John
Higgins' family and the Bournes family were acquainted long
before the young people became aware of each other Social
life in Mayo was largely confined to the area in which one
lived and the Higgins of Ballina and the Bournes of Crossmolina were only a few miles apart

John Higgins. born in May 1819 and baptised 14 May
1819 in the Parish of Kilmoremoy, was the eldest son of James
Higgins,[130] Gentleman of Ballina, and Frances Atkinson,

---

[127] Actually Rossport House faces the Sruwaddacon (Sruth Fada Con), at one time a
large channel Sruwaddacon means the Long Current of the Hound and may be the
reason why the family knew it as "The Greyhound River"

[128] Nettie Palmer, *Henry Bournes Higgins, A Memoir*, (London 1931), p 7

[129] *Ibid*, p 8

[130] James Higgins (1792-1857) was the only son of John Higgins, or O'Higgins, of
Ballina, Co Mayo and Fanny de Misset He married Frances Atkinson (1792-1844)
and had seven children, all born in Ballina John Higgins George Higgins, born 25 Aug
1821, was baptised 29 Aug 1821 and died 1 Oct 1873 without surviving issue, James
Higgins, no date of birth known, who died unmarried, William Higgins, born 14 Jan
1829, was baptised 16 Feb ' 1829 and died 15 Sept 1829, aged 9 months, Julia Anne
Higgins, born 25 July 1830, was baptised 19 Aug 1830 and married Robert Gildea, Esq.
of Her Majesty's Customs They migrated from Ireland to Cardiff, Wales in Oct 1850,
Charles Higgins, baptised 10 April 1834, migrated to the United States in 1858, Frances
Higgins who also migrated to the United States in 1853 or 1854 and was deceased by
1906 (Sources Register of the Parish of Kilmoremoy, Higgins family letters, "The
Gildea Family Records," compiled by G P Gildea in 1906)

daughter of Charles Atkinson, Esq [131] For a short time after completing his education, John was employed by the Bank of Ireland He then decided, against his father's wishes, to enter the ministry and became a Methodist clergyman in 1842 John was disinherited by his father, who refused to communicate with him from that point on It would appear that the father had some remorse as "the old man was proud of his son, at a distance, and received his wife and children when they visited Mayo, advising her to encourage her husband to write, as he had a gift of expression."[132]

John Higgins enjoyed music, often playing an old Dutch violin As a Connaught man he knew all the Irish airs that other fiddlers played but his music was eventually put to a more serious purpose in training the young people of the Church.[133]

Anne Bournes and John Higgins were married the 17th of May 1848 at the Wesleyan Chapel in Crossmolina. As their marriage was the first to be performed in the Chapel, the Trustees presented them with a bound copy of the Oxford Bible and Wesley Hymns.[134] Anne's "dowry" was a charge against the lands of Rossport amounting to £351 4 6

During their married life in Ireland, Anne and John Higgins lived in many Irish towns. Newtownards, Borrisokane, Killarney, Fermoy, Abbeyleix, Newry, Clonmel and Wexford were at one time or another home to the Higgins family. No matter where they lived, John Higgins always taught his young sons to plant a good garden, to help their mother and to be diligent in their religious reading. Their writing was his special concern and he, with precise instructions, taught the children the art of exquisite penmanship.

Anne's chores were endless for in addition to household

[131] Charles Atkinson, Esq of Ballina married Miss McCarthy Cormack and they had Robert Atkinson, Lieutenant R N , the only son, who died unmarried, Frances Atkinson who married James Higgins and Diana Atkinson who married Anthony Joynt of Ballina (Source "The Gildea Family Records," op cit)

[132] Palmer, op cit , p 5

[133] Palmer, op cit , p 6

[134] *Tirawley Herald*, issue of 18 May 1848

tasks, such as candle making and sewing, she helped the children with their lessons and later even took in a dozen or so little girls as day students She covered her many responsibilities with the help of one devoted and beloved servant, Margaret, who was affectionately called "Bawdit" by the family. In spite of her busy life, she never allowed the young ones to shirk their household chores and she always found quiet moments to instruct them in the New Testament, or to urge that good poetry be memorized "Like the soundest mothers of her generation, she made time for whatever she believed in "[135]

Some years later her son, Henry Bournes Higgins, wrote in his journal recalling memories of this remarkable mother

"A clear, capable brain, a strong will, strong affection, absolutely unselfish, devoted to family! She had a sweet voice for singing, but not forcible When we were children she showed us how to use water-colour paints, when we were lucky enough to have a paint-box (worth a shilling or two) In her old age men who knew her frequently came to enjoy her strong, racy direct talk, and to hear her playing on the piano from memory Not from ear memory—so she always assured us—but from memory of the notes as they stood before her mental eye Some of her old Irish folk-airs were wonderful I recollect in particular her rendering of the *Coolin*, the old lament The pauses in the air, in my mother's setting, were far more impressive than in the setting of Moore's Melodies Until her later years she certainly believed in the banshee of her family (banshee means white lady) who use to come and shriek in the bogs when some one of the family was going to die She had heard the banshee just before her Uncle George died but in her later years she disliked any allusion to it "[136]

John and Anne Higgins sent their four eldest sons to Wesleyan Connexional School. As each son reached his tenth birthday, he left home to begin a formal education within the strict confines of the church boarding-school in Dublin A preacher's child for approximately £20 per annum, exclusive of washing and extras, received a sound education, including the required study of Greek and Latin. These classical subjects were prerequisites for Trinity College and it was taken for

[135] Palmer, op cit , p 9
[136] Palmer, op cit , pp 234-235

granted in those days that all parents desired their sons to enter this school in order to prepare for a profession [137] It was a spartan existence relieved by boxes of homemade food and letters of parental encouragement

The Higgins children looked forward to their vacations from school Returning to the family circle was a welcome change from austerity and strict discipline, and there often was the excitement of a new town to explore as the place of their home varied frequently They also looked forward to occasional visits to Mayo with their mother These trips were no small undertaking and John Higgins usually gave his wife detailed and beautifully written instructions before she embarked on the long tiring journey. Before one such excursion, she was counseled to proceed by train to Dublin, then by one coach or jaunting-car after another, returning the same way "The advice was emphatic never to pay a tip until sure the luggage was aboard, and the final injunction 'Trust in Providence!' was written in the fairest, clearest script of all "[138]

The final stage of many trips to Erris was the long ride from Crossmolina, or Ballina, to Rossport. Bianconi coaches connected these towns with Belmullet so it was necessary, when the coach reached Glenamoy, to leave the comparative comfort of this mode of transportation for a jaunting-car. The car took the family the last miles to their destination. The complete journey of approximately 50 miles lasted eight or nine hours [139]

A trek to Mayo usually included a visit at Crossmolina and a stop with Grandfather Higgins in Ballina The longest stay, however, was at Rossport in western Erris The familiar warm surroundings of Rossport and the opportunity to see

---

[137] Palmer, op cit , p 23

[138] Palmer, op cit , p 6

[139] Charles Bianconi, an Italian, came to Ireland in the early part of the nineteenth century to establish a mail and coach service connecting the principal towns of this country He was extremely successful and subsequently expanded his services In 1840 a mail and coach run began to operate, and continued for approximately twenty years, between Ballina and Belmullet The Bianconi name is still remembered in Ireland and it is not unusual to find this Italian name gracing the sign of a Grill or Pub

close friends and relations drew the Higgins family back time
and again to this remote part of Mayo. Although Anne Higgins was devoted to her father it was not easy to visit his
Crossmolina home and the contrast between the strained
atmosphere there and the congenial environment of Rossport
was great indeed

The days in Erris passed all too quickly and Anne's
children grew to love the rugged coast line, as had their mother
since she was a child Bathing was a special treat, but not
always possible because of the changeable Irish climate There
were, however, many hours spent with the Rossport Bournes
and in visiting friends and distant relations, for the O'Donel,
Carey, Hearne, McCormick and Joynt families all lived in or
near the Rossport community

The ties that bound Anne Higgins and her family to Ireland, especially to Connaught, were strong ones and it was
with reluctance that, in the sixties, they began to think of
migrating to a new country There had been talk of various
places for some time, America was dismissed after a son related
stories of the extreme cold during his stay in New York [140]
Delhi, India was a possibility, as was Natal, South Africa
where several of the Wallace family had previously migrated
Finally, after their eldest son died in 1869, Anne consulted a
Dublin physician about the fragile health of the other children
The doctor stressed that a warmer, drier climate would be
beneficial and the decision to migrate was not to be postponed again Victoria, Australia was decided upon and plans
were made to leave the country of their birth.

A charge on the Rossport lands, settled on Anne at the
time of her marriage, was now paid by her cousin, George
Smith Bournes, and the necessary funds were provided for the
trip John Higgins, unable to leave until he had completed his
year on the Wexford circuit, remained behind with their son,
John Jr Anne, with the six other children, undertook the long

[140] Some of the letters written by John and Anne Higgins' son to his parents may be
found in the Appendix, pp 221-282

trip to Melbourne, sailing from Liverpool in February of 1870 on the cargo vessel "Eurynome " Her husband and son, along with Margaret, joined them the following year

When the "Eurynome" was within a few days of reaching Australia, the baby, Charles, became ill and died at sea. The exhilaration of reaching a new country was dampened by this unhappy event, and Australia, the land of promised health and fresh opportunities must have seemed quite dismal when Anne and the five children viewed it for the first time

"Anne Higgins was not one to take lightly the loss of their adored and youngest child her grief was overwhelming, and she could not hide it None the less, her spirit was indomitable, and she never forgot why they had come to Melbourne, never cast regretful looks behind "[141]

Australia did, however, become all they had hoped The family's health was restored and each child found his own niche, guided, one may be sure, by the energetic and devoted mother John Higgins became a home missionary in Australia until his death 1 February 1895 in Melbourne Anne Bournes Higgins died in 1917 at 92 years of age

Reverend John Higgins and his wife, Anne, had the following children, all born in Ireland

    i James Henry Higgins, the eldest son was born 26 Feb 1849 in Newtownards, Co Down He was educated at the Wesleyan Connexional School, 78-79 St Stephen's Green Dublin and in 1866, at 17 years of age, migrated to the United States He settled in New York City where he found employment [142] Due to poor health, a source of concern to his family, he was forced to return to his parents' home, then in Wexford, Co. Wexford He died in June 1869 and was buried in Selskar Abbey, Wexford

    ii. Henry Bournes Higgins, born 3 June 1851 in Newtownards, Co Down was educated at the Wesleyan Connexional School and in 1870 migrated to Victoria Australia with his mother, three brothers and two sisters In Australia, he attended the University of Melbourne and graduated in 1875, LL B, M A, was called to the Victorian Bar in 1876 and admitted to the English Bar this same year In 1894, he entered politics as M L A for Geelong in the Federal Convention of 1897-1898 and was a member of the

[141] Palmer, op cit, p 57
[142] Higgins Papers, National Library of Australia, Canberra, Australia, MS 1057.

Anne Bournes. Painted in Ireland ca. 1835. Artist unknown. Reproduced from the Palmer Collection, National Library of Australia, Canberra, Australia.

Nettie (Higgins) Palmer, author of *Henry Bournes Higgins, a Memoir.*
Courtesy, Misses Helen and Aileen Palmer.

judiciary committee He represented North Melbourne in 1901
in the first Commonwealth Parliament and, in the second
Parliament, was appointed Attorney-General in J. C Watson's
Labour Ministry of 1904 Two years later, he became Justice of
the High Court, with special duty of presiding over the Federal
Court of Conciliation and Arbitration, in which he established
the principles on which Federal arbitration awards should be
based In 1922, he resigned from the Presidency of the Court but
retained his seat on the High Court Bench He married Mary
Alice, daughter of Dr George Morrison of Geelong, Victoria in
Dec 1885 and they made their home at Malvern, Melbourne
Their house was called "Doona," named after the ancient castle
of Grace O Malley which once stood on the coast of western
Ireland Henry Bournes Higgins died at Dromana, Victoria 13
Jan 1929 They had issue

(1) Mervyn Bournes Higgins, the only child, was born in Melbourne, educated at Oxford University, England and became
a Barrister with a practice in Melbourne During World War
I he was a Captain in the Australian Army and was killed in
action at El Maghdabe, Turkey in 1916 He was unmarried

iii. John Higgins, born in Feb 1853 in Newtownards, Co Down, was
educated at the Wesleyan Connexional School and migrated to
Australia with his father in 1871 He became an accountant and
married Catherine McDonald (Katie) in 1914 They had issue

(1) Janet Gertrude Higgins (Nettie), born 18 Aug 1885 in
Bendigo, Victoria, graduated from the University of Mel-
bourne, B A , M A She married 23 May 1914 in London,
Edward Vance Palmer, born 23 Aug 1885 in Bundaberg,
Queensland, Australia, the son of Henry Burnett Palmer by
Mary Church Carson Edward V Palmer and his wife,
Nettie, were writers by profession She was the author of
"Henry Bournes Higgins, A Memoir " He died 15 July 1959
in Melbourne and his wife died 18 Oct 1964 in Kew, Victoria
They had issue

a Aileen Palmer, born 6 April 1915 in London, was educated,
with her sister, Helen, at a "one-teacher" state primary
high school in Petrie, Queensland Aileen also attended
the Presbyterian Ladies College, Melbourne and graduated
from the University of Melbourne, B A She is a writer
and resides in Kew, Victoria

b Helen Palmer, born 9 May 1917 in Melbourne, graduated
from the University of Melbourne, B A , Dip Ed , B.Ed
She is a writer, editor and school teacher and resides in
Sydney

(2) Esmonde McDonald Higgins, born ca 1900 was educated
at Scotch College, Australia He enlisted in World War I at
the age of 18, married Joy_____ and had issue

       a Chris Higgins

       b Lee Higgins

iv. George Higgins, born Feb 1856 in Borrisokane, Co Tipperary, was educated at the Weslevan Connexional School and migrated to Australia in 1870 with his mother He became an engineer, married Beatrice Shoeter and had issue

    (1) Ormsby Higgins

    (2) Charles Higgins

v Samuel Higgins, born ca 1858 probably in Killarney, Co Kerry, migrated to Australia in 1870 with his mother He became a doctor and practiced in Geelong, Australia

vi Frances Georgina Watts Higgins (Ina), born Sept 1860 in Fermoy, Co Cork, migrated to Australia in 1870 with her mother She became a landscape gardener and died unmarried in Melbourne

vii Anna Higgins, born ca 1862, probably in Abbeyleix, Queen's Co, migrated to Australia in 1870 with her mother She graduated from the University of Melbourne, M.A and married Egbert Reeves They had no issue

viii Charles Higgins, born ca 1864 in Newry, Co Down, migrated to Australia in 1870 with his mother He died at sea shortly before they arrived at the Port of Melbourne

ix William Higgins, born ca 1866, probably in Clonmel, Co Tipperary, died in infancy.

V. Stonefield

Stonefield,[1] in northwestern Erris, is adjacent to the townlands of Carrowteige, Portacloy and Kilgalligan and a short
distance from Rossport A mountain, or coastal range, and
majestic, rocky cliffs, towering from five hundred to over eight
hundred feet above the Atlantic, give this area an austere
beauty Stonefield may best be described, however, in the
words of a native writer as "a land of mist and sunshine .
moorland and meadow, brown heather and green bent, shaggy
bogs and sandy dunes, barren hills and fertile lowlands   "[2]

Kid Island, or Oilean Mionnán, off the shores of Stonefield
consists of approximately thirty acres and was once used by
the Bournes family for grazing sheep Originally named for
Manaan Mac Lir, the pagan sea-god, Kid Island had a more
colorful history in the distant past when it was the site of
piratical and smuggling operations [3]

As noted in the chapter devoted to the Castleconnor family,
Stonefield was leased on the 10th of June 1707 by Sir Arthur
Shaen, Baronet of Kilmore, Co Roscommon to "Andrew
Bourne of Straid in the County of Mayo, farmer   ."[4] The

---

[1] Stonefield is the translation of the Irish, Ceathrú na gCloch The Anglo-Irish
spelling varies considerably, two examples are Lecarrowneyglogh and Carrownaglough

[2] *Western People*, issue of 14 March 1936

[3] *Ibid.*

[4] Land Commission, Dublin The name of Andrew Bourne's residence is not entirely
legible on this old lease Later leases indicate that it was "Straid " There was, and is, a
Straid in Co Mayo, near the town of Castlebar

land was described as consisting of "three score and three acres of profitable land being part and parcel of the cartion of land called Lecarrownaglough and one thousand and forty acres of unprofitable or mountain land such as cattle might graze upon being part and parcel of the same lands as the same by meais and bounds were then divided and then lately surveyed   "

The Stonefield lease was made for three lives· "Andrew Bourne, Mary a daughter of Andrew Bourne and Sidney another daughter of Andrew Bourne . . ." The name of Elias Bourne(sic) is found once more as the occupier of Stonefield given "full power and authority to give livery and seizin   . in the name of the whole unto Andrew Bourne . "[5] Thus we appear to have the same situation as in the Castleconnor lease in that Elias (the occupier) was the link to the ancestry of the Bournes of Stonefield Unfortunately, no subsequent renewals of lease have been located and it is seemingly impossible to prove the relationship, if any, between Elias and Andrew Bournes, and later between Andrew and the descendants of his daughters It is not until the latter part of the eighteenth century that we can, with any degree of accuracy, re-create the Bournes family of Stonefield.

On the back of the Stonefield document we find that the lease was witnessed by three persons· one an Anthony Barry;[6] the second witness surname of Bourke is legible and the third witness name is completely unreadable Following the customary signing and witnessing, four memoranda were made and although some of the writing has faded through the years most of these early memoranda are quite easily deciphered

"Memorandum livery and seizin of all and singular the land within mentioned was given and delivered by the within named Elias Bourne unto the within named Andrew Bourne this seventh day of June Anno Domini 1707 according to the tenor of the within written indenture in the presence of us "

---

[5] Elias Bourne(sic) is found on the Castleconnor family's lease given "power and authority .   in the name of the whole unto Thomas Bourne .   "

[6] A witness to the Castleconnor family's lease as well

The signatures of four witnesses follow but only the first is clearly discernible as "Thomas Bourne."

"Memorandum on sealing hereof it is agreed that the within named Andrew Bourne shall have liberty of taking sea weed for manuring the lands within written from off the lands of Kilgalligan."[7] Signed, "Art Shaen."

"Elias Bourne   herein named Andrew Bourne and Henry Bourne both of Balbinconine[8] . . . doth hereby assign and alien for life and make over unto Thomas Bourne of Castleconnor the written lease with our rights and title for ever from the twenty ninth day of Sept last as witness our hand and seal this 30th(?) day of Dec 1707(?)" The memorandum was signed by Andrew Bourne and Henry Bourne and witnessed by four persons, one of whom is decipherable as "James Hendry."

"Memorandum livery and seizin of all and singular the lands within mentioned . . by Andrew Bourne and Henry Bourne and Thomas Bourne of Castleconnor the 20th day of Dec 1710 (or 1740?)   ." The name of one witness can be identified as "William Bourne", the signatures of the other witnesses have faded entirely.

At this point, it should be said that, according to the Stonefield family tradition, an Andrew Bournes came to Erris on the 6th day of June 1603 and acquired the lands of Stonefield. This, of course, is a century earlier than the Andrew Bourne(sic) who is clearly identified with Stonefield in the above paragraphs. In the absence of supporting documents there are at least three possible interpretations of the tradition. First, there may indeed have been an "Andrew Bournes" who came to Erris in 1603, and he may thus have been the progenitor of subsequent families in the area whose records have been lost. Second, the cogs of history may have slipped a

[7] The small strand northwest of Rinroe, Rinroe itself, and the strand to the east were the "lands of Kilgalligan" where the seaweed could be taken

[8] Balbinconine is the closest translation of this place-name that is possible Unfortunately, there is no land that can be so identified with the possible exception of Ballingonnie (Ballinconnie), a part of Elly, near Barrack North, in the Mullet peninsula

hundred years or so, and the 1603 Andrew of family tradition
may be the 1707 Andrew who acquired land from Sir Arthur
Shaen Or thirdly, an Andrew Bournes who was a predecessor
of the Stonefield family may have come to Northern Ireland
in 1603, and his descendants may later have migrated to
Erris The latter is quite plausible as many English and
Scottish settlers were planted in Ulster in the early years of
King James I, and we have, for example, found records of an
Andrew Bourne(sic) who resided at Coleraine in Co London-
derry, ca 1620-1641 [9]

Although no land conveyance has been located to assist in
bridging the years between 1707 and the latter part of this
same century, renewals, recitations of the land's history as
well as other sources, have enabled us to learn more about the
Bournes of Stonefield in the late eighteenth century A John
Bournes who resided at Stonefield by 1790 apparently lived,
prior to that time, at Carrick-on-Shannon, Co Leitrim He is
named in an indenture dated 10 July 1780 as holding land in
Co Leitrim by lease from Richard St. George [10] The description given in this indenture of John Bournes, his wife, Jane,
and his daughter Elizabeth, gives ample proof that the John
of Carrick-on-Shannon was the same John who ten years later
was of Stonefield, as will be shown subsequently

The deed, or indenture, from which the above information
was drawn primarily concerned the Bournes family of Ardglass
If the reader will glance at the Castleconnor pedigree once
again, he will see that David Bournes of Ardglass was a
brother of Thomas Bournes "the elder" of Castleconnor. The
assumption that John Bournes of Carrick-on-Shannon, and
later of Stonefield, was a brother of these two men, i e David
and Thomas Bournes, seems quite justified on the basis of the
above material and other records to be cited.

Returning to the land of Stonefield, we are aware that the
original lease of 1707 was renewed several times and the

[9] P R O Belfast, Rental of Coleraine, Co Londonderry #T724, p 7
[10] Registry of Deeds #1841 15 134

tenants' interest eventually became vested in John Bournes [11] He thereby became entitled to the right of renewal, pursuant to the usual covenants and conditions, and on the 23rd of January 1790, John Bournes, his daughter, Eleanor, and Thomas Bournes (the elder) of Castleconnor were "inserted" in place of the former lives on the Stonefield lease. [12]

The "former lives" were, of course, the names of those unknown persons who held the land of Stonefield prior to the above mentioned renewal It is disappointing not to be able to name these "lives," although it is quite possible that descendants of Andrew Bournes' daughters, Mary and Sidney Bournes, held the land until the time when John Bournes assumed ownership, or the tenants interest

A deed of release made the 14th of December 1792 between the Right Honorable Robert, Lord Clonbrock, Denis Bingham, Esquire and John Bournes of Stonefield, Gentleman, reveals that the lands of Carrownaglough (Stonefield) were granted to John of Stonefield for the sum of £240 [13] This deed is disappointingly brief and we only learn further that one full moiety of the lands of Garter was also granted Garter, it was said, "was formerly held and enjoyed by Walter Burke, Esq" At least, it has now been firmly established that John Bournes was of Stonefield

In the years that followed John Bournes' arrival at Stonefield, he acquired other lands in Erris—Kid Island, Garter Hill and Cornboy (Corán Buí), to name a few. These acquisitions are noted in subsequent deeds and their recitations of past events He acquired, as well, an interest in certain lands of the townland of Rosserk in the Parish of Ballysakeery, some forty-five miles from Stonefield and near the market town of

---

[11] Land Commission, Dublin Indenture dated 5 March 1827, between William Henry Carter of Castle Martin, Co Kildare and John Bournes of Stonefield, grandson and devisee of John Bournes, late of Stonefield, deceased

[12] Land Commission, Dublin Indenture dated 5 March 1827, op cit

[13] Registry of Deeds #504 470 334437 Denis Bingham was a direct descendant of Sir Arthur Shaen, Baronet, by his wife, Susanna Shaen The Right Honorable Robert, Lord Clonbrock was a descendant of Susanna Shaen by her second husband, Robert Dillon

Ballina, Co. Mayo Rosserk has not been mentioned heretofore, except in the Foreword to this book—it is the "Rosserieke," referred to in our family legend.[14]

Apparently, Rosserk was acquired sometime prior to 21 May 1742 by the Right Honorable James, Baron of Tirawley and Kilmaine On this date he demised five cartrons of Rosserk to Hubert Synott and later this same land was legally vested in Thomas Cowan Green, Esq of Hammersmith, Middlesex, England.[15]

On the 13th of May 1811, Thomas Cowan Green leased certain lands of Rosserk, specifically Cloonerly, alias Bowlirac(sic), to Matthew Bournes Jr, merchant of Ballina [16] Matthew Bournes Jr, Thomas Cowan Green and John Bournes of Stonefield, as we shall see, had much in common, beyond their mutual interest in Rosserk Although the author has been unable to establish the exact relationship between Matthew Bournes Jr. and John Bournes, it is believed these two men were nephew and uncle [17] There may have been some family connection between Thomas Cowan Green and the Bournes in the early part of the nineteenth century; there definitely was later, as will be shown.

Matthew Bournes Jr, the lessee of 1811, was to hold the lands of Rosserk for, and during, the life of Richard John Cowan Green, only son of Thomas C Green, and for the lives of James and Thomas Bournes, eldest and second sons of the said Matthew

Thomas Cowan Green died before 6 July 1814 when his Will was proved He left his estates in England and Ireland to his widow, Elizabeth Cowan Green, and named her as the sole Executor [18]

[14] Robert C Simington, *Book of Survey and Distribution, Co Mayo* (1956), p 220 Rosserk, or Rosserieke, as our family called it, is given as ' Rossericke" in this instance Combined with the land of Lygan, it was held prior to 1641 by the Earl of Cork There is no clue as to whom it was distributed during the Acts of Settlement

[15] Registry of Deeds #636 133 436512, #1849 20 139

[16] Registry of Deeds #636 133 436512

[17] See Appendix for chart pedigree, p 296

[18] Somerset House, London PCC Will 413 Bridport Thomas Cowan Green, according to his Will, dated 22 Oct 1805, was formerly known as Thomas Cowan

On the 18th of May 1818, Elizabeth Green, and her son, Richard John Cowan Green, leased certain lands of Rosserk to John Bournes of Stonefield [19] The lands were identified as "the Abbey half quarter, the small islands off the shore in the River Moy (Inishdugh, Carrigeens and Inishportan), Goose Island, also in the Moy, and the town and lands of Upper and South Deaghmean, all lately held by Robert Maturin Crofton, Esq , deceased " The lives inserted on the Rosserk lease of 1818 were of mutual concern to Matthew Bournes Jr of Ballina and to John Bournes of Stonefield, as will be seen in the pedigree which follows shortly

Since few sources are still available that pertain to the history of Erris, and more specifically to the personal history of the people, it is especially gratifying to be able to have a glimpse into the past through Michael Corduff's manuscript A seanchas (folktale) entitled, "The Abduction of Young Women,"[20] gives us some conception of life in Erris in the latter part of the eighteenth century

"About one hundred and fifty years ago.[21] the abduction or kidnapping of young women was a feature of the social life of Mayo and possibly of places outside of it [22] At that time there lived in Stonefield, a landlord who was locally known as Jack a Bán Bournes [23] He was a man of high social position in this part of the country and highly esteemed and respected He received information in confidence that one at least of his three beautiful daughters, or perhaps two of them, would be abducted, and that plans were being laid by the kidnappers to

[19] Registry of Deeds #716 417 507953, #716 418 509954 Actually there were two leases made by the Greens, 18 May 1818, to John of Stonefield Four of the six lives inserted on these leases were grandchildren of John Bournes, two lives presumably were related, but how is not known One was Edward Howley, son of Edward Howley of Ardnaree, Co Sligo, aged about 13, the other was William Rutledge, eldest son of David Rutledge of Newcastle, Co Mayo, Esq , aged about 14

[20] Michael Corduff, "Notes on Erris,"*Irish Folklore Commission*, Vol VI, pp 518-524

[21] Probably the latter part of the eighteenth century, about 1790, or later

[22] See *Matters of Felony*, by Marjery Weiner (1967) for another eighteenth century story of an abduction in Co Kilkenny

[23] John Bournes, or Jack a Bán meaning white or fair-haired He was also known as Jackie Bawn

carry them off as soon as a suitable opportunity arose A strong force of kidnappers was to come from Ballycroy, about forty miles away, some night on this unlawful expedition The young ladies were intended by the kidnappers to be married to members of an aristocratic family named O'Donnell, some- where near Westport.[24] The Ballycroy men were selected for this hazardous operation on account of their characteristic daring and determination, and their local knowledge of the territory of Dún Caocháin[25] in which Bournes lived

"Jack a Bán Bournes was an equally determined man who kept firearms and was not loath to use them if necessity arose But as his business and official duties necessitated his rather frequent absence from home, he was placed in some difficulty concerning the protection of his daughters during his absence As the kidnappers would come to hear of the time he would be away, they would almost certainly swoop down on the unde- fended citadel at Stonefield . .

"Jack a Bán Bournes was aware of the intentions and plans of his enemies and so long as he was at home he had no fear of them, but in his absence he had no great confidence in the 'garrison' he would leave behind to defend the fort . .

"For a time, things were in a state of tension. Jack a Bán apprehended attack any night, and he had made his plans and preparations to meet it, but time was passing and yet there was no sign of an 'invasion.' It was still in the offing and the danger was not receding one bit. Jack a Bán had his secret agents working and they kept him posted and informed of every move and development in the enemy camp Doubtless too, the enemy had their agents at work and were watching the movements of Jack a Bán, especially of any prolonged absence from home Conditions between the parties had developed into what is known in modern parlance as a 'cold war,' each side watching the other.

[24] Westport, Co Mayo was probably an error Newport, Co Mayo was the Seat of the O'Donnell (O'Donel) family

[25] The territory of Dún Caocháin is comprised of Kilgalligan, Stonefield and Cai- rowteige However, this name has not been used in recent years

"Then Jack a Bán had very important business in Dublin to attend a conference or convention of landlords, or perhaps some legal business concerning his estate. It was a duty which could not be postponed and it was imperative that he should attend. In those days a journey to and from Dublin cost time and trouble as compared with modern standards Jack a Bán's absence on the occasion would be at least of a fortnight's duration, and as the matter was of the utmost importance he could not possibly abstain from attending the meeting He considered the advisability of taking his daughters with him to Dublin in the interests of their security but, as this project was in the circumstances of the occasion and times somewhat impracticable, he decided to leave them behind.

"To some of his local advisors, he proposed the idea of transporting them to Kid Island (Oileán Mionnán), an island on his own estate lying off the coast of Dún Caocháin, and making provisions there for food and shelter   . until his return from Dublin While on the island they would have the attendance and service of a maid and there would be a few men as a guard stationed on the island for the duration of the temporary exile The island is quite large and has an area of about thirty acres, is uninhabited and given over to sheep grazing. A landing on the island can be affected only in calm weather and even in fine weather landing is sometimes impossible owing to ground swell, or surf (in Irish, called bruth), and the craft used was the curragh, the only available sea craft on the coast down to the present day [26] But there was a snag in this proposal If after the transportation was carried out a prolonged storm came on, as often did, the little island colony would become marooned, and it might be impossible to reach it by any means   . It was decided that the project was not feasible, and therefore abandoned

"On the coast of Portacloy there is a high plateau of land about twelve acres in extent which is almost cut off from the

---

[26] As this story was written quite a few years ago, this statement is no longer correct Today modern, twenty foot, or more, motor boats are widely used in Erris for fishing and other purposes

mainland The only remaining connection being a narrow
neck of ground, the upper part of which has been washed away
by coast erosion From this little isthmus one has to climb the
rocky precipice to the high ground of the Dhoona (Dúna),[27]
by which this semi-detached feature of the coast was known.
The Dhoona up to very recent times was a venue for the
congregation of the young people of northwest Erris on Gar-
land Sunday (Domhnach Chrom Dubh). Here the Sunday
afternoon was spent in picking heath berries, fun and merri-
ment, accompanied by music and dancing.

"It was on this locale that Jack a Bán with the approval
of his advisors finally decided to settle his daughters, pending
his return from Dublin At the time there lived in the locality
a man known as Séan Caoch Ó Tuathail (Blind Jack
O'Toole)[28] Séan was known for his herculean physique and
strength which was only equalled by his determination and
fearlessness in any crisis or danger It was suggested that
Séan Caoch be requisitioned to keep ward over the Bournes
ladies while in retreat on this coastal headland When approached and told of his remuneration for this duty, he was
delighted beyond measure

"Then the three ladies and their maid were helped up the
precipice of the Dhoona and stores and provisions were laid in
Séan Caoch had the time of his life He was monarch of the
Dhoona and of all he surveyed. A cairn of stones that he had
built was his sole ammunition, in case of enemy attack His
position was absolutely impregnable and no one dared assail it

"When the Ballycroy men heard of the protective measures
which had been taken by landlord Bournes, they wisely
decided to abandon the project and nothing further was heard
about it It was said a young woman was abducted near
Killala instead

"When Jack a Bán Bournes returned home from Dublin

---

[27] Fort or fortified place

[28] Séan Caoch Ó Tuathail though called Blind Jack O'Toole was actually only blind
in one eye

after about a fortnights absence, he found his women folk safe
and well and he brought them home and gave a great feast at
which the indomitable Séan Caoch was the guest of honor . "

Another story about John Bournes of Stonefield but from a
different source,[29] concerns an incident that occurred during
the period that followed the French invasion at Killala, Co
Mayo in August of 1798

Catholic Priests, at that time, as in most nationalist movements, were very active in assisting the French and in protecting their own people Protestant Loyalists of the area
were equally busy, as they were engaged in conveying secret
information to the English, while pretending to be neutral One
Catholic Priest, Father Owen Cowley of Crossmolina was
largely responsible for seeing that many of these Loyalists
were captured and imprisoned for their actions

Following the defeat of the French, the English began a
vindictive manhunt for the capture of the Priest A £300
reward was offered and no doubt he would have been executed
had he been caught

However, Father Cowley managed to escape his pursuers,
but was forced to flee from one place to another in order to
avoid detection He eventually made his way to the western
most part of Erris where he was given sanctuary in the home
of a Protestant landlord, John Bournes of Stonefield When
the yeomenry came to search this area, John Bournes led the
weary Priest to the coast Here he carried Father Cowley up
the face of a steep and dangerous cliff near Portacloy and hid
him on the Dhoona, the same Dhoona that had sheltered his
own daughters.

The remarkable part of this feat was that John Bournes
was over sixty years of age at the time he scaled the cliff
carrying the Priest. Fortunately, his efforts were not in vain,
because Father Cowley escaped the yeomenry in Erris For
some six months, the Priest continued to avoid apprehension

---

[29] *Ballina Herald,* issue of 4 Sept 1948, Stonefield family records

but he finally died while hiding in a mountain cave near Enniscrone, Co. Sligo [30]

The Bournes of Stonefield

I. John Bournes of Stonefield, possibly 'a son of Elias Bournes of Castleconnor, Co Sligo, was born ca 1738 [31] He married Jane Lloyd, born ca 1747, who died 11 January 1845, aged 98, in the Parish of Killala [32] John Bournes died 23 September 1826 at Stonefield and was buried in Kilgalligan Cemetery His Will was dated 29 July 1826, Codicil dated 1 August 1826 and the Will and Codicil were proved this same year [33]

Although John Bournes' Will and Codicil are among the Stonefield family records, much of the writing is now illegible However, with these old documents and with the assistance of the Land Commission and Registry of Deeds, the following has been pieced together.[34]

In 1826, John of Stonefield bequeathed his Erris property to his grandson, John, eldest son of John and Eleanor Bournes, then of Rosserk. This bequest included the lands of Stonefield, New Garter, Bog Town, the house division, Portacloy, Old Garter and Kid Island. He also named his granddaughter, Jane Celia, but the provisions made for her cannot be deciphered In the Codicil, he provided for two of his daughters, Celia (Cecelia) and Alicia Bournes. The name Denis Bingham of Bingham's Castle, Co Mayo is clearly discernible as an Executor It appears that Robert Fawcett and Robert D

---

[30] A detailed account of Father Cowley's activities, including his flight to Erris, may be found in *The Last Invasion of Ireland or When Connaught Rose* (1937) by Richard Hayes

[31] Stonefield family records John Bournes is said to have been over 60 years of age in 1798

[32] Register of the Parish of Killala

[33] Land Commission, Dublin Indenture dated 21 June 1860, Stonefield family records, Will of John Bournes, P R O , Dublin Will Index

[34] Land Commission, Dublin Deed dated 5 March 1827, Registry of Deeds #1838 16 28, dated 15 April 1836

Bournes M D may have been Executors as well The witnesses names are illegible

John and Jane Bournes had issue

    i Thomas Bournes, who died without issue

    ii Eleanor Bournes q v

    iii Elizabeth Bournes, born ca 1785, married (M L B Killala and
        Achonry) in 1810, David son of David Bournes of Carrick on
        Shannon by Celia Lloyd (see Ardglass family)

    iv Alicia Bournes who married 29 June 1819, Robert Fawcett of
        Ballinglen, Co Mayo in the Parish of Killala [36] He presumably
        died 2 Sept 1855 at Allegheny, Penn at which time he was
        called Robert Fawcett late of Moyne House, Co. Mayo [36] They
        had issue

        (1) Anne Fawcett, baptised 7 July 1823 in the Parish of Killala

        (2) John B Fawcett who died 13 Aug 1853, aged 30, in Penn
            and was called son of Robert Fawcett, late of Moyne, Co
            Mayo [37]

        (3) Richard Fawcett, born ca 1830, married Ellen born ca 1830,
            daughter of Matthew Bournes of Newtownwhite, Co Mayo
            2 Nov 1852 in the Parish of Killala Witnesses to the mar-
            riage were James Walton and John Selchow [38]

    v Cecelia (Celia) Bournes who married Rev Malachi Maxwell
       (see Part Two)

II Eleanor (Ellen) Bournes, born ca 1783, was called the
daughter of John Bournes of Stonefield in a renewal of lease.
dated 23 January 1790 [39] She married (M L B Killala and
Achonry) in 1804, John, possibly the son of Matthew Bournes,
merchant of Ballina, and his wife, Margaret [40] John Bournes,
born ca 1774, was also a merchant and he and his family
resided in Ballina but later lived at Rosseik Eleanor Bournes
died and was buried in the Parish of Kilmoremoy 27 September
1839, aged 56 John Bournes, her husband, was buried in this
same parish 14 March 1834, aged 60 [41] They had issue

    [35] Alicia Bournes was recorded as being ' of Erris" in the marriage register of the
Parish of Killala

    [36] *Connaught Watchman*, issue of 19 Sept 1855

    [37] *Tirawley Herald*, issue of 22 Sept 1853

    [38] Registers of the Parishes of Killala and Ballysakeery

    [39] Registry of Deeds #822 25 533158

    [40] Eleanor (Ellen) and John Bournes and their nine children are the family referred
to in our family legend

    [41] Register of the Parish of Kilmoremoy.

    i John Bournes q v

    ii Matthew Bournes, born ca 1807, was named as a son of John Bournes, merchant of Ballina, in a lease for the lands of Rosserk, dated 18 May 1818 [42] He was educated in Ireland and England becoming a member of the Royal College of Surgeons in 1829 [43] In 1838 and 1839, he was listed as a member of the R C S I and his residence was given as Rosserk, Co Mayo However, in 1834 Dr Bournes, according to the Tithe Composition taken that year, had land in Belmullet, Co Mayo and by 1836 was the doctor for the Erris area [44] In 1853, he was M O of the Belmullet Poor Law Union and in 1855 he was residing at Carter Square, Belmullet [45] It is possible that he may have been the "Mathew Bourns" who married Anne Matthews, 26 Feb 1832 in the Parish of Kilmoremoy [46] Dr. Bournes died 28 July 1859[47] in Belmullet and left issue

    (1) Nanette Bournes, or Nanny as she was known, was the daughter of Dr Matthew Bournes of Belmullet She married 4 April 1852 at St Mary's Church, Dublin, Zachariah, born ca 1822, son of Joseph Wallace by Anne Dillon [48] Zachariah Wallace was the Proprietor and Editor of *The Anglo-Celt*, a Cavan newspaper, from 1847 to 1856 Mr Wallace's activities as a newspaper man are worth noting, especially during the 1852 general election (the first tenant-right contest), for he was sympathetic toward the sufferings of the tenants and courageously outspoken in his editorials [49] As a result of the latter, he was brought before the Court Magistrate in Dublin on charges that an editorial written in August 1852 was libelous [50] He was subsequently fined £50 and sentenced to six months imprisonment in Cavan gaol His sentence commenced 22 April 1853 [51] Although his friends, relatives and numerous supporters circulated petitions in 1853 for his release the Lord Lieutenant refused to intervene [52] A moving

---

[42] Registry of Deeds #746 417 507953 Matthew Bourns(sic), aged 11, was one of the lives added to the lease

[43] Medical Register of 1859

[44] Patrick Knight, *Erris in the Irish Highlands* (1836), p 129

[45] Thom's Directory of 1853, Griffith's Valuation of 1855

[46] Register of the Parish of Kilmoremoy

[47] General Medical Council Records

[48] Register of St Mary's Church, Dublin Zachariah's father was called Joseph Wallace, Gent, Nanny's father was called Mathew Bourns M Ch The marriage was witnessed by Daniel Mooney, Curate of St Mary's Chapel of Ease, William Dunbar S F T C D and Elizabeth Snowe, *Sligo Chronicle*, issue of 17 April 1852 See the Appendix p 220

[49] Rev Terence Cunningham, "The 1852 General Election in County Cavan," *Breifne*, Vol III, no 9 (1966), p. 112

[50] *Ibid*, p 131

[51] Cunningham, op cit, pp 132-133

[52] Cunningham, op cit, p 133, State Paper Office, Dublin Castle, #W 10/1853 Many of the signers were from the Ballina area Among them were James Bournes Sr of Knockroe House, Castleconnor and James Bournes Jr of Castleconnor, Co Sligo, Richard J C Green of Rosserk, Co Mayo Thomas C G Bournes, Esq of Rosserk and a Matthew and Thomas Bourns, not identified by occupation or by residence.

and direct appeal to Queen Victoria was written by Nanny
Bournes Wallace 30 Aug 1853, asking for her husband's
pardon and release [53] This dramatic step did not however,
succeed in abridging Wallace's full sentence He finally left
Cavan gaol 22 Oct 1853 and died approximately three years
later, 1 Feb 1857, aged 35, at his residence on Main St ,
Cavan [54] He was buried in the cemetery attached to Coolock
Church, Co Dublin [55] In his Will he named Charlotte and
Alicia Bournes as guardians of his two children [56] Nanny
Bournes Wallace survived her husband as she was residing
in Cavan Oct 1857 [57] They had issue

a   Child who died 2 Feb 1853 [58]

b   John Martin Wallace, born 22 March 1854, was baptised
3 Dec 1854 in Cavan [59] He was a printer residing at 34
Upper Rutland St , Dublin where he died 4 June 1887,
aged 33, unmarried [60]

c   William Wallace, born 5 June 1855, was baptised 15 July
1855 in Cavan [61]

iii   Jane Celia Bournes, born ca 1808, was named as a daughter of
John Bournes, merchant of Ballina, in a lease for the lands of
Rosserk, dated 18 May 1818 [62] She married 26 Aug 1837, William
Bournes of Portacloy (see Carrowteige and Portacloy family)

iv   William Lloyd Bournes, born ca 1812, was named as a son of
John Bournes, merchant of Ballina, in a lease for the lands of
Rosserk, dated 18 May 1818 [63] He married in Feb 1833, Hannah
Maria, daughter of Rev Malachi Maxwell by Cecelia, daughter
of John Bournes of Stonefield (see Part Two)

v.   Margaret Eleanor Bournes, baptised in the Parish of Castleconnor, 24 March 1814, died unmarried 8 Dec 1840 at Rosserk,
aged 24, buried in the Parish of Kilmoremoy She was called the
second daughter of John Bournes, Esq of Rosserk [64]

[53] See Appendix, pp 283-287
[54] Cunningham, op cit , pp 133-134
[55] Coolock Cemetery gravestone inscription See Appendix, p 220
[56] Anglo-Celt, issue of 10 Sept 1857
[57] Ibid, issue of 22 Oct 1857
[58] Ibid, issue of 3 Feb 1853
[59] Coleraine Chronicle, issue of 8 April 1854, Register of the Parish of Cavan
[60] Custom House Register Ellen Bournes, an aunt, of this same address was present
at time of death
[61] Register of the Parish of Cavan
[62] Registry of Deeds #746 417 507953 Jane Celia Bourns(sic), aged 10, one of the
lives added to the lease
[63] Registry of Deeds #746 418 509954 William Lloyd Bourns(sic), aged about 6
years, one of the lives added to the lease
[64] Western Star, issue of 11 Dec 1840

vi Eliza Bournes named as a daughter of John Bournes of Rosserk in our family legend Although no records have been located to substantiate this it is possible that she was the "Eliza Burns" found in the McLean family records (see Part Two)

vii Mary Anne Bournes, baptised 4 June 1818 in the Parish of Kilmoremoy, was called the fourth daughter of John Bournes, Esq of Rosserk [65] She married 15 June 1853, in the Ballysakeery Church, Richard John Cowan Green of Rosserk, born ca 1791, only son of Thomas Cowan Green, deceased, formerly of Hammersmith, Middlesex England, by Eliza_____ The marriage was performed by Rev James Meehan and witnessed by W Holliday and Robert Rogers [66] Richard John Cowan Green, landholder of Rosserk, had, by July 1852, released part of his lands to Annesley Paul Gore [67] By a deed of conveyance, dated 16 March 1853, Richard J C Green assigned lands and premises of Rosserk, for a sizable consideration, to Francis Arthur Knox Gore of Belleek Manor, Co Mayo [68] He died 31 Oct 1859, aged 68,[69] at Albion Place, Hemel Hempstead, near London, but nothing further is known about his wife, Mary Anne They had issue of at least one child, a son who died in infancy 9 May 1859 at Rosserk [70]

viii Alicia Barbara Bournes, baptised 9 Nov 1823 in the Parish of Ballysakeery, was called the daughter of John and Eleanor Bournes of Rosserk [71]

ix Thomas Cowan Green Bournes, born ca 1827, married Margaret _____ They lived in the Parish of Ballysakeery, Co Mayo, residing at Rosserk where several of their children were born He died 24 Feb 1892, aged 65, at Smithstown, near Kilfian[72] but was buried in the Parish of Kilmoremoy [73] Margaret Bournes, his

---

[65] *Tirauley Herald*, issue of 16 June 1853

[66] *Ibid*, Register of the Parish of Kilmoremoy

[67] Registry of Deeds #1852 25 237

[68] Registry of Deeds #1853 9 2 For the lives of "Richard John Cowan Green, His Royal Highness, Prince George of Cumberland and His Royal Highness Prince George of Cambridge'

[69] *Tirawley Herald*, issue of 15 Nov 1859, General Register Office, Somerset House, London

[70] *Tirawley Herald*, issue of 14 May 1859

[71] Register of the Parish of Ballysakeery

[72] Custom House Register John and Eleanor Bournes, according to family information, did have a son called Thomas Although it has not been possible to establish that the above mentioned Thomas Cowan Green Bournes was this son we feel he may have been and for the following reasons The name of Green, as stated in our legend, was a family name It has already been demonstrated that the land of Rosserk was acquired by the Bournes from a Thomas Cowan Green, Esq His son, Robert, subsequently became a son-in-law to John and Eleanor Bournes and the two families were closely united

[73] The Kilmoremoy Parish Register states that he was buried 27 Feb 1892, aged 64 In the Ballysakeery Register, there is a record of a Thomas G Bourns(sic) of Smithstown, buried 26 Feb 1892 It would appear that we either have two men by the same name or a clerical error

wife, died 9 Dec 1883, aged 47, at Smithstown and was also buried in the Parish of Kilmoremoy [74] They had issue [75]

(1) Thomas Cowan Green Bournes, born 3 April 1846, was baptised 28 June 1846 in the Parish of Ballysakeery and died shortly thereafter [76]

(2) William Thomas Cowan Bournes born 22 May 1847, was baptised 6 June 1847 in the Parish of Ballysakeery

(3) John Bournes was baptised 15 May 1849 in the Parish of Ballysakeery.

(4) Matthew Bournes was baptised 11 June 1851 in the Parish of Ballysakeery

(5) William Bournes was baptised 16 March 1853 in the Parish of Ballysakeery

(6) Richard Bournes, born 2 July 1854, was baptised 13 Aug 1854 in the Parish of Kilmoremoy [77] He resided at Smithstown and on 17 March 1883 married, Rebecca J Farrell, daughter of Francis Farrell in the Ballinglen Presbyterian Church Witnesses to this marriage were Ellen Wilkin and Bridget_____ [78]

(7) Francis Bournes was baptised 13 Feb 1859 in the Parish of Ballysakeery

(8) Elizabeth Bournes was baptised 13 April 1864 in the Parish of Ballysakeery

(9) Robert Bournes was baptised 3 Sept 1865 in the Parish of Ballysakeery

(10) Samuel Bournes was baptised 6 Oct 1867 in the Parish of Ballysakeery

x Charlotte Bournes, born ca 1829,[79] was named, with Alicia Bournes, as a guardian of Zachariah Wallace's children [80] She was residing in Cavan by 1855 and became the Proprietor and

---

[74] Custom House Register

[75] The birth and baptismal records are found in two parish registers The parents, Thomas C G Bournes and Margaret were of Rosserk when the first six children were born, they later were of Magherablack The father in some records is called a Gentleman farmer

[76] A notation beside this entry indicates the child was dead by 3 Jan 1847

[77] At the time of Richard Bournes' baptism, he was called son of "Thomas and Margaret Bourns of Castle Road, Rosserk, farmer "

[78] Register of the Ballinglen Presbyterian Church

[79] Our original assumption was that Charlotte must have been a daughter of Dr. Matthew Bournes, since there was no reference to her in our family legend An article in *The Meath Herald*, issue of 4 July 1857 (report of Rolls Court case "Wallace v Bournes") identifies her, and Alicia Bournes, as aunts of Nanny Bournes Wallace (Dr Bournes' daughter) Granting the fallibility of newspaper items, this is nevertheless the only written evidence that we have been able to uncover and we have been guided by it in spite of the silence of our family legend on this matter

[80] *Anglo-Celt*, issue of 10 Sept 1857

Editor of *The Anglo-Celt* by March 1857, following Zachariah's
death After being with this paper for a brief period, she established *The Cavan Observer*, 11 July 1857 This latter paper, according to the leader of the first issue, was established for the
benefit of the Wallace children [81] Charlotte died 25 Oct 1864,
aged 35, unmarried at Cavan [82] Her Will was proved 8 Dec
1864 [83]

III   John Bournes, eldest son of John and Eleanor Bournes,
was born ca 1805 [84] He married 22 June 1830 in the Church of
Ardnaree, Margaret, born ca 1812 at Rappa Castle, Co
Mayo,[85] youngest daughter of Francis Knox of Ardnaree,
Co Mayo John Bournes was of Stonepark, Co Mayo at the
time of his marriage The ceremony was performed by Rev.
James Huston and witnessed by William Bournes and William
West [86]

The articles of agreement made prior to the marriage of
John and Margaret Knox were dated 16 June 1830 and were
between "John Bouins of the first part, Francis Knox of the
second part, Margaret Knox, daughter of Francis Knox of the
third part and Richard John Cowan Green and Annesley
Knox Jr of the fourth part "[87]

John Bournes died 18 May 1843, aged 37, in Ballina and
was buried in the Parish of Kilmoremoy.[88] In his Will, dated
19 June 1842, he named his four children [89] Margaret Knox
Bournes died in Dublin and was buried 6 August 1842, aged
30, in the Parish of Kilmoremoy

Following the death of John and Margaret Bournes, their

[81] *Cavan Observer*, issue of 11 July 1857

[82] Custom House Register, *Cavan Observer*, issue of 29 Oct 1864

[83] P R O Dublin Will Index, Cavan Registry

[84] Registry of Deeds #746 117 507953, dated 8 May 1818, in which John Bournes,
aged 13, was one of the lives added to the Rosserk lease

[85] Stonefield family records

[86] *Ballina Impartial*, issue of 22 June 1830, Register of the Parish of Kilmoremoy
Stonepark is near Togher and Castlebar in Co Mayo

[87] Registry of Deeds #1865 35 270

[88] *Ibid* Although our family legend indicated that John Bournes was a solicitor of
Castlebar no records have been found to substantiate this It is interesting, however,
that his eldest son was a Barrister and practiced law in Dublin In this instance the
legend and the records are in complete agreement

[89] Registry of Deeds #1865 35 270

"Rosserk Abbey." Artist, Frank Egginton, R.S.A., F.I.A.L. Reproduced from the original, owned by Mary A. Strange. Rosserk Abbey seen in the background of this picture stands on the lands of Rosserk, near Ballina, Co. Mayo. In the foreground is the Moy River and Castleconnor, Co. Sligo.

John Bournes, Barrister at Law, ca. 1870. Courtesy, John P. Bournes

two daughters were brought up by their aunts, Miss Maria Knox and Mrs Anne Nash of Binghamstown House, Binghamstown, Co Mayo The two boys were reared by Helena Knox, wife of Dr MacAulay of Garden St, Ballina.[90]

i   Anne Jane Bournes, born in April 1831, was baptised 2 Jan 1832 in the Parish of Kilmoremoy She died unmarried and intestate 6 Jan 1868 in Binghamstown, Co Mayo The administration of her estate was granted to her brother John Bournes of 26 Lower Gloucester St, Dublin [91] She was buried in the Belmullet Cemetery, near Binghamstown [92]

ii John Bournes, the eldest son was born 20 Aug 1834 at Stonefield and educated in Dublin He was admitted as a student in the Michelmas Term to King's Inn 1860, to the Society of the Middle Temple in Great Britain, Michelmas Term 14 Nov 1863 and he became a Barrister at Law King's Inn 1865 [93] He resided in Dublin at 26 Lower Gloucester St, but returned to Stonefield where he died unmarried, 1 Jan 1893, aged 60 [94]

iii Francis Bournes q v

iv Elizabeth Eleanor Bournes, born 10 Feb 1837, was baptised 14 April 1837 in the Parish of Kilmoremoy She resided in Binghamstown, but moved to Dublin where, in 1884, she lived at 96 Lower Mount St [95] By 1896, she was residing at 3 Upper Gloucester St, Dublin unmarried [96]

IV Francis Bournes, born ca 1836 at Stonefield, married Sarah McCabe. He resided at Barrack Lodge, Belmullet, Co Mayo in 1874 but by 1896 was of Stonefield [97] He died 15

[90] Stonefield family records

[91] P R O Dublin, Consolidated Wills, Administration Index 1858-1877

[92] Belmullet Cemetery gravestone inscription

[93] Registers of Admission to the Middle Temple in Great Britain 1782-1902, Vol II, King's Inn Register of Admission Trinity Term 1865, Memorial of John Bournes "The Memorial of John Bournes of Stonefield sheweth that he is the eldest son of John Bournes, Esq, late of Stonefield in the Co of Mayo deceased and of Margaret Bournes orse Knox, his wife That he was admitted student in Michelmas Term 1860 and into the Society of the Middle Temple in Great Britain in Michelmas Term 1863 That he attained the age of 30 years on the 20th day of August last, and that he now requests admission to the Honorable Society, and to the degree of Bachelor at Law Signed, John Bournes, 2 May 1865"

[94] Custom House Register

[95] Registry of Deeds #1896 52 282

[96] Ibid

[97] Ibid

June 1909, aged 74, at Stonefield [98] His Will was dated 11 May 1901 and proved in 1919.[99] They had issue [100]

   i   Francis Bournes q v

   ii Matilda Bournes, born 8 Dec 1861, died in 1867, aged 6 years.

   iii Elizabeth Bournes, born in 1864, died 22 Aug 1945 at Stonefield, unmarried

   iv John Bournes, born 3 March 1867, died in infancy

V. Francis Bournes, the eldest son, was born ca. 1860 and married Mary McGuinnis in 1892. He died 4 September 1927 at Stonefield and left issue, all born at Stonefield.[101]

   i   John Francis Bournes q v

   ii Elizabeth Bournes, born ca 1896, died in March 1919, aged 23 She married Thomas McGarry in 1917 and had issue

      (1) John McGarry, born 1 July 1918, resides at Rossport, unmarried

   iii Thomas Bournes, born 16 Nov 1897, married 12 June 1927, Sabina, born 11 Nov 1902, daughter of Anthony Philibin They had issue

      (1) William Patrick Francis Bournes, born 8 Nov 1942 at Stonefield, married 11 Sept 1968, Evelyn, daughter of Thomas Naughton They reside at Stonefield.

   iv Mary Bournes born in 1899, married Patrick Connolly and resides in Co Kildare

   v   George Bournes (twin), born ca 1901, resides in British Columbia, Canada

   vi Jane Bournes (twin), born ca 1901, died 16 June 1909, aged 7½ years [102]

   vii Annie Bournes, born ca 1904, died 6 June 1920

   viii Ellen Bournes (twin), born 22 July 1909, resides in New York, New York, unmarried

   ix Sarah Bournes (twin), born 22 July 1909, married Ernest Smith 13 Aug 1933, and resides in North Arlington, New Jersey They had issue

      (1) Donald Joseph Smith, born 12 Nov 1935, graduated from St Peter's College, Jersey City, New Jersey with a B S

[98] Custom House Register
[99] P R O Dublin Will Index
[100] Stonefield family records
[101] *Ibid*
[102] Custom House Register

degiee in 1958 He did giaduate woik at New Yoik University, New Yoik, is piesently with the Celanese Coip as Coipoiate Personal Managei, and is mai ried to Katherine Langan They had issue

a Brian Donald Smith, boin 13 Feb 1960

b Gregoiy Einest Smith, boin 12 Nov 1963

(2) Richard Edward Smith, boin 6 June 1938, giaduated from St Petei's College, Jeisey City with a B A degiee in 1960 He is a teachei and woiking toward his Mastei degiee at Newaik Teacher's College

(3) Maureen Jean Smith, boin 18 Nov 1944, giaduated fiom Caldwell College foi Women. Caldwell, New Jersey with a B A degree in 1966 She is a stewaidess with T W A

x Alice Bouines, born ca 1910, married Matthew Brady and iesides in New Yoik, New Yoik

xi Eleanor Bournes (triplet), boin ca 1913, died in infancy

xii Jane Bournes (triplet), born ca 1913, died in infancy

xiii Ceceiia Bouines (tiiplet), boin ca 1913, died in infancy

VI. John Francis Bournes, the eldest son, boin 20 December 1894, was baptised 23 December 1894 in the Parish of Aughoose, Co. Mayo. He married 3 January 1920, Maria, born 10 March 1892, daughter of John Mills. John Francis Bournes died 13 February 1957; his wife died 29 September 1962 and they both were buried in Kilgalligan Cemetery. They had issue, all born at Stonefield

i John Patiick Bournes, born 19 Dec 1920, resides at Stonefield, unmarried

ii Mary Teresa Bouines, boin 16 Dec 1924, iesides at Stonefield, unmaiiied

iii Bridget Eileen Bouines, born 15 July 1927, married Alexander Corcoian They reside at Crossmolina, Co Mayo and had issue.

iv Annie Elizabeth Bournes, born 15 Nov 1931, married in Sept 1949, John O'Sullivan They ieside in Dublin and had issue.

VI. Carrowteige and Portacloy

Carrowteige and Portacloy,[1] part of the estate acquired in the seventeenth century by Sir James Shaen, are townlands characterized by rolling hills, a rugged coast line and a good harbor at Portacloy. Port a' Chlóidh, the Harbor of the Rampart, is well named, for it is a snug little port lying between towering cliffs Directly west of the harbor lies Benwee Head, some 830 feet above the Atlantic, where one finds a magnificent south-westerly view of Mullet country and the other townlands so closely connected to the Bournes families of Erris. Northward from Benwee Head are five pinnacles of rock, known as the Stags of Broadhaven These ancient sentinels, guarding the Atlantic approach to northern Mayo and to Erris, are familiar to Irish fishermen, for here is found some of the finest coastal fishing of Ireland

In 1641, prior to the Shaen era, Carrowteige or Lecarrow mcteige, as it was then recorded, was held by Erevanc Mc-Phillip [2] Portacloy, however, was not included on any early list of Erris land and not until 1707 was it identified, insofar as the author has been able to determine, as a distinct and separate townland

[1] Carrowteige and Portacloy are translations of the Irish words, Ceathrú Thaidhg and Port a' Chlóidh
[2] Robert Simington, *Book of Survey and Distribution*, Vol II, Co Mayo (Dublin 1956), p 203

83

On the 10th of June 1707, Sir Arthur Shaen, Baronet of Kilmore, Co Roscommon granted the townlands of Carrowteige and Portacloy to Elias Bourne(sic), of Castleconnor, Co Sligo. The land granted was described as follows "All that cartron of land called or known by the name of Lecarrowteige containing by estimation 80 acres of profitable land and 80 acres of unprofitable or mountain land being part of the same lands and 325 acres of unprofitable being part and parcel of the land called Portacloy containing in the whole by estimation 80 acres of profitable and 405 acres of unprofitable situate in the half barony of Erris, Co Mayo aforesaid with all the rights members and appurtenances thereunto belonging to hold for the lives of the three persons therein mentioned and the survivors of them . ."[3]

In separate leases, also executed on the 10th of June 1707, Arthur Shaen conveyed additional property to Elias Bourne. The lands of Rossport and Stonefield were involved in these transactions which are described in some detail in the chapters dealing with the Castleconnor and Stonefield families Unfortunately, the original document covering the Carrowteige and Portacloy land is no longer in existence and we have no information on the identity of the "three lives" that are cited in the foregoing paragraph. It would seem, however, that we are entitled to make a few "educated guesses" with respect to the situation

Let us begin with the demonstrable fact that the Carrowteige and Portacloy lease was executed on the same day and that the two principal parties (Shaen and Elias Bourne) were the same. We know that Elias Bourne of Castleconnor had three sons, namely, Thomas, William and George Bourne. It has been fully established that Thomas remained at Castleconnor and George became the landlord of Rossport [4] The question now is, what became of William, the third son?

Nothing has been found in any of the old deeds relating to

---

[3] Registry of Deeds #1867 35 86
[4] See the Castleconnor Bournes family

the lands of Castleconnor, Rossport or Stonefield that places
William in these areas But what about the land that his
father acquired called Carrowteige and Portacloy? When our
searches uncovered a marriage settlement, dated 29 July
1752,[5] naming a William Bourne of Carrowteige, we began to
speculate about the possibility of this "William" being the
third son of Elias Bourne of Castleconnor There is rather
strong evidence to support this conjecture

In the first place, the chronology is right The marriage
settlement of 1752 involved a son of William Thus William
himself would have been old enough to have been a son of
Elias of Castleconnor Second, William's son was named Elias,
and it was quite customary in those days to name the eldest
boy after his grandfather. Finally, the marriage settlement
was witnessed by Alexander MacKensie and Elias Bourne,
Esquires, both of Castleconnor The latter would appear to
establish an additional cross-linkage between the children of
Elias "the elder," and we therefore have three Elias Bournes,
the original Elias of Castleconnor and two grandsons of the
same name, one the son of William and the other the son of
Thomas In the absence of contrary evidence, we are therefore
quite certain that William of Carrowteige was the son of Elias
Bourne of Castleconnor and that he probably was one of the
"three lives" named in the missing Carrowteige and Portacloy
lease.

Returning to the marriage settlement, William Bourne
(Bournes or Bourns as he and other members of the family
were thereafter known) and his son were parties to this settlement made prior to the marriage of Elias and Marjerry(sic),
daughter of James Hendry[6] of Atticree, Co Sligo Provision
was made in the settlement for Elias to inherit two-thirds of
his father's estate but the remaining one-third was to be held
during the lifetime of his "uncle," Garret Bourne(sic). Sur-

[5] Registry of Deeds #256 291 166155
[6] James Hendry was a witness to a memorandum affixed to the original Stonefield
lease

prisingly, Garret Bourne is only mentioned in this one eighteenth century source,[7] presumably he was another brother of
William's, but the name "Garret" is not perpetuated in the
family identified as the Bournes of Carrowteige and Portacloy.

William Bournes of Carrowteige and his wife, Jane Clynes,[8]
had at least one other child, a daughter, Shuana(sic) Shuana
married John Kerin of Bunnefinglass, Co Mayo, a townland
in the Parish of Attymas The articles of agreement (or
marriage settlement) being executed 30 October 1759 By
1770, The Kerins were residing at Carrowkeribly, Co Mayo
in the same parish.[9]

William of Carrowteige died shortly before 2 September
1777 At this time a renewal of lease was made in which it was
noted that William, the last of the three original lives, had
died [10]

The history of the family from this period until well into
the next century is obscured, perhaps forever, by the loss of
many valuable records. No family legend endured to fill in
the missing years but one small folktale is still recalled.

Jane Clynes Bournes, wife of the landlord, was a kindly,
charitable woman who frequently helped her less fortunate
neighbors. On one occasion, and unknown to her husband,
she gave away all of the oat seed that William had stored for
the coming Spring sowing. Sacks of chaff, however, remained
in the Bournes storehouse for in those days chaff was frequently used for bedding Sowing time came and the land was
prepared for the Spring planting William was called away
from home and he instructed his foreman to begin the planting in his absence The foreman soon discovered there was no
seed at all, only light sacks of chaff Jane Bournes begged him
not to tell her husband what she had done but to take the

---

[7] In the seventeenth century a Garret Bourne is found on an Army list According
to the record, he was discharged from duty in 1686 (Ormond MS, 418)
[8] Registry of Deeds #256 291 166155 in which Jane Clynes is called the wife of
William of Carrowteige
[9] P R O Belfast, #T 1021/8, p 62, Chancery Bill abstract In 1770, William Bournes,
the father, was of Carrowteige but Elias, his son, was residing at Attyan(sic), Co Sligo
[10] Registry of Deeds #180 604 123282, #466 11 29567

chaff and harrow it into the ground. This he did and it is tradition that such a crop of oats never grew before or since in Carrowteige [11]

Before continuing with the pedigree of the family it is interesting that the available records for the eighteenth century refer to William Bournes as "of Carrowteige " In the next century, another William resided in this same area but he was known as William Bournes of Portacloy.

The Bournes of Carrowteige and Portacloy

I. William Bournes, landlord of Portacloy, according to family sources, was originally a school teacher in Ballina, Co. Mayo He married 26 August 1827, Jane Celia, born ca 1808, the eldest daughter of John Bournes of Rosserk[12] and the granddaughter of John Bournes of Stonefield [13] Jane Celia was also a teacher and presumably quite proficient in languages When she and her husband eventually made their home in Portacloy, she became known in that Erris community as "the lady with seven tongues."[14]

The articles of agreement made prior to their marriage were dated 23 August 1827 but unfortunately give no clue as to William Bournes' parentage.[15] This agreement was made between William Bournes of the first part, John Bournes (Jane Celia's father) of the second part, Jane Celia Bournes of the third part and John Bournes, the younger, (presumably Jane Celia's brother) of the fourth part [16]

Exactly when the Bournes came to Portacloy and made their residence there is not known, but it probably was some

---

[11] Related to the author by John and Thomas Bournes of Stonefield

[12] *Ballina Impartial*, issue of 22 Aug 1827

[13] Stonefield family records Jane Celia was named as granddaughter in the Will of John Bournes of Stonefield, dated 29 July 1826

[14] Michael Corduff, "Notes on Erris," *Irish Folklore Commission*, Vol I, p 72

[15] A descendant of the McCormick family of Erris indicates that William Bournes was a first cousin of George Smith Bournes of the Rossport family

[16] Registry of Deeds #1867 35 86 The original articles of agreement have not been located However, a reference to this document is made in a deed made some years later in 1867

time after 23 June 1842, the date their son, Richard John
Cowan Green Bournes, was baptised in the Parish of Killala,
Co Mayo Very little is recalled about the Bournes during
their years in Ballina, or later in Portacloy, but we have been
told that William Bournes was cautioned by the family, as
the time came to move to Erris, against taking a "city bred"
girl so far from her friends and home

William Bournes was a respected landlord and in 1869 he
became a member of the Mayo Grand Jury.[17] He apparently
died prior to his wife, for when Jane Celia died at Portacloy
5 April 1889, aged 79, she was called a widow [18] They both
were buried in Kilgalligan Cemetery and left issue [19]

   i John Bournes, born ca 1828, died in Jan 1857, aged 29 [20]

  ii Ellen Bournes, baptised 21 Nov 1831 in the Parish of Ballysakeery, died unmarried 4 July 1910, aged 75 She was buried in
Kilgalligan Cemetery [21]

 iii William Bournes q v

 iv Robert Bournes named as a "Gentleman and son of William and
Jane Celia Bourns" in an indenture, dated 17 April 1877 [22]

  v Richard John Cowan Green Bournes, baptised 23 June 1842 in
the Parish of Killala, died ca 1882, aged 40, unmarried [23]

 vi Mary Anne Sarah Bournes named as a daughter of "William and
Jane Celia Bourns" in an indenture, dated 17 April 1877 [24] She
was born ca 1851 and died unmarried in 1916, aged about 65,
at Portacloy [25] Her Will, dated 23 Oct 1913, was proved in 1920
In the Will, she named her niece, Anne Bournes, daughter of
"my late brother Matthew," as Executrix and residuary legatee [26]

vii. Matthew Bournes who emigrated to the United States and died

---

[17] *Ballinrole Chronicle*, issue of 10 July 1869

[18] Custom House Register

[19] According to descendants of William and Jane Celia Bournes, they had seven
children

[20] Higgins Papers, National Library, Canberra, Australia, MS 1057

[21] Register of the Parish of Kilcommon Erris, 1879-1947 This register is in the possession of the Rector of Crossmolina, Co Mayo and is the earliest register for Kilcommon
Parish that exists today

[22] Registry of Deeds #1877 21 79

[23] Portacloy family records

[24] Registry of Deeds #1877 21 79

[25] Portacloy family records

[26] P R O Dublin, Ballina District Registry

prior to 1913 He had issue of at least one child, a daughter, Anne, who was unmarried and living in Whitehaven, Penn [27]

II William Bournes Jr , the eldest son, born ca. 1828 (or 1829) was a landlord of Portacloy. He married first, Jane McGuiness and second, Mary Harken. On the 15th of April 1903, he died at Portacloy, aged 75 [28]

By Jane McGuiness, William Bournes had issue

    1. William Samuel Bournes q v

By Mary Harken, William Bournes had issue [29]

    ii Mary Bournes, born ca 1874, died 28 April 1893, aged 19, at Portacloy, unmarried [30]

    iii Charlotte Bournes, born ca 1881, died 1 Dec 1963, aged 82, at Portacloy, unmarried

    iv John Bournes, born ca 1882, married Nora Reilly and resided at Portacloy He survived his wife and died 7 April 1967, aged 85, at Portacloy They had issue

        (1) Michael Bournes, born 21 Sept 1921, resides at Portacloy, unmarried

    v Matthew Bournes, born ca 1886, died 30 March 1887, aged 7 months

    vi Anne Bournes, born ca 1889, died in 1921, aged 32, at Portacloy, unmarried

    vii Richard Bournes, born 1 May 1897, resides at Portacloy, unmarried

III William Samuel Bournes, born ca 1861 in Rossport, Co. Mayo,[31] was reared and educated by his grandmother, Jane Celia Bournes, following the death of his mother William Samuel Bournes was locally known as Sonny Mór (Big Sonny), or as Sonny Billy, and was the spokesman for the Portacloy community, being able to converse in both English and Irish. From the Corduff manuscript, previously mentioned, one learns that William Samuel Bournes was the

[27] P R O Dublin, Ballina District Registry
[28] Custom House Register
[29] Portacloy family records
[30] Custom House Register
[31] According to his daughter, Mary Anne Bournes Collins

foremost poet in Erris and many of his early poems were composed with the help of his grandmother, Jane Celia [32]

His poems, or songs as they are called in Ireland, were concerned primarily with local history or nature He also used his verse to chide young people whom he felt sought only pleasure or amusement, and he frequently censored the trend of modern culture [33] Although he occasionally had cause to be provoked, he never used his writings for personal retaliation [34] He was a prolific author and yet today only four of his poems still exist [35]

William Samuel traveled with four of his children to the United States, via Canada, in the early part of the twentieth century settling in Denver, Colorado for seven years Presumably, he had hoped his wife, Elizabeth Naughton, would join them after they were settled She, however, preferred to remain in Ireland and he subsequently returned to Portacloy where he died in 1944, aged 83 Elizabeth Naughton Bournes died in July 1919 at Portacloy They had issue [36]

i   John Bournes who died in the United States in 1961

ii Jane Celia Bournes who came to the United States at the age of 16 years She resides in San Francisco, California, unmarried.

iii Mary Anne Bournes who came to the United States at the age of 14 years She married John Collins and resides in Los Angeles, California They had issue

   (1) Betty Collins who married Dr Coleman

   (2) John Collins

   (3) William Collins

   (4) James Collins

iv Richard Bournes who came to the United States at the age of 13 years He died in 1954

v   Thomas Bournes (called Tommy Mór) who resides in Portacloy, a widower

---

[32] Corduff, op cit , Vol III, p 489
[33] *Ibid*
[34] Corduff, op cit , Vol III, p 486
[35] See Appendix, pp 289-293
[36] According to Mary Anne Bournes Collins, their daughter

   vi William Bournes who resides in the United States, unmarried

  vii Robert Bournes who resides in San Francisco, California, un-married

viii. Ellen Bournes who married John Doherty and resides in Porta-cloy. They had issue of four children

  ix Nora Bournes who married and resides in Oakland, California They had issue of two children

   x George Bournes who resides in Portacloy, unmarried

  xi Henry Bournes who married and resides in Portacloy They had issue of five children

VII. Ardglass

The townland of Ardglass is in the Parish of Ardcarne, county of Roscommon. The river Shannon flows near this townland, forming a natural boundary between the counties of Roscommon and Leitrim Across the Shannon is Carrick-on-Shannon, a sizeable market and post town in Co Leitrim. Carrick-on-Shannon is rather important to the story of at least three Connaught Bournes families It was the very early residence of the Ardglass, the Hatley and the Stonefield Bournes

Insofar as is known, the Ardglass family originated with a David Bournes, who was residing in Carrick-on-Shannon by 10 June 1780 At this time, Richard St. George demised land in Leitrim to David Bournes,[1] who also, presumably, acquired Ardglass from the St. George family Although no record has been located to verify this, it is known that by the mid-1800's

---

[1] Registry of Deeds #1841 15 134 On this same day, 10 July 1780, Richard St George also demised land in Carrick-on-Shannon to a John Bournes of this same place The land was demised for and during John Bournes life, the life of his wife, Jane Bournes, and for the life of John Roddy(sic), son of John Roddy of Carrownaglough (Stonefield), Co Mayo John Bournes, according to this deed, is said to have died on or about 1826 having made his last Will and Testament He is also said to have bequeathed the said demised premises to his daughter, Elizabeth, the wife of David Bournes of Ardglass This reference to John of Carrick-on-Shannon and to his wife and daughter identifies him as being the same John Bournes who was later known as John of Stonefield

Ardglass was leased by Richard St George's son to the son of David Bournes [2]

David Bournes was residing at Ardglass by 12 October 1801 when he was a party to a marriage settlement When the settlement was made, prior to the marriage of Thomas Bournes, the younger, of Castleconnor, Co Sligo and Hester O'Brien, David Bournes was recorded as being "of Ardglass "[3] After David's death in the early nineteenth century, his sons and later their sons continued to live in this area Descendants of David Bournes were at Ardglass as recently as 1912 [4]

Although very little is known about David Bournes himself, he presumably inherited land in Co Mayo from his father, Elias Bournes of Castleconnor Elias had been granted the townland of Tawnynaboll by Charles Atkinson of Rehins, Co Mayo on the 9th of December 1761 [5] Tawnynaboll, consisting of slightly more than 451 acres of land, was in the Parish of Dunfeeny and not far from Killala, Co Mayo

The Bournes of Ardglass

I David Bournes of Ardglass, son of Elias Bournes of Castleconnor, Co Sligo,[6] married Celia (Cecelia) Lloyd and had issue of four children, all named in an indenture of demise [7] According to this indenture, he died intestate on or about 1809 His wife died at Ardglass and was buried in the Parish of Ardcarne, 29 October 1820 [8]

   1 Thomas Bournes, the eldest son, died intestate and without issue in April 1821

[2] In 1641, Ardglass was in the possession of Tumultagh McHugh but was later acquired by Sir Oliver St George during the Acts of Settlement Charles Manners St George, Richard's son and a descendant of Sir Oliver's, leased Ardglass to David Burns (sic) ca 1858 (Book of Survey and Distribution, Vol I, p 134, Griffith's Valuation, 1858)

[3] Registry of Deeds #848 204 547704, #880 563383

[4] Land Commission, Dublin

[5] Registry of Deeds #251 428 162789

[6] Registry of Deeds #466 11 295267.

[7] Registry of Deeds #1841 15 134

[8] In the parish register, she is called Mrs Cecelia Bournes

ii William Bournes, the second son, was born ca 1774 and died intestate, without issue, in June 1837, aged 64

iii David Bournes q v

iv Eliza Bournes who was born ca 1778

II David Bournes of Ardglass, the third eldest son, was born ca 1781 and came into possession of his father's estate following the death of his two brothers He married (M L B Killala and Achonry) 1810, Elizabeth, born ca 1785, daughter of John Bournes of Stonefield, by Jane Lloyd [9] David Bournes was buried 22 December 1865, aged 84, in the Parish of Ardcarne His wife, Elizabeth, was buried in this same parish 6 August 1860, aged 75.[10] They had issue.

i David Bournes q v

ii Jane Bournes who married Dec 1837[11] Henry Bournes of Attichee, Co Sligo at the Killanley Church in the Parish of Castleconnor They had issue

(1) Eliza Bournes, born 19 Dec 1838, was baptised in the Parish of Ardcarne 24 Dec 1838

iv. Sarah Bournes, born 23 Dec 1821, was baptised in the Parish of Ardcarne 26 Dec 1821

III David Bournes of Ardglass born 1 June 1825, was baptised 15 June 1825 in the Parish of Ardcarne as David Oldfield Bournes [12] On the 16th of December 1850, "David Bourns, Gent, then of Danesford, Co Roscommon, married Mary, daughter of Thomas Roycroft, Gent, of Danesford" The witnesses to this marriage, performed in the Killuken Parish Church, Co. Roscommon, were Thomas Roycroft and George W Brown [13]

[9] Registry of Deeds #1841 15 134, Stonefield family records

[10] In the Custom House Register, David Bournes' date of death is given as 5 Jan 1866 He died at Ardglass, son David present

[11] *Mayo Constitution*, issue of 12 Dec 1837 in which Jane is called the daughter of David Bournes, Esq of Ardglass However, in the Castleconnor Parish register, the marriage of a Jane Alicia Bournes, daughter of William Bournes of Ardglass to Henry Bournes of "Attichee," Co Sligo 13 Nov 1837 is recorded John Bournes, brother of the bride, and William Bournes, the father were witnesses

[12] The name of "Oldfield" insofar as is known, was not a family name There was, however, a clergyman by the name of Oldfield in the Ardcarne Parish about 1825

[13] Custom House Register

David Bournes died 8 February 1910 at Faus, Co Roscommon, aged 84, and the Administration of his estate was
granted to his son, Elias [14] Mary Bournes, his wife, died 23
December 1884 at Ardglass, aged 60, and she was buried in
the Killuken Cemetery [15] They had issue.

    i   Elias Bournes, the eldest son, was born 14 Oct 1854 and baptised
       3 Jan 1856 in the Parish of Ardcarne He was a party, with his
       father, to an indenture made 13 Sept 1878 in which the lands of
       Tawnynaboll were to be demised to Thomas Hailey Monck [16]

    ii Elizabeth Barbara Bournes, born 17 Sept 1855, was baptised 3
       Jan 1856 in the Parish of Ardcarne

    iii David Bournes, who was living at the time of his mother's
       death [17]

    iv Robert Bournes, born 7 April 1870, was baptised 19 April 1870 in
       the Parish of Ardcarne

    v Hans (John) Bournes

    vi Anne Bournes

    vii Molly Bournes, her brother, Hans, and sister, Anne, were named
       with the other four children as the surviving heirs to their father's
       estate, 1912 [18]

[14] Custom House Register, P R O , Dublin, Index to Wills

[15] Custom House Register The Ardcarne Parish Register shows that Mary Bournes
was buried 20 Dec 1884, aged 60, or three days before her death was registered!

[16] Registry of Deeds #1878 44 140

[17] Custom House Register

[18] Land Commission, Dublin Family settlement dated 9 January 1912

VIII.   Hatley

The lands of Hatley are located in the Parish of Kiltoghart and in the barony and county of Leitrim Hatley, a part of the St George family's estate, was leased to members of the Bournes family through the years [1] The earliest known representative to reside there was a John Houston Bournes who lived at Hatley Manor, near Carrick-on-Shannon, in 1814 [2]

The history of this particular family branch is difficult to reconstruct because there are so many records missing Although it would be more conservative, from a genealogica standpoint, to avoid any reference to those whose lineage has not been deciphered, we have preferred to engage in speculation. It seems better to record all known facts about a family than to withhold information that has been insufficiently collated.

Thus the pedigree of the Hatley Bournes family is presented, even though certain assumptions have been made We hope that, in spite of this, it will be of interest to a reader, and perhaps of some assistance to other genealogical researchers

The Bournes of Hatley

I Robert Bournes, probably son of Elias Bournes of Castle-connor, Co. Sligo, was a Surgeon of Carrick, Co. Leitrim. His

---

[1] Griffith's Valuation, 1856, Registry of Deeds #1875 47 117
[2] Leet's Directory of Gentlemen's Seats (1814)

name appears as a party to a settlement made prior to the marriage of Thomas Bournes, the younger, of Castleconnor and Hester O'Brien, 12 October 1801 [3] Robert Bournes married (M L B. Elphin) 1782 Catherine Davis, and it is believed they had the following issue

    i John Houston Bournes q v

    ii Robert Davis Bournes, Surgeon of Carrick-on-Shannon, Co Leitrim, presumably married several times as he, or a man by this same name, is found in various marriage records The following account is presented, therefore, only to record known facts, rather than to interpret them Robert Davis Bournes married (M L B Elphin) 1802, Jane Lockhart On 13 Jan 1812, he married Olivia Grattan in the Parish of Boyle, Co Roscommon [4] And on 18 June 1818, he was married to Celia Bournes of Ardglass in the Parish of Ardcarne, Co Roscommon [5] From other records, it is known that he was residing in Killala, Co Mayo by 1822 and in 1824 was officially recorded as a Surgeon of this town [6] A Robert Bourns(sic) was buried 11 March 1826, aged 38, in the Parish of Killala, but there is no apparent way to prove that this "Robert" and Robert Davis Bournes were the same person However, Dr Bournes was deceased prior to 1853, for Celia was then residing on Hudson Ave , Brooklyn N Y and called a widow She presumably had migrated to America ca 1853 for this was the first time her name appeared in the Brooklyn City Directory Subsequent directories, called her Celia, or Jane Celia, as did census enumerations, and she was always referred to as a widow [7] When she died 28 July 1871, aged 79, at 240 Court St , Brooklyn, she was called "the relict of Robert D Bournes, M D of Co Mayo "[8] Celia, or Jane Celia Bournes was buried in The Green-Wood Cemetery, located at 5th Ave and 25th St , Brooklyn [9] The following children, all baptised in the Parish of Killala, may possibly have been issue of Dr Robert D Bournes and his wife Celia

        (1) Catherine Davis Bournes, baptised 4 March 1818, was called the daughter of Robert and Jane Bournes.

        (2) Jane Celia Bournes, baptised 17 Oct 1819, was called the daughter of Robert and Jane Celia (Bournes) Bournes She

[3] Registry of Deeds #848 204 547704 #889 383 563383

[4] Witnesses to this marriage were "William Grattan, Freeman and many others "

[5] In the Elphin M L B , Robert D Bournes is recorded as marrying Jane C Bournes, 1815 Is it not possible that this record and the 1818 marriage were the same? Thus either the M L B or the Parish record was incorrectly copied

[6] He was a witness to the marriage settlement, in 1822, made prior to the marriage of Henry Bournes and Fanny Watts, (see Rossport family), Pigot's Directory (1824)

[7] Brooklyn City Directories, 1853-1870, Kings Co , N Y Census Enumeration, 1870, 10th Ward, p 14 (taken June 17, 1870)

[8] G Barber, *Abstracts of Deaths from the Brooklyn Eagle*, Vol 15, p 74

[9] The Green-Wood Cemetery records

may possibly be the same Jane C Bournes who died unmarried 25 Aug 1871, aged 46, at 231 Court St , Brooklyn,
and was buried in The Green-Wood Cemetery [10]

(3) Eleanor Bournes, baptised 25 Feb 1821, was called the
daughter of Robert and Jane Celia (Bournes) Bournes She
may possibly be the Ellen (Eleanor) Bournes who was residing with Mrs Jane C Bournes in 1870 [11] An Eleanor
Bournes died unmarried 26 May 1884, aged 63, at 503 Hicks
St , Brooklyn, and was buried in The Green-Wood Cemetery [12]

(4) Alicia Bournes, baptised 9 Aug 1823, was called the daughter
of Robert and Jane Celia (Bournes) Bournes

II John Houston Bournes of Hatley Manor, Carrick-on-
Shannon, Co Leitrim[13] married 3 April 1804[14] Elizabeth
Henderson, also of Carrick-on-Shannon He presumably died
before 1850,[15] and it is believed that he and his wife had the
following issue

i   Robert Wilson Bournes q v

ii Arthur Henderson Bournes of Carrick-on-Shannon was born ca
1808 and married, 4 May 1835, Jane Elizabeth Browne in the
Parish of Kiltoghart Witnesses to this marriage were D H
Browne, Evans B Grose and R W Bournes [16] From 1837
Arthur H Bournes was listed as Postmaster in the Kiltoghart
Parish Register He died 31 Aug 1894, aged 86, at Carrick-on-
Shannon and his wife died 6 Oct 1882, aged 74, at the same
place [17] They had issue all baptised in the Parish of Kiltoghart

(1) Mary Catherine Bournes was baptised 27 March 1836 She
was residing at 70 Amiens St , Dublin when she married, 18
June 1859, James Imrie, merchant, of 23 Suffolk St Dublin,
the son of George Imrie, merchant The marriage, performed
at St Thomas' Church, Dublin, was witnessed by Arthur H
Bournes and William Hughes [18]

(2) John Houston Thomas Bournes was baptised 20 Oct 1837

[10] Barber, op cit , Vol 15, p 82, The Green-Wood Cemetery Records
[11] Census Enumeration 1870, op cit
[12] The Green-Wood Cemetery Records
[13] Leet's Directory of Gentlemen's Seats (1814), Tithe Book, 1834
[14] *Faulkner's Journal of Dublin,* issue of 10 April 1804
[15] *Sligo Chronicle,* issue of 17 April 1850 in which he was called the "late John Bourns
of Hatley '
[16] Register of the Parish of Kiltoghart
[17] Custom House Register
[18] *Ibid*

(3) David Browne Bournes was baptised 18 Feb 1839 He was known as a Gentleman farmer of Carrick-on-Shannon and he died there, 25 May 1883, aged 44, unmarried [19]

(4) Elizabeth Henderson Bournes was baptised 19 Jan 1843

(5) Susanna Adelaide Bournes was baptised in Dec 1844

(6) Jane Alicia Bournes was baptised 28 July 1848

iii Eliza Bournes who died 28 Dec 1850 at Hatley and was called the daughter of the "late John Bourns of Hatley "[20]

iv Susan Davis Bournes, born ca 1805, was named in the Will of Robert Wilson Bournes (to be cited) as "aunt" to his children She died 2 May 1875, aged 70, unmarried[21] at Hatley Manor

v Mary Anna Bournes who was named as "aunt" in the Will of her niece, Margaret Susan, eldest daughter of Robert Wilson Bournes

vi Alicia Whitelaw Bournes, born ca 1821, was called the daughter of John Houston Bournes and Elizabeth Henderson [22] She migrated to New York from Ireland in 1857 and resided at 9 East 64th St When she died, unmarried, 23 March 1908, aged 87 years, 7 months and 3 days, her home was at 49 East 73rd St Alicia W Bournes was buried in The Green-Wood Cemetery, Brooklyn [23]

III Robert Wilson Bournes of Summerhill, Co Leitrim was of Hatley Manor by 1852 [24] He held the title and interest in "the lands of Hatley, Grove Hop, Bolly Parks and Kilbodery" by lease under Charles Manners St George, Esq Also the lands of Lisernaron in the Parish of Aughrim, Co Roscommon by lease under Arthur French Lloyd, Esq and the lands of Dromagh by lease under Charles Peyton, Esq On the 26th of May 1834, he married Frances Margaret Grose in the Parish of Kiltoghart Witnesses to this marriage were A Grose and Arthur Browne [25]

Robert Wilson Bournes dated his Will 18 January 1855, and he died this same year.[26] In his Will he expressed a desire

[19] Custom House Register
[20] *Sligo Chronicle*, issue of 17 April 1850.
[21] Custom House Register
[22] Death Certificate
[23] *Ibid*, The Green-Wood Cemetery Records
[24] Register of the Parish of Kiltoghart
[25] Custom House Register
[26] P R O , Dublin Index to Wills

to be interred in the family burial ground at Killuken, Co
Roscommon [27] He bequeathed all his right, title and interest
in the "lands of Ballyghart in the Parish of Kiltoghart" to
his three daughters, Margaret Susan, Elizabeth Henderson
and Frances Eliza Bournes To his eldest son, Robert Whitelaw Bournes, he left his right, title and interest in the lands of
"Hatley Manor, Lisernaron, Grove Hop, Boly Parks, Kilbodery and Dromagh " Although he referred to his seven sons,
he only made specific bequests to his eldest son, Robert
Whitelaw, and to his fourth son, Arthur Henderson Bournes
He instructed his eldest son to care for his aunt, Susan Davis
Bournes, and she was also named as one of the Executors to
his Will. Hugh Church, Inn Keeper, George Church. Shopkeeper and Arthur Bournes, Postmaster. all of Carrick-on-
Shannon, were named as Executors, as were Charles Grose of
Rose Bank, farmer and Robert Whitelaw Bournes of Hatley
Manor The Will was witnessed by William Whitelaw, Gentle-
man, Newcomen Whitelaw, Gentleman and Thomas Church,
in business, all of Carrick-on-Shannon, Co. Leitrim.

Frances Margaret Grose Bournes presumably died before
her husband as she was not named in his Will They had issue

    i Margaret Susan Bournes, born ca 1835, died unmarried, 15
       June 1897 at Westhill, Oxted, Surrey, England She and her two
       sisters inherited the lands of Ballyghart, Co Leitrim from their
       father Her Will was dated 10 June 1897 and proved 17 Nov
       1897 by her brother, Dr Newcomen Whitelaw Bournes [28]

    ii Elizabeth Henderson Bournes was baptised 28 Sept 1836 in the
       Parish of Kiltoghart She married 5 Jan 1859 in this same parish,
       Marmaduke, son of Thomas Church of Carrick-on-Shannon,
       merchant Witnesses to this marriage were Michael Mitchell and
       James Toptown [29]

    iii Robert Whitelaw Bournes q v

    iv Frances Elizabeth Bournes was baptised 17 Nov 1840 in the
       Parish of Kiltoghart She was residing at 26 Charlemont Place,
       Dublin[30] when she married 21 Feb 1865 at St Peter's Church,

    [27] Killuken burial ground was also used by the Ardglass Bournes family

    [28] Somerset House, London

    [29] Custom House Register

    [30] Although this address was given at the time of her marriage, she was also said to
be of Hatley Manor, Co Leitrim

Dublin, Thomas, son of Hugh Church, of Cloonbrian, Ardnanse, Co Roscommon Witnesses to this marriage were George Church and Robert Bournes [31]

v Daniel Charles Grose Bournes (twin), born 25 April 1843 at Hatley Manor, was baptised 13 April 1843[32], in the Parish of Kiltoghart He was a licentiate of the Royal College of Surgeons and Physicians, Edinburgh, Scotland in 1864[33], Assistant Surgeon Army Staff, 30 Sept 1864, 85th Regiment of Foot, 12 Aug 1870 and served in South Africa in 1879 and Egypt in 1882; a Fellow of the Faculty of Physicians and Surgeons, Glasgow, Scotland [34] Dr Bournes died unmarried, 9 July 1892 at Hall Hill, Oxted, Surrey at which time he was a Lieut. Colonel Surgeon [35] His Will was dated 31 Aug 1891 and proved 9 Aug 1892 by "his brother Charles Bouins, licentiate of the King's and Queen's College of Physicians, Ireland "[36]

vi John Houston Bournes (twin) was baptised 13 April 1843 in the Parish of Kiltoghart

vii Arthur Henderson Bournes was baptised 2 July 1845 in the Parish of Kiltoghart In his father's Will he was called the "fourth son," and he inherited the lands of Clonsher and Bally-mamoney

viii Charles Wilson Bournes, born 2 July 1847, was baptised 2 Aug 1847 in the Parish of Kiltoghart He was admitted a licentiate 13 July 1870 to the Royal College of Surgeons and Physicians in Ireland, a licentiate of King's and Queen's College of Physicians, Ireland 1870[37] and he graduated from the University of Edinburgh, Scotland, M O in 1912 at the East District Godstone Union [38] He resided from 1878 through 1894 at Oxted Surrey, England but his specific addresses there varied in the medical registers [39] He married, wife's name unknown, and had three daughters who were named in the Will of his brother,[40] Dr Newcomen White-law Bournes

(1) Margery Bournes, unmarried in 1927

(2) Florence Bournes, who married _____Walker

(3) Kathleen Bournes, unmarried in 1927

[31] Custom House Register

[32] Dr Bournes' birth date comes from the Roll of Army Medical Service, 1727-1898 (#6196) and his baptismal date from the parish record Obviously one is in error

[33] Medical Register, date of registration, 8 July 1864

[34] Roll of Army Medical Service, op cit

[35] Ibid

[36] Somerset House, London

[37] Medical Register, date of registration 5 Sept 1870

[38] Records of the Royal College of Surgeons and Physicians in Ireland

[39] From 1878 through 1885 he was of Oxted, Godstone, Surrey, in 1888 of Hall Hill, Oxted, Godstone, Surrey and in 1894 of Westhill, Oxted, Surrey

[40] Will of Newcomen Whitelaw Bournes, dated 19 March 1927

ix Evans Bournes was baptised 3 June 1850 in the Parish of Kiltoghart

x Newcomen Whitelaw Bournes was baptised 20 Dec 1852 in the Parish of Kiltoghart He was educated privately at Hatley Manor and became a member of the Royal College of Surgeons in England in 1879, licentiate of the Royal College of Physicians, Edinburgh, Scotland 1880 and M D University of Brussels, Belgium 1880 In 1881 he was at the Cancer Hospital, London.[41] He resided in 1883 at 449 Fulham Road, West Brompton, London[42] and died 2 Oct 1927[43] at Churchfield, Wincanton, Somerset, England In his Will, dated 19 March 1927 he mentions his wife, Alice Bournes who predeceased him 11 April 1922 A Codicil was made 29 Sept 1927 and the Will and Codicil were proved 6 Dec 1927 [44] Presumably he died without issue for no children were named in his Will, or Codicil

IV   Robert Whitelaw Bournes of Hatley Manor was a land agent and a law clerk He was baptised 14 September 1838 in the Parish of Kiltoghart and as the eldest son, inherited most of his father's estate On 6 October 1875, he married Marion, the daughter of James Francis Moore of Carrick-on-Shannon

The marriage settlement dated 6 October 1875 was made between Robert Whitelaw Bournes of Hatley Manor, Esq. of the first part, Marion Moore of Carrick-on-Shannon, spinster of the second part and James Francis Moore of Carrick-on-Shannon, Esq and Charles Bournes of Hall Hill, Oxted, Surrey, Esq , Medical Doctor of the third part [45]

Robert Whitelaw Bournes died 16 November 1909, aged 71,[46] and was buried in Killukcn Cemetery His Will was dated 28 April 1908 and proved in 1909 [47] They had issue

i   Robert Wilson Bournes who died 30 Nov 1876 aged 5 months, at Carrick-on-Shannon [48]

---

[41] Medical Register, date of registration 26 Feb 1879

[42] Ibid, issue of 1883

[43] Who Was Who (1916-1918 ed)

[44] Somerset House, London

[45] Registry of Deeds #1875 47 117

[46] Custom House Register He was called a widower and a law clerk

[47] P R O Dublin, Cavan District Registry

[48] Custom House Register

ii. Lydia Mary Bournes, born 13 Aug 1877, was baptised 20 Sept 1877 in the Parish of Kiltoghart She married David Clarke [49]

iii Frances M Bournes, unmarried in 1927 [50]

iv Marion May Bournes, born 26 May 1883, was baptised 29 June 1883 in the Parish of Kiltoghart She was unmarried in 1927 [51]

[49] Stonefield family records She was named as "daughter of Robert Whitelaw Bournes, my brother," in Will of Newcomen W Bournes, 1927
[50] Will of Newcomen W Bournes, 1927
[51] *Ibid*

Part Two

Hannah Maria Bournes
and
Her Descendants

IX. Hannah Maria Bournes, née Maxwell

Our great grandmother, née Hannah Maria Maxwell, was born ca 1809, probably in Ballina. Co Mayo, the only child of Reverend Malachi Maxwell and Cecelia, daughter of John Bournes of Stonefield

Very little is known about Hannah Maria's parents, and some of the information with respect to her father, Reverend Maxwell, is quite puzzling There is conflicting evidence about his christian name, and we are not certain as to when and where he died

Family tradition identifies Hannah's father as "Malachi," and this is substantiated by the records of Trinity College, Dublin which carry the following entry "Malachi Maxwell, sizar, (his father), matriculated 7 June 1803, aged 18 Son of Matthew Maxwell (agricola), born Cork "[1]

The confusion over Malachi's christian name is caused by the record of Hannah Maria's second marriage (subsequently cited) which states that she was the daughter of "Reverend Henry Millick Maxwell " This is the only reference that has been found to "Henry Millick" and in view of the Trinity record, family tradition and other available sources, we must assume that "Henry Millick" is a phantom caused by a

[1] *Alumni Dublinenses*, op cit

clerical aberration One can imagine that "Millick" is a
perversion of "Malachi," but "Henry" seems to be an un-
witting bonus! At any rate it would seem that Hannah Maria's
father was, indeed, the Reverend Malachi Maxwell and, although it would have been simpler for this story not to include
"Henry Millick," we have preferred to mention him in the
interest of completeness and for the benefit of anyone who
may care to retrace our searchings.

Malachi Maxwell's Trinity College record furnishes sound
evidence that he was born ca 1785 in Cork, the son of Matthew
Maxwell, a farmer (agricola) The father, who provided his
son's pre-college education, obviously was a person of modest
means as the entry "sizar" meant that Malachi had obtained
financial assistance, or a scholarship, from Trinity

We suspect Malachi met Cecelia Bournes during the time
he was a student and perhaps married her before completing
his college career [2] There is some evidence that Malachi did
not receive a formal degree from Trinity,[3] but there is no
record of his marriage to Cecelia Bournes

By 1812, Reverend Maxwell had become vicar of the
Parishes of Kilmore and Kilcommon, Erris and he remained
in that area for a least a year [4] Curiously, another clergyman,
Patrick Maxwell, served these two parishes from 1770 to
1807, but we have no reason to suspect that these two men
with a common surname were in any way related There are
no references providing the name of the clergyman (or clergy-
men) who served this area for the intervening years, 1807-
1812 Other than disclosing that a clergyman in Erris received
approximately £150 per annum from the tithe and Glebe,[5]
available records have given us no further insight

---

[2] This is contrary to our family tradition (related in the Foreword to this book)
which states that Rev Maxwell's daughter, Hannah Maria, met and married William
Bournes while William was a student at Trinity As there are no records at T C D , or
elsewhere, to substantiate this, or to indicate that William Bournes was a clergyman,
it does not seem likely that tradition is correct

[3] Canon J Leslie, *Biographical Succession of the Diocese of Killala and Achonry*,
op cit

[4] *Ibid*

[5] James M'Parlan, *Statistical Survey of the County of Mayo*, (1802), pp 155-156

Reverend Malachi Maxwell presumably died soon after 1813, for his name disappears at that time from the clerical records of the church Placing his death soon after Hannah Maria's birth would be in agreement with our family tradition, but would be at variance with a holographic commentary found at the church office Leslie's *Biographical Succession of the Diocese of Killala and Achonry* is an authoritative source for the clergy, and Reverend Maxwell's parishes of Kilcommon and Kilmore were within this Diocese However, in Leslie's printed account, a handwritten entry is found opposite the name of Malachi Maxwell stating briefly and without further comment, "died in Canada " We have been unable either to identify the author of this annotation or to determine why it remains in the clerical records

Tradition tells us that after Reverend Malachi's death, his widow, Cecelia, and her daughter, Hannah Maria, lived with the Reverend's brother who was a bachelor and also a clergyman From this point forward, we have no further information regarding Cecelia Bournes Maxwell, and our attention is thus directed to her daughter, Hannah Maria

We are able to pick up the threads of Hannah Maria's story in 1833, for in the *Ballina Impartial*, issue of 18 February 1833, a small notice appeared "A few days ago at Easkey Church by the Rev Mr Stokes,[6] William Bourns Esq , third son of John Bourns Esq of Rosserk was married to Miss Maxwell, daughter of the late Rev Mr Maxwell of Erris."[7] William, baptised William Lloyd Bournes, was born ca. 1812 in Ballina, Co Mayo [8] He was the son of John Bournes, merchant

---

[6] Easkey Church is in the town and Parish of Easkey, Co Sligo near the North West coast of the barony of Tyreragh Rev Mr Stokes was Gabriel Stokes, Rector of Skreen (near Easkey) 1814-1835 The Skreen Parish Register for the year 1833 is no longer in existence and although the Easkey Register is available, beginning with the year 1824, the marriage of William Bournes and Hannah Maria Maxwell is not recorded

[7] One is inclined to wonder about the meaning of 'late'' as applied to Rev Maxwell If the Rev died in 1813, this is reaching back twenty years, a longer span than is normally embraced by this adjective It would be a mistake, however, to attribute too much precision to journalistic reporting

[8] Registry of Deeds #746 418 509054 in which William Lloyd Bournes, aged 6 years is named as a life to the Rosserk lease of 1818 William's parents resided in Ballina at that time

of Ballina, later of Rosserk, and Eleanor, daughter of John Bournes Esq. of Stonefield, Co. Mayo

Newspaper articles have contributed small items of interest about the Bournes family of Connaught, but nothing was found in these stories, or elsewhere, to explain why Hannah Maria married William Lloyd Bournes in the Easkey Church It is evident, however, that they resided at Rosserk where William had a stable of horses When his mare "Coquet" was given credit by a local paper for winning fifth place at the Mount Falcon race course, he seemed to feel it was sufficiently important to write a correction to this story. In his letter to the paper, he emphasized that "Coquet" had captured fourth, not fifth place in the recent race[9] Although this small sidelight gives one the impression that William Lloyd Bournes was a country gentleman, the parish register in 1837 stated that William was a police officer.[10]

William and Hannah Maria had four daughters presumably all born at Rosserk, their parents' home in the Parish of Ballysakeery, near Ballina, Co Mayo The family consisted of Cecelia Maxwell Bournes, born in 1833; Ellen Bournes, born in 1835, Margaret Bournes, born in 1836 and Hannah Bournes, born in 1837 [11]

The father died at the age of 33 and was buried 27 January 1837 in the Parish of Ballysakeery, the day before his youngest daughter was baptised.

Hannah Maria, now a widow with four young daughters, probably remained at Rosserk for awhile Sometime, however, within the next ten years she moved to Cork City, as this was the site of her second marriage in 1847. There is no way of determining exactly when or why Hannah Maria left Mayo for southern Ireland. Possibly she had kin there because, it will be recalled, this is where her father was born. At any rate,

---

[9] *Ballina Impartial*, issues of 21 May 1832, 28 May 1832, 28 Sept 1835

[10] Register of the Parish of Ballysakeery

[11] An account of Hannah Maria's children, and their descendants, is given in subsequent chapters

it was in Cork that Hannah Maria became the wife of Patrick Nowland.

Tradition tells us that Patrick Nowland was a "Civil Engineer" of Irish birth who moved to western Ireland during the famine years It is fortunate for our research that Ireland, beginning in 1845, required that marriages be registered Among those recorded at the Custom House in Dublin is that of Patrick Nowland to Hannah Maria Bournes, 27 November 1847

According to the record, Patrick and Hannah Maria both resided on Leitrim Street in the Parish of St Anne's Shandon, Cork City The marriage, a civil ceremony, was performed at the Registrar's Office, possibly suggesting a mixed marriage Hannah Maria was described as a widow, the daughter of Reverend Henry Millick Maxwell, clergyman Patrick Nowland, or Nowlan, as stated in the record, was a bachelor and labourer, the son of Michael Nowlan, miller Witnesses were John McCarthy, James Redmond and John F. Enright.[12]

Two daughters were soon born to Patrick and Hannah Maria Nowland on the 26th of March 1850 and Emily Nowland in January 1851 [13] We assume these births occurred in Cork City, but no baptismal records have been located in the registers of the Catholic or the Established Churches of that area.

The years immediately following the marriage of Patrick and Hannah Maria were difficult ones for Ireland. Weakened by the terrible famine and its consequences, thousands of families migrated to other parts of the world, particularly to North America The Nowlands and Hannah Maria's children by her former marriage were a part of this exodus

Margaret Bournes, Hannah Maria's third daughter, migrated to Canada, prior to 1850, with her uncle, Thomas

---

[12] It was customary in Ireland for witnesses to be related to the bridal couple In this instance, there is no evidence that the three witnesses were other than casual acquaintances

[13] Municipal Archives and Records Center, New York City, Death Certificate, E B Fitzgerald collection, Bible record.

Bournes and his family Cecelia Maxwell Bournes, the eldest daughter, according to family tradition, attended a Dublin boarding-school and migrated to the United States after she had completed her education The Nowlands, with Ellen and young Hannah Bournes, journeyed to Liverpool, England where they remained until passage was secured for America

In April of 1853, they sailed from Liverpool to New York, with 627 other Irish born passengers, aboard the "Middlesex," captained by H B Parmenter The ship's manifest described the family as follows "Patrick Nowlan, aged 40, Engineer, Mrs. Nowlan, aged 40, wife; Ellen Nowlan, aged 16, daughter; Anna Nowlan, aged 14, daughter, Maria Nowlan, aged 4, child and Emily Nowlan, aged 2, child " Their destination was given as Canada, they carried four pieces of baggage [14]

The "Middlesex" arrived in New York City, 20 April 1853, where the Nowland's third daughter, Elizabeth Whately, was born, 26 May 1853

Although the Nowlands may originally have planned to go to Canada, they did not do so Instead, they remained in New York, residing at first with Patrick's sister, Mrs Prendergast Later they had an apartment of their own When Emily Nowland died, 8 October 1854, aged 3 years and 9 months, her parents' residence was given as 268 W. 32nd St , New York. She was buried in the cemetery of the Trinity Episcopal Church, located at 153rd St and Broadway [15]

Soon after Ellen Bournes became the wife of Alpheus Jones Tynes, on the 22nd of June 1857 in New York City,[16] the Nowlands and young Hannah Bournes moved to Nashville, Tennessee It is quite probable that Patrick was attracted by the expansion of railroad companies in this area and the consequent demand for engineers and skilled labor

When Hannah, the youngest Bournes daughter, married David Anderson McGredy in August of 1857, the Nowland

[14] National Archives, Washington, D C Passenger List #279, Reel #124, no 23-28
[15] Municipal Archives and Records Center, op cit Trinity Episcopal Church itself is located at 74 Trinity Place, New York
[16] E B Fitzgerald Collection, family records

family were residing in South Nashville Hannah Maria became a communicant this same year at the Episcopal Church
of the Advent in Nashville, the church in which her daughter
was married

During the next three years, it is believed that Hannah
Maria lived in Nashville with Maria and Elizabeth, or Lizzie,
as she was called Patrick's work frequently took him away
from home and, just prior to the Civil War, he joined
the Confederate forces.[17] Hannah Maria became a teacher
in order to augment the family's slender income Although
she had no formal training to teach, she did have a fine educational background, particularly in French which she spoke
fluently By 1860, she was living with the Robert L Vanner
family in Cheneyville, Louisiana.[18]

Shortly before Louisiana seceded from the Union, 26
January 1861, Hannah Maria wrote a letter to her eldest
daughter, Cecelia M Bournes Thompson, in Nashville The
complexities and strain of residing in a State that was to
separate from the Union are revealed in the mother's letter.[19]

Cheneyville
Monday 21st Jan

My dear Cecelia

    I feel very uneasy at the prospect of not being able to hear from you
all, nor you from me as of course all mails will be stopped in *this* State
after it secedes which it is to do tomorrow or next day! It is a sad state
of affairs in this country It is hard to say how it will end—I shall be
wretched when I am shut out altogether from my children I write this
on the chance of its reaching you, it never may, but if it does, the only
way I see for you to write to me is (after the mails are stopped) to send
your letters in the way of a parcel to "Payne & Harrison" Merchants,
New Orleans for R L Vanner Esq Cheneyville La Put that on the
outside cover and my name on an inside cover, well sealed—and when

---

[17] Although our family legend had indicated that Patrick Nowland was a Confederate
soldier, we have been unable to locate his service record Existing records show that
there were at least three men by this name but the information given is not sufficient to
establish if one of them was our Patrick Nowland There was Patrick A Nowlan attached to Co G , 3rd North Carolina Artillery Patrick Noland with Co A , 48th
Mississippi Infantry and finally Patrick Nolan with the 26th Georgia Infantry

[18] 1860 Census, Cheneyville, La , pp 207-209, House 1474, no 1466 "Robert L
Vanner, aged 62, born in South Carolina, Mary, his wife, aged 49, H Nowland, aged 35,
female schoolteacher, born in Ireland, Lizzy Nowland, aged 7, born in New York "

[19] E B Fitzgerald Collection, family letters

you write in this way get a letter from Ellen too and make one parcel
of it, but I chiefly depend on you for communications as you understand how to manage Enquire particularly about the *Post Office
Department* and let me know what you learn Tell Ellen she may not
be able to hear from me for some time, but I shall depend upon her to
take care of Maria I think Richard will manage about getting letters
to me through Payne & Harrison even if the mails are stopped it will
be more difficult for me to send letters but after I hear from you and
know how matters stand, I shall (D V) try I have not been at all well
for a short time past I am working hard, the days are short and of
course little time for recreation Give my love to Richard, take care
of yourself, and I also give my love to Ellen, Hannah and Maria, not
forgetting their *husbands*—Lizzie is very well—I feel rather depressed
but I should not, I know for these Political Troubles God Bless you all,
in haste your fond mother

H M Nowland

Hannah Maria's other daughters were in Nashville at this
time, with the exception of Margaret who by 1861 was married
to Alexander McLean and resided in Canada. Ellen, wife of
Alpheus J Tynes, operated a Millinery and Dry Goods Store
with her husband Maria Nowland, her step-sister, lived
with them Hannah, wife of David A McGredy, also resided
in Nashville

Hannah Maria and Lizzie remained in Cheneyville for
several years, returning to Nashville via river packet about
1863 or 1864 By December of 1864, they were living in the
Tynes' Hillsboro home, three miles outside of Nashville, when
the war was literally brought to their doorstep One of the
early engagements during the Battle of Nashville took place
on the Tynes property, the setting and the people involved in
this event were witnessed by a small child. Lizzie Nowland,
about 11½ years of age, never forgot December of '64 and
years later, as a mother, then a grandmother, she frequently
related the story of the battle on Hillsboro Turnpike.

The Tynes' one story, newly built home overlooked approximately twelve acres of well cultivated land with a large
orchard The house was substantial, consisting of a hall, parlor,
dining room, pantry and five bedrooms The kitchen was in an
adjacent building, as was customary during that era Prepara-

tions had been made for the winter months, and there was an ample supply of food on hand for the Tynes family and for their livestock On the 14th of December, Hannah Maria, her daughter, Lizzie, David McGredy (young Hannah's husband) and Miss O'Keefe (an employee in the Tynes business) were all in the house

The 4th Army Corps of the Federal Army was poised on the outskirts of Nashville while the Confederates, commanded by General John B Hood, were advancing from nearby Franklin, Tennessee Under the directives of Brigadier General Thomas J Wood, the 4th Army Corps established pickets to the east of the Tynes property, other pickets were placed close to the house itself The occupants of the house were ordered to remain inside As the Federal soldiers waited for the Confederates, they stripped the farm of its provisions and used the fences as kindling for their campfires

When the northern and southern forces met on Hillsboro turnpike road, cannon ball and shot occasionally pierced the walls of the home The fighting continued for two days and two nights and the Confederates slowly gained ground The four persons within the Tynes house, fearing for their safety, finally stepped outside carrying a white flag attached to a stick Fortunately, General Wood of the Federal Army saw this small flag of "surrender" and ordered a temporary cease fire Hannah Maria, Lizzie, David McGredy and Miss O'Keefe returned safely to Nashville

After their departure, General Wagner, acting under General Wood's orders, set fire to all the Tynes buildings Although the newly built house and adjacent buildings at first resisted the flames, a volley of shells destroyed them completely What seemed to be a rather unnecessary action on the part of the northern soldiers was actually a means of preventing the oncoming Confederates from taking lodgement behind the buildings, either for their own safety, or for their sharpshooters

The efforts of the Confederates were unsuccessful On the

16th of December 1864, General Hood surrendered and the Battle of Nashville was over

The years that followed the Civil War constituted a period of tragic and difficult adjustment in the South and for those who lived there The Tynes as well as Hannah Maria and Lizzie, lost most of their personal possessions in the destruction of the Hillsboro home A J Tynes filed several unsuccessful claims against the United States Government for financial restitution in both 1864 and 1865 Subsequent claims were made by members of the family, the last being filed as recently as 1909 [20]

Following the war, Hannah Maria joined the staff of the Athenæum, an Episcopal Church school for girls, in Columbia, Tennessee, approximately 45 miles south of Nashville Her daughters, Maria and Lizzie, received the final years of their education there

Patrick Nowland was wounded during the Civil War but was able to return to civilian life and to his profession as an engineer Continuing to travel through the southern states, Patrick visited his family briefly and intermittently Little is actually known about him during these post-war years, but on the 6th of July 1870 a letter indicated he was working at White River, Jackson County, Indiana and ultimately headed for Louisville, Kentucky [21] After the death of his wife in 1872, Patrick presumably made his home with a brother in Hopkinsville, Kentucky, and it is believed that he died in this town

Through the remaining years of the sixties and into the next decade, Hannah Maria continued to teach school She was determined that her two young daughters would have the same educational advantages that their step-sisters had enjoyed Her perseverance and courage had already seen her family through many difficult years; nothing was more important to her now than their security and welfare

---

[20] House of Representatives, Congressional No 14322
[21] E B Fitzgerald Collection, family letters

Existing letters, written in 1868, from Hannah Maria to
Maria and Lizzie, contained paragraphs admonishing them
for occasional frivolities and urging them to "make every
opportunity count."[22] No doubt, Hannah Maria was well
pleased to have her two young daughters marry and "settle
down." Her pleasure would have doubled had she lived to see
all her daughters enjoying enduring marriages with closely knit
families

Shortly after her youngest daughter Lizzie was married,
Hannah Maria Nowland died 14 February 1872, aged 63, in
Nashville She was buried at Mount Olivet Cemetery,
Lebanon Road, Nashville [23]

Six of Hannah Maria's seven daughters lived to maturity
and were, according to our genealogical arithmetic, four
generations removed from John Bournes of Stonefield, Co
Mayo, Ireland A brief account of these six daughters and
their descendants may be found in the following pages.

[22] E B Fitzgerald Collection, family letters
[23] Christ Episcopal Church records, Mt Olivet Cemetery records, E B Fitzgerald
Collection, Bible record

X. Cecelia Maxwell Bournes

IV Cecelia Maxwell Bournes was born ca 1833, probably at Rosserk, near Ballina, Co Mayo When her mother and stepfather, Patrick Nowland, journeyed to America in 1853, she remained in Ireland to complete her education A picture taken of Cecelia in Dublin about this time would seem to indicate that she may have attended a school in that city

A search to find the exact date that Cecelia came to America has not been entirely successful The manifest of the "City of Mobile" which sailed from Liverpool to New York in 1856[1] does show a name that could possibly be hers. The rather illegible writing might be interpreted as "Cecelia Burns, age 20, female, spinster, born in Ireland" We are certain, however, that Cecelia was in Nashville on the 25th of December 1858 because she became a communicant on that day at the Episcopal Church of the Advent She resided in West Nashville, presumably in the Nowland's home [2]

Cecelia M Bournes married prior to July 1860, for she is listed in the census of that date as the wife of Richard H

---

[1] National Archives, Washington, D C , passenger list no 271, page 8 The "City of Mobile" arrived in New York, 3 May 1856

[2] Register of the Church of the Advent

Thompson.[3] They resided at North Market St with the family of Richard's brother. Richard H. Thompson was born 1837 in Ireland, according to this same census He was a communicant of the Church of the Advent 2 February 1858, with the word "Transferred" following his name Cecelia Thompson died 18 February 1878, at their residence on South Spruce St and her husband died 6 April 1883, at the home of his brother [4]

They had issue of ten children all born in Nashville but only one child lived to maturity The records of four of their children have been found [5]

    i Richard Fielding Thompson was baptised 28 March 1861 by Rev C T Quintard in the Church of the Advent The sponsors were Robert, Richard and Elizabeth C Thompson

    ii Cecelia Maxwell Thompson q v

    iii Angela Thompson was born 17 May 1867 and baptised 18 June 1867 by Rev James Moore in the Church of the Advent

    iv Althea Elliott Thompson was born 4 June 1873 and baptised 28 Dec 1873 by Rev Edward Bradley in the Church of the Advent The sponsors were Robert Thompson, Mrs Ellen Tynes and Miss Julia Elliott

V Cecelia Maxwell Thompson, the only surviving child, was born 12 August 1865 [6] In 1880 she was living with her aunt and uncle, Ellen and Alpheus Tynes, at their home 24 South Summer St , Nashville and she continued to live with them until her marriage 22 April 1891 to Archibald Bonner Munn.[7] The Munns moved to New Jersey, residing first at Boonton and then Montclair where Cecelia died, 15 October 1955 They had issue.

    i Archibald Bonner Munn Jr was born 19 Dec 1894 in Boonton, New Jersey He married 8 Feb 1923, Margaret Chestor Baker,

---

[3] 1860 Census of Davidson Co , Tenn (taken 26 July 1860) second ward, Nashville, page 63, no 338-376 A notation beside the names of Cecelia and Richard Thompson signifies that they were married within the year

[4] *Daily American*, issues of 19 Feb 1878 and 7 April 1883 Richard H Thompson's obituary indicates that he was born in 1839

[5] Three of the children's records were found in the Register of the Church of the Advent

[6] E B Fitzgerald Collection, Bible record

[7] Marriage Certificate, State of Tennessee, Davidson Co

born 10 April 1896, daughter of Henry Franklin Baker of Philadelphia Pa He died 18 Jan 1952 in Montclair They had issue

(1) Margaret Chester Munn was born 10 May 1925 in Bryn
Mawr, Pa She married Gardner Bowne Miller in 1945 and
had issue

    a Gardner Bowne Miller Jr , born 22 Dec 1947

(2) Franklin Bonner Munn was born Oct 1927 in Montclair,
New Jersey He married Virginia Warren Aug 1953 They
had issue

    a Bruce Bonner Munn, born 20 June 1955

    b Warren Slater Munn, born 20 Jan 1960

    c Avery Wistar Munn, born 20 Oct 1962

(3) Barbara Maxwell Munn was born 5 April 1929 in Red Bank,
New Jersey She married A Lloyd Kitchin May 1953 They
had issue

    a A Lloyd Kitchin III, born 22 July 1954

    b Jeffrey Bonner Kitchin, born 2 Oct 1957

Mrs. John W. Morton, née Ellen Bournes. Copy of a portrait appearing in *Forrest's Artillery*, John Watson Morton, Nashville, Tenn., 1909.

XI. Ellen Bournes

IV Ellen Bournes was born in 1835,[1] probably at Rosserk, Co Mayo She accompanied her mother and step-father, Patrick Nowland, when they came to New York in 1853. On the 22nd of June 1857, she married Alpheus Jones Tynes in that city [2]

Alpheus Jones Tynes, born 19 July 1831, was baptised 9 November 1831, by the Reverend Lightbourne, at Christ Church, Parish of Devonshire, Bermuda He was the son of William Clarke Tynes and Frances Gilbert Dill, the daughter of Richard Gilbert Dill and Mary Dill [3] Alpheus J Tynes left his father's home in 1850 and came to New York Eventually, he became a citizen of the United States [4]

Following their marriage in 1857, Alpheus and Ellen Tynes journeyed to St. Paul, Minnesota where they were residing by November of that year [5] Sometime prior to 1860, the Tynes joined the Nowlands and Ellen's sister, Hannah Bournes, in

---

[1] E B Fitzgerald Collection, Bible and other family records

[2] Ibid

[3] E B Fitzgerald Collection, Tynes family Bible From the Colonial Archives, Hamilton, Bermuda it was found that William Clarke Tynes, son of William and Catherine Tynes, died in Devonshire Parish 6 Jan 1867, aged 73 His wife, Frances, died in 1885, aged 88 The Tynes families of Bermuda apparently descended from a Steven Tynes who came to this island in the mid-seventeenth century They were planters, mariners and master mariners and toward the close of the nineteenth century, merchants in Hamilton, Bermuda

[4] United States census enumerations

[5] Territorial Census, Ramsey Co, Minn (taken 11 Nov 1857) page 74, no 1464. Living in the same household were P Lynch and Bridget Lynch, both born in Ireland and both 23 years of age The relationship between the two couples, if any, is not known.

Nashville, Tennessee They subsequently became the owners of a "Millinery Cloaks and Fancy Goods" store[6] and also acquired property in and near Nashville Land on the Murfreesboro Road, outside of Nashville,[7] became the site of a home that was destroyed during an engagement of Federal and Confederate troops in December 1864

Alpheus Jones Tynes died 20 November 1881 in Philadelphia Pennsylvania, while on a business trip He was brought to Nashville and buried in Mt Olivet Cemetery [8]

Ellen Bournes Tynes married secondly Captain John Watson Morton on the 6th of August 1901 in Nashville [9] He was born 1843 in Williamson County, Tennessee, the son of John Watson Morton Captain Morton was previously married to Annie Payne Humphreys who died 14 July 1899 and left issue Although Captain Morton had been educated to be a doctor he is best known in Tennessee history for his Army and public service Captain Morton served during the Civil War as Chief of Artillery in the Cavalry Corps under General Nathan B Forrest and later became the Commissioner of Agriculture of Nashville From 1901 through 1909, he was Secretary of State in Tennessee [10] Captain Morton died 23 November 1914 in Nashville and was buried in Mt Olivet Cemetery [11]

Ellen Morton died 21 August 1912 at "Mansfield," their home on Murfreesboro Road, Nashville and was buried in Mt Olivet Cemetery [12]

---

[6] 1860 Census, Davidson Co , Tenn. (taken 26 July 1860) page 40, no 267-331, Nashville City Directories 1869-1880

[7] Registry of Deeds, Nashville Book 33, pp 73, 81 and Book 34, p 543

[8] Mt Olivet Cemetery records E B Fitzgerald Collection, family records

[9] E B Fitzgerald Collection, family records

[10] John Watson Morton, *Forrest's Artillery* (Nashville, 1909), Confederate Veteran s Magazine

[11] Mt Olivet Cemetery records

[12] Mt Olivet Cemetery records, *Nashville Banner,* issue of 22 Aug 1912, Will of Ellen Tynes Morton, dated 2 June 1910, probated 26 Aug 1912, E B Fitzgerald Collection, family records

Although she left no issue by either marriage, Ellen had virtually been a mother to her niece, Cecelia Thompson, who had lost both parents as a child. Maria Nowland also spent many years with her step-sister, and it is evident from family stories that Ellen played an important role in guiding and protecting her younger sisters, Maria and Elizabeth W. Nowland and Hannah Bournes

XII. Margaret Bournes

IV. Margaret Bournes was born 20 March 1836 at Rosserk in the Parish of Ballysakeery, Co Mayo.[1] There are at least two versions of the manner in which she migrated to Canada and the United States. One of these versions is based on family stories derived from Margaret's older sister, Ellen The other is based on stories from descendants of Margaret, herself The research problems involved in reconciling these two legends, and the ultimate disclosure that both versions may have "telescoped" two generations, afford an interesting vignette of the kind of "puzzlements" that can make genealogy such an intriguing undertaking

The stories derived from Margaret's sister, Ellen, claim that Margaret came to Canada with her uncle, Thomas Bournes. The opposing legend is that Margaret was brought to Canada, presumably by a governess or a companion, and joined her Uncle Thomas and his family there. The difference would seem to be quite unimportant except for the striking coincidence that both legends probably have erred in their treatment of "Uncle Thomas." The details of this relationship will be explored later. For the moment we shall simply record the fact that in 1859, Margaret Bournes married Alexander McLean in Canada [2]

[1] *Western Star*, issue of 30 March 1836
[2] McLean family records

127

Alexander McLean, born 1832 in Glasgow, Scotland, migrated to Nova Scotia and to Prince Edward Island about 1850 with his father, John McLean [3] In 1851, Alexander lived briefly in Quebec, Canada[4] and later, presumably following his marriage, in Brantford, Ontario Subsequent residences were Winnipeg, Manitoba, Fort Erie, Ontario and St Paul, Minnesota He was employed by the Grand Trunk and Canadian Pacific Railways and held responsible positions with these railways for several years

In 1886, the McLean family, consisting of the parents and five children, moved to Puget Sound in the State of Washington Here, Alexander McLean became the Master Mechanic of the Fairhaven and Southern Railway, then under construction He died in 1903 in Bellingham, Washington,[5] and his wife, Margaret, died 12 March 1912 in Penticton, British Columbia [6] They had issue.

    i William John McLean, born 1861 in Fort Erie, married ca 1902, Edna Ross in Stratford, Ontario He was a Master Mechanic for the Bellingham and British Columbia Railway and died 28 April 1945 in Bellingham They had issue

      (1) Donald John McLean, born 1906 in Bellingham, married Helen McKenzie He is an engineer with the Standard Oil Company of Portland and resides in Lake Oswego, Oregon They had issue

        a Mary Helen McLean who married 22 June 1963, Steven Arnold Windall in Lake Oswego They reside in Brookfield, Illinois

        b John McLean, a student

    ii Elizabeth Green Burns McLean,[7] born 18 July 1865 in Brantford, Ontario, married Fred N Culver 1 Sept 1896 in Bellingham

---

[3] John McLean, a graduate apprentice of a marine engineering school in Paisley, southwest Scotland, was the son of Alexander McLean and Janet Cameron Among the McLean family records is a photostatic copy of an Indenture between Alexander Vallance and John McLean showing that John had completed four years apprenticeship on the 24th of April 1815 and was now free from bond

[4] A letter written by Alexander McLean while he was in Quebec to his father at Prince Edward Island indicated that he had been in Quebec "three months and that was too long"

[5] McLean family records Bellingham was formerly Fairhaven, Washington

[6] Death certificate

[7] It is possible that Elizabeth was named for the aunt with whom her mother had lived prior to her marriage See pp 131-132

They resided in Friday Harbor, Washington On 6 June 1899, she died at her parents' home in Bellingham, aged 33 years 10 months and 19 days She was buried in Bayview Cemetery, Whatcom, Washington They had issue

(1) Margaret Burns Culver, born 1897 in Friday Harbor, Orcas Island, married James McKim 1921 in Seattle They both were graduates of the University of Washington, Seattle James McKim's profession as a mining engineer took his family to Paris, France, later to South America After his retirement, they moved to Water Isle St Thomas, Virgin Islands They had issue

   a Elizabeth Ann McKim, born in 1922, married Scott Allen Peterson and resides in Fort Collins, Colorado They had issue

   b Edward Culver McKim who married Marilyn_____ and resides in Heyburn, Idaho They had issue

   c Susan McKim, born Oct 1936 in Salt Lake City Utah, was educated in Europe, married and resides in New York City

iii Rosala Fanning King McLean, born 1866 in Fort Erie, Ontario, married 1895, James T Gander in Orcas Island, San Juan County, Washington She died 1914 in Bellingham and left issue

(1) McLean Thomas Gander, born 2 Dec 1898 in Bellingham, married 12 Oct 1921, Helen Hadley He graduated from the University of Washington, served in World War I and later became associated with the bonding firm of Dominick and Dominick, New York City They had issue

   a Lindley Hadley Gander, born in Seattle, married Linda Butler of Lewiston, Idaho They reside in Wilton, Conn and had issue

   b James Thomas Gander, born in Seattle, graduated from Colorado University He married Phyllis_____ and resides in Lancaster, Ohio

   c Roderick Gander, born in Bronxville, New York, married Isabelle_____ in 1955 He resides in New York City where he is Assistant to the Editor of News Week They had issue

iv Alexander Robert McLean who died at fourteen years of age

v Archibald McLean born 21 Nov 1869 in Erie Co, New York, married Clarice Witter 2 July 1901 in Bellingham He died 1 June 1954 in Tacoma, Washington Archibald McLean followed his father and brother in the mechanical field and in 1892 was appointed Superintendent of Motive Power for the Georgia Northern Railway, Pitcock, Georgia From 1902 to 1904, he was owner and manager of the Bellingham Machine Works Later, he was appointed Chief Engineer of The Western State Hospital

and made Supervising Engineer of Washington State Institutions
They had issue

(1) Archibald Marshall McLean, born 21 Aug 1906 in Seattle,
married first, Margaret Krull in 1929 He graduated from the
University of Washington and is now President and owner of
McLean and Co Investment Brokers, Tacoma By his first
wife, he had issue

    a Archibald Marshall McLean, born 1930 in Seattle, mar-
ried 1955, Bonnie Lundgren in Las Vegas, Calif He
graduated from the University of Washington in 1952,
and served as a 1st and 2nd Lieut in the Korean Conflict,
1953-1954 He is now with his father's investment firm
They had issue

      1 Scott McLean
      2 Mark McLean
      3 Marshelle McLean

    b Patricia Ann McLean, born 7 July 1934 in Tacoma,
graduated from Washington State University, Pullman,
Washington She studied voice in Vienna and later taught
music at Michigan State University and at DePauw University, Greencastle, Indiana

(2) Bruce Maxwell McLean, born 3 June 1910 in Fort Steilacoom, Washington, married 17 Aug 1940 in Seattle, Lois
Diveley, born 1910 in Seattle He attended the University
of Washington and is now part owner of the General Hard-
ware Co , Tacoma They had no issue

(3) John (Jack) Witter McLean, born 17 April 1918 in Fort
Steilacoom, married 7 April 1955 in Tacoma, Hazel North-
rop, born 1924 in Eugene, Oregon He enlisted in the Army in
1940 and served overseas until 1945 He is now a salesman
with the Wholesale Builders Supplies They had issue

    a Douglas Northrop McLean
    b Victor Ford McLean

Returning now to Margaret Bournes and Uncle "Thomas,"
we shall not try to resolve the question of whether Margaret
journeyed to Canada with her uncle or whether she joined him
there More important is the question of Uncle Thomas'
identity. Was there indeed an Uncle Thomas and, if not,
what was the true relationship between Thomas and Margaret?
In our effort to answer these questions we must now refer to
the McLean legend and to supporting documentation from
various sources in this country

Briefly, the McLean story is that Margaret joined her Uncle Thomas Burns[8] and his wife, Eliza, in Canada The Burns had two sons, James and Thomas, and it was believed that they lived in Fort Erie, Ontario, Canada In 1901 they moved to Bellingham, Washington to join Margaret and Alexander McLean while their eldest son, James, remained behind Thomas Burns, according to the McLeans, purchased an iron foundry in Bellingham which he managed until his death in that city

In a Whatcom County History,[9] a sketch of "Thomas Burns of Bellingham, Washington" appears wherein the truth about Margaret's "uncle" is revealed With the assistance of the Whatcom History, as well as other sources, the following story emerges

About 1850, a Robert Burns, born ca 1825, and his wife, Eliza, born ca 1819, emigrated from Ireland to Canada, where Robert followed the blacksmith's trade as a life's work Three children were born to this couple while they lived in Canada Prior to 1889, the Burns moved to St Paul, Minnesota[10] and in 1901 traveled further west to Bellingham, Washington

James, their eldest son, was born ca 1859 and was a machinist He moved to Minnesota in 1882 and had settled in St Paul by 1889 where he presumably died Their youngest child, a daughter, Matilda, was born ca 1871.[11]

Thomas, the second son of Robert and Eliza Burns, was born 1860 in the Province of Ontario He was educated in the Ontario public schools and afterwards served an apprenticeship to the machinist's trade. Thomas proved to be an apt pupil and became the Master Mechanic at Sioux City, Iowa for the Chicago, Milwaukee and St Paul Railroad, remaining with the railroad for eighteen years In 1883, he was residing

8 The McLean family spelled the Bournes' name as "Burns "

9 History of Whatcom Co (1926), Vol II, p 382

10 1895 Minnesota State Census, St Paul precinct 14, Ward 5, Family #94

11 Ibid

in St Paul and on the 24th of December 1897, Thomas Burns became a citizen of the United States in that city [12]

He moved to Bellingham with his parents in 1901 where he purchased the Bellingham Iron Works, and in 1911 married Mrs. Alma Vail, a Canadian born widow Thomas Burns in a quiet and unassuming way did a great deal for Bellingham "He stimulated its development along commercial lines and as one of the city's self-made men is well deserving of the respect accorded him "[13] Thomas Burns continued to reside in Bellingham until his death [14] He and his wife left no issue [15]

Those who are interested might well inquire who, then, were Robert and Eliza Burns? Which one of the many Connaught Bournes families did they belong to? It is difficult, perhaps even impossible, to answer these questions However, it is believed that Eliza Burns was Margaret's aunt, and if this is correct, she would then be a member of the Stonefield Bournes family. William Lloyd Bournes, Margaret's father, did have a younger sister, Eliza, according to our family stories More elusive though is the identity of Robert Burns Was he actually a Burns, or was he a member of the Bournes family who had assumed the Burns name?

As we try to trace the threads that form this part of the Bournes' family tapestry, it seems reasonable and plausible to associate both Robert and Eliza with the Stonefield branch. Some future researcher may uncover more concrete evidence with respect to Robert, and, if so, it will probably be found within that particular geography and context

[12] 1895 Minnesota State Census, op cit , District Court, Ramsey Co , Minn
[13] *History of Whatcom Co* , op cit
[14] His name appears in the Bellingham City Directory as recently as 1926
[15] McLean family records

XIII. Hannah Bournes

IV. Hannah Bournes was baptised 28 January 1837 in the Parish of Ballysakeery, Co Mayo [1] She came to America in 1853 with her mother and step-father, Patrick Nowland, residing first in New York City and later in Nashville, Tennessee On the 24th of August 1857, she married David Anderson McGredy at the Nowland's home in South Nashville Her parents and W Wynne were witnesses to this marriage performed by Rev. W. D. Harlan [2]

David Anderson McGredy, according to census enumerations, was born in Ireland ca 1826. He became the owner of the McGredy Nursery on the Hillsboro Pike, near Nashville, and died in March 1899 in Nashville He was buried in Mt. Olivet Cemetery Hannah Bournes McGredy died 10 September 1902 at her home, 1711 No Johnston Ave., Nashville and was buried with her husband [3]

They had issue, all born in Nashville [4]

   1 Hannah Maria McGredy, born 1858, was baptised 25 Jan 1859 by Rev C Harris in the Church of the Advent Sponsors were Cecelia Bournes and David Anderson McGredy She married

---

[1] The Register of Ballysakeery states that she was the daughter of William and Hannah Bournes of Rosserk, Co Mayo

[2] Register of the Episcopal Church of the Advent, Nashville.

[3] 1880 Census of Davidson Co, Tenn (taken 17 June 1880), page 154, no. 442, Church of the Advent Mt Olivet Cemetery records and various newspaper obituaries, (names of papers unknown)

[4] *Ibid*

Edward Moore, died 28 Dec 1937 and was buried in Mt Olivet Cemetery They had issue, born in Nashville

(1) Nina Moore who married William Anderson and had issue
    a William Anderson Jr , born 1918 in Nashville, married and now resides in Melbourne, Australia

(2) Edna Moore who married Frank Harper and had issue
    a. Cecile Harper, born in 1913

ii David Anderson McGredy Jr , born ca 1861, married in 1877, Eleanor Ennis, born 1862, of Worcestershire, Dudley, England He died 3 Aug 1936 at his home, 308 Twentieth Ave , N Nashville, and she died there in Feb 1945 They were buried in Mt Olivet Cemetery and had issue, all born in Nashville

(1) Annie McGredy, born in 1880, died in infancy

(2) Frank G McGredy, born in 1882, graduated from Vanderbilt University, Nashville and died unmarried, 7 July 1906

(3) Elizabeth Alsted McGredy, born in 1884, graduated from Vanderbilt University She married 29 June 1910 in Nashville, Henry Rodenhauser, born 1883 in Nashville, son of Jacob and Mary Rodenhauser She died July 1954 in Nashville and he died there in Dec that same year They were buried in Mt Olivet Cemetery, leaving issue, all born in Nashville

    a Frances Rodenhauser, born 3 Feb 1912, married 27 April 1935, Ned Lentz, son of Dr J J Lentz and Eliza Davis They had issue

        1 John David Lentz, born 7 Jan 1942, married 22 Dec 1962, Phyllis Gray, daughter of Warren and Nancy Gray

        2. Eleanor Ennis Lentz, born 14 Sept 1944

        3 Allen Davis Lentz, born 29 Sept 1946

    b Mary Eleanor Rodenhauser, born 29 Aug 1913, married 20 May 1936, Maury Calvert, son of C W and Media Calvert They had issue

        1 Eleanor Calvert, born 17 Sept 1939 in New Orleans, La , married Sept 1962, James Crowder in Miami, Fla

        2 Elizabeth Calvert, born 28 Sept 1940 in New Orleans, married, Richard Voelker II and had issue

        3 Maury Calvert Jr , born 3 June 1945 in Atlanta, Ga

    c. David Rodenhauser, born 11 June 1915, married 21 Nov 1940 in Nashville, Frances Wilkenson, daughter of Morgan and Florence Wilkenson They had issue

        1. Judith Rodenhauser, born 24 Dec 1942

        2 Florence Elizabeth Rodenhauser, born 15 Oct 1946

iii Ellen Rutledge McGredy, born ca 1863, married Dr Shirley Cox
  She died Aug 1959 and was buried in Mt. Olivet Cemetery. They
  had issue

  (1) Hannah Maxwell Cox

  (2) Elizabeth Cox

iv William John McGredy, born ca 1866, married and died without
  issue Jan 1955 He was buried in Mt Olivet Cemetery

v. Martha McGredy, born ca 1868, married Joseph Sidney Johnson
  who was born in 1870 and died Nov 1926 She died 9 May 1932
  at their residence 2313 Murphy Ave , Nashville They were buried
  in Mt Olivet Cemetery and had issue

  (1) Joseph Sidney Johnson Jr.

  (2) Nell Johnson

  (3) Fred M Johnson

vi Louis McGredy, born ca 1872, married Nora Warner He died in
  1912 and they had issue, all born in Nashville

  (1) Eleanor McGredy

  (2) Katherine McGredy

  (3) Christine McGredy

  (4) Esther McGredy

  (5) Louis McGredy Jr who died without issue

vii Emily Mayfield McGredy, born 16 June 1873, married John W
  Blevins, born 9 Dec 1878 They resided on Old Hickory Blvd ,
  Whites Creek, Tenn He died in May 1949 and she died in Oct
  1952 They were buried in Mt Olivet Cemetery and had issue.

  (1) Emily Blevins

  (2) Helen Blevins

  (3) Anna R Blevins

  (4) Dorothy Blevins

viii Maxwell McGredy, born ca 1877, married Josephine Meadows
  He died in Nashville in Sept 1930 and was buried in Mt Olivet
  Cemetery They had issue.

  (1) Maxwell McGredy Jr who married but died without issue

XIV. Maria Nowland

IV. Maria Nowland was born 26 March 1850 in Ireland, probably in Cork,[1] and came to America with her parents in 1853. They resided first in New York and later in Nashville, Tennessee. In 1860, while her mother was in Louisiana, Maria lived with her half-sister, Ellen Bournes Tynes in Nashville.[2] She received her education in Nashville and married Lewis Lever Losey there 22 September 1868.[3] Lewis L. Losey was born in Goshen, Ohio, 22 September 1839, the son of Abiel Losey and Barbara Lever.[4]

For several years following their marriage, the Loseys resided in Nashville, where he was a deputy sheriff, lawyer and a stock agent for the North Carolina and St. Louis Railroad. In July of 1890, they moved to Chicago and lived at 2322 Calumet Avenue. He continued the practice of law and also represented the Illinois Central Railroad. They died in Chicago, he

[1] E. B. Fitzgerald Collection, Bible record, Death Certificate. It is believed that Maria was born in Cork, as her parents had married there in 1847. However, a search of the parish registers of that city did not reveal a birth or baptism record. A search was also made without success through the birth registrations at Somerset House, London

[2] 1860 Census, Davidson Co., Tenn. (taken 26 July 1860), Ward 8, page 40, no 267-331

[3] State Library and Archives, Nashville, Christ Church marriage record, Nashville

[4] E. B. Fitzgerald Collection, family records supplemented by official sources indicate that Abiel Losey was born in Goshen, Ohio, 22 Feb 1814 and died in Nashville, 17 April 1898. Barbara Lever Losey, born in Goshen, 25 Feb 1812, died in Nashville, 18 Aug 1883

on the 25th of June 1915 and she on the 16th of February 1930[5] and were both buried in Mt Olivet Cemetery, Nashville. They had issue, born in Nashville.

   1 Lewis Lever Losey Jr, born 3 Oct 1877, was baptised 20 Nov 1877 in the Church of the Advent by Rev C T Quintard [6] Sponsors were his parents and Mr and Mrs Tynes He married Anna Frera 29 April 1933 in Chicago, as her third husband [7] She was born 26 Dec 1878 and died 3 April 1966 in Evanston, Ill Lewis L Losey Jr was a lawyer and he and his wife resided in Chicago, Ill He died 26 Jan 1959 and he and his wife were buried in Mt Olivet Cemetery, Nashville They had no issue

  [5] *Nashville Banner*, issues of 28 June 1915 and 19 Feb 1930, Death Certificates, E B Fitzgerald Collection, family records

  [6] Register of the Episcopal Church of the Advent, Nashville

  [7] E. B Fitzgerald Collection, family records Anna Frera had married (1) William F Bottinger and had issue of one daughter, Alice M Bottinger, who married Ernest Schumacher and resides in Wilmette, Ill Anna Frera married (2) Ernest Flagg in Dec 1916

XV.
Elizabeth Whately Nowland

IV. Elizabeth Whately Nowland was born in New York City 12 May 1853,[1] shortly after her parents arrived in America. She was named after Elizabeth Whately, the wife of Richard Whately, Archbishop of Dublin [2]

Elizabeth received her education primarily in Nashville, Tennessee where she taught school before her marriage 5 September 1871 to Hans Peter Alsted [3] Hans Peter was born 5 March 1848 in Alsted Mark, Vaile Amst, Denmark and was baptised in the Parish of Sönder-Ornme [4] He was the son of Jens Peter Jacobsen and Ane Margrethe Hansdatter, daughter of Hans Madsen and Volborg Jørgensdatter.[5]

Hans Peter Alsted was an apprenticed watchmaker, and, during the controversies following the Danish and Schleswig-Holstein War (King Christian IX reign), he served briefly in the army. After he incurred wounds of sufficient severity to terminate his army service, he emigrated to America, debarking at the Port of Buffalo, New York 15 October 1868

---

[1] E B Fitzgerald collection, Bible and family records, Death Certificate
[2] Richard Whately (1787-1863) was ordained at St Patrick's Cathedral, Dublin 23 Oct 1831 He married 18 July 1821, Elizabeth, (who died 25 April 1831) third daughter of William Pope of Uxbridge, Middlesex, England
[3] State Library and Archives, Nashville, Christ Episcopal Church records
[4] E B Fitzgerald Collection, family records which include information from Personalhistorisk Institut, Plantanvej 30, Copenhagen, Denmark v Hans Peter was baptised Hans Jens Peter Jensen Alsted
[5] Ibid

Upon arrival in America, Hans Peter presumably journeyed directly to Kenosha, Wisconsin and resided for a short period with a brother, Jacob Alsted [6] By 1870, he had moved to Nashville, Tennessee where he was employed by the Calhoun Jewelry Co as a watchmaker [7] After marriage and the birth of two children, he and his family moved to Texas [8]

Hans Peter Alsted and his family, according to family stories, remained in Texas very briefly. In 1880, they lived in Chicago, Illinois and five years later moved again, this time to Milwaukee, Wisconsin In both Chicago and in Milwaukee, he was a travel agent and it was not until 1887 that he returned to his chosen profession as a watchmaker. He was employed then at the C Preusser Jewelry Co and some years later, in 1899, became an owner of the Alsted-Kasten Jewelry Co in Milwaukee. Hans Peter also acquired his United States citizenship in Milwaukee 17 February 1908 [9]

Elizabeth Nowland Alsted died 5 May 1924 in Pasadena, California where she and her husband had been visiting. Hans Peter Alsted died 7 October 1924 in Milwaukee and was buried with his wife in Forest Home Cemetery, Milwaukee. They had issue, born in Nashville

    i   Ellen Marguerite Alsted q v

    ii   Lewis Losey Alsted q v

V Ellen Marguerite Alsted, born 15 December 1872, was baptised 29 March 1874 in the Episcopal Church of the Advent by Reverend Edward Bradley. Sponsors were Alpheus Jones Tynes, Ellen Bournes Tynes and Maria Nowland Losey

She was educated in Milwaukee, Wisconsin attending Milwaukee Female College which subsequently became Milwau-

---

[6] E B Fitzgerald Collection, family letters from Edward P. Alsted, (son of Jacob and nephew of Hans Peter Alsted) to Lewis L Losey Jr

[7] Nashville City Directories 1869-1875, 1870 Census, Davidson Co, Tenn (taken 17 June 1870)

[8] Episcopal Church of the Advent, Nashville, Communicant Lists

[9] Chicago City Directories 1880-1885, Milwaukee City Directories 1885-1887, E B Fitzgerald Collection, Certification of Citizenship and other family records

kee Downer College On the 14th of November 1895, Ellen
Marguerite married Frank Rogers Bacon. He was born 28
September 1872 in Milwaukee, the son of Edward Payson
Bacon and Emma, daughter of George Rogers and Fanny
Baxter Lothrop [10] Frank R Bacon was educated at Lake For-
est Academy, Lake Forest, Illinois and at Princeton Univer-
sity, Princeton, New Jersey. During World War I, he was a
Major in Army Ordinance. He was the founder, long-time
President and Chairman of the Board of Cutler-Hammer Inc ,
Milwaukee.

Ellen Marguerite and Frank R. Bacon died in Milwaukee;
he on the 6th of October 1949, she on the 29th of April 1953
They were buried in Forest Home Cemetery, Milwaukee and
left issue, all born in Milwaukee.

1 Edward Alsted Bacon, born 24 June 1897, died 5 Oct. 1968 in
   Boston, Mass , and was buried in Forest Home Cemetery He
   married 17 Feb 1920 in Philadelphia, Pa , Lorraine Goodrich
   Graham, born 15 May 1898 in Philadelphia, the daughter of
   Dr Edwin Eldon Graham of Philadelphia and Lorraine Goodrich
   of Milwaukee Edward A. Bacon graduated from Harvard Univer-
   sity, Cambridge, Mass in 1919, served in the Marine Corps during
   World War I, in World War II was a Commander in the U S.
   Navy During the Eisenhower administration, he was appointed
   Deputy Assistant Secretary of the Army and resided in Washing-
   ton, D C In his later years, he resided in Martha's Vineyard,
   Mass and in Miami Beach, Fla They had issue.

   (1) Lorraine Graham Bacon, born 25 June 1925 in Philadelphia,
       married 17 Sept 1948 in Washington, D C David Bethune
       Holdsworth, Commander, British Royal Navy, Retired He
       was born 5 June 1922 in Nutley, N J , the son of Hugh
       Reginald Holdsworth of Halifax, Yorkshire, England and
       Dorothy Ann Frances Bethune They had issue

       a Lorraine Lindesay Graham Holdsworth, born 5 Feb 1950
          in Northcote, New Zealand

       b Mary Caroline Stuart Holdsworth, born 21 Sept 1953 in
          Washington, D C

       c David Crispian Alsted Bethune Holdsworth, born 7 Oct
          1955 in Washington, D C

   (2) Edward Alsted Bacon Jr , born 27 Sept. 1927 in Milwaukee,

[10] After George Rogers died, his widow married Henry Hobbs The daughter was
adopted by her stepfather and thereafter was known as Emma Rogers Hobbs

married 1 Dec 1952 Louise Olsen in Washington, D C She was born 7 Aug 1922 in Salt Lake City, Utah, daughter of Oliver Smith Olsen and Pauline Ryser They had issue

    a   Ann Louise Olsen Bacon, born 4 Oct 1954 in New York City

    b   Lorraine Ryser Bacon, born 31 Jan 1957 in New York City

(3) Ellen Alsted Bacon, born 9 June 1929 in Milwaukee, married 16 June 1951 in Edgartown, Mass, Richard Smallbrook McKinley III He was born 8 Oct 1926 in Bryn Mawr, Pa, the son of Rowland Paull McKinley and Ethel Dori They had issue

    a   Richard Smallbrook McKinley IV, born 10 April 1952 in Baltimore, Md

    b   Ellen Graham McKinley, born 7 Feb 1954 in Baltimore, Md

    c   David Todd McKinley, born 14 Aug. 1956 in Washington, D C.

    d   Edward Bacon McKinley, born 14 May 1962 in Washington, D C

ii   Elizabeth Bacon, born 22 Nov 1900, married 26 Oct 1921, Edmund Fitzgerald in Milwaukee He was born 1 March 1895 in Milwaukee, the son of William Edmund Fitzgerald and Jessie Lenox Blackburn, daughter of James Blackburn and Georgiana M. Cooke of Ottawa, Canada Elizabeth Bacon was educated at Milwaukee Downer Seminary and the Guild and Evans School, Boston, Mass, graduating in 1919 Edmund Fitzgerald graduated from the Sheffield Scientific School of Yale University, New Haven, Conn Ph B. 1916, LL.D., Marquette University, Milwaukee, LL D, University of Wisconsin, Madison, Wis During World War I he served as a Capt 328 Field Artillery He was President of the Northwestern Mutual Life Insurance Co 1947-1958, Chairman of the Board 1958-1960 They had issue, born in Milwaukee

(1) Elizabeth Fitzgerald, born 28 Dec 1922, married 18 Oct 1947, Richard Woolsey Cutler in Milwaukee He was born 9 March 1917 in New Rochelle, N Y, the son of Charles Evelyn Cutler of Westport, Conn and Amelia Shaw Mac-Donald Elizabeth Fitzgerald graduated from Smith College, Northampton, Mass, B A 1944, during World War II she was with the Office of Strategic Services, Washington, D C and later with the War Crimes Commissions, Nurembergh, Germany. Richard W Cutler graduated from Loomis Institute, Windsor, Conn 1934, Yale University, B A 1938, LL B 1941, served during World War II as a Capt U S A F and was with the Office of Strategic Services He is a partner in

the firm of Brady, Tyrrell, Cotter and Cutler, Milwaukee
They had issue

a Marguerite Blackburn Cutler, born 26 March 1949 in
New York City

b Alexander MacDonald Cutler, born 28 May 1951 in
Milwaukee

c. Judith Elizabeth Cutler, born 14 April 1954 in Milwaukee

(2) Edmund Bacon Fitzgerald, born 5 Feb 1926, married 6
Sept 1947 Elisabeth McKee Christensen in Milwaukee She
was born 12 Jan 1926 in Milwaukee, the daughter of Clarence
A Christensen and Eugenia Greer Edmund B Fitzgerald
graduated from Deerfield Academy, Deerfield, Mass 1943
and the University of Michigan B EE 1946 He served
during World War II as a Lt in the Marine Corps and was
a Capt , Marine Corps in the Korean War In 1965, he became the President of Cutler-Hammer Inc , Milwaukee.
They had issue all born in Milwaukee

a Karen Fitzgerald, born 9 June 1951

b Kathleen Fitzgerald, born 30 Aug 1954

c Edmund Greer Fitzgerald, born 28 Dec 1955

d Rogers Christensen Fitzgerald, born 6 Dec 1959

iii Frank Rogers Bacon Jr , born 30 June 1909, was educated at Exeter
Academy, Exeter, Mass and graduated from Harvard University, Cambridge, Mass in 1931 He married first in June 1931,
Elizabeth Howe Donham in Framingham, Mass and they resided in Milwaukee where the following children were born

(1) Elizabeth Bacon, born 8 July 1932

(2) Gregory Bacon, born 24 Nov 1935, married Terance K Hoke
in Oct 1963

Frank Rogers Bacon Jr moved to California where he married
second, Susan Dette Holbrook in 1939 and had issue

(3) Nancy Bacon, born 30 July 1940 in San Mateo, Calif ,
married Michael Sandback Aug 1962

He married third, Elizabeth Mapes in 1953, and 3 May 1963,
he married fourth, Thea Bicker There was no issue by these
marriages.

V. Lewis Losey Alsted, born 3 January 1875, was baptised
by the Reverend Edward Bradley 25 April 1875 in the Episcopal Church of the Advent. Sponsors were Alpheus Jones
Tynes, Ellen Bournes Tynes and Hans Peter Alsted:

Lewis L Alsted was educated in Milwaukee's public schools and the University of Wisconsin, Madison, obtaining his B A. degree in 1896 and his LL D. in 1898 After being admitted to the Wisconsin Bar, he practiced law in Milwaukee for a number of years In 1922, he moved to Appleton, Wisconsin to become the President of the Combined Locks Paper Co

On the 26th of May 1907, Lewis L Alsted married Mary Van Nortwick in Appleton. She was born 17 January 1882 in Batavia, Illinois, the daughter of John Smith Van Nortwick and Bina Totman, daughter of Edsel Totman and Mary Jane Allen

Lewis L. Alsted died 21 May 1938 in Chicago, Illinois; his wife, Mary, died 10 July 1960 in Appleton. They both were buried in Forest Home Cemetery, Milwaukee, and left issue.

1 Mary Van Nortwick Alsted, born 21 Dec 1915 in Chicago, Ill, married John Giffin Strange 19 Sept 1939 in Appleton He was born 17 Sept 1911 in Neenah, Wis, son of Hugh McGregor Strange and Carolyn Giffin, daughter of Dr Leverett Giffin and Amelia (Burroughs) Fuller Mary Van N Alsted was educated at Baldwin School, Bryn Mawr, Penn and graduated from Northwestern University, Evanston, Ill, B S 1938 John G Strange was educated at St John's Military Academy, Delafield, Wis and graduated from Lawrence College (now Lawrence University), Appleton, B A 1932 He joined The Institute of Paper Chemistry, Appleton immediately following graduation becoming President of this educational and research institution in 1955 During World War II, he served as Chief, War Products Development Section, War Production Board, Washington, D. C He received a LL D from Beloit College and a D Sc from Ripon College and is the author of various papers and articles on science and education They had issue, born in Chicago, Ill

(1) Mary Alsted Strange, born 10 Aug 1940, was educated at Wayland Academy, Beaver Dam, Wis and Lawrence University She resides in Appleton, unmarried

(2) Peter Alsted Strange, born 20 July 1942, was educated in the Appleton public schools and graduated from Carroll College, Waukesha, Wis, B S 1964, Columbia College, Chicago, B A 1966 and has been with the A R N G since 1964 He resides in Chicago, unmarried and is affiliated with WFLD-TV

(3) John David Strange, born 25 Jan 1947, was educated in the
Appleton public schools and is presently attending Lawrence
University He married 7 June 1968 in Appleton, Shirley Ann
Wanty, daughter of Alfred Charles Wanty of King, Wis and
Edna Boushley.

Part Three

The Bourne Family

XVI. Introduction

The following account of the Bourne families of Burren and Clooncallabeg, Co Cork and of Taney Hill, Co. Dublin is based primarily on pedigrees compiled by the late Dr. Lorton Wilson These may be seen at the library of the Irish Genealogical Research Society, 82 Eaton Square, London, England [1] Miscellaneous records of the Bourne(s) families were also collected by Dr Wilson and deposited at the Public Record Office, Belfast, Northern Ireland.[2] These latter records contain references to the Bournes of Connaught

Neither of the two pedigrees compiled by Dr Wilson reveals, unfortunately, where the first members of the family were born, nor is there any clue to their ancestry We have been unable to find the answers to these questions and, presumably, like Dr Wilson, have found no actual proof that the Burren and Clooncallabeg Bourne family and the Taney Hill family were related. It may be reasonable to assume that as more records are located future researchers will discover "missing links," and, for this reason we have, when possible, noted various items that might offer clues to this relationship.

The extensive work done by Dr Wilson was brought to our attention after we had become aware of these two family

---

[1] Deposited with the I G R S in 1958

[2] Deposited with the Public Record Office, Belfast, Northern Ireland in 1958 and indexed under T 1021/25-32

groups and had, in fact, compiled pedigrees for the Cork and Dublin Bourne families Although Dr. Wilson's work was done with original source material in Ireland and England, we were able to find many of the same references in published material in United States repositories. Additional information was obtained from the Public Record Offices in Dublin and Belfast, the Registry of Deeds in Dublin and other repositories in Ireland and London Two societies that have outstanding collections of Irish books and records in this country are the American-Irish Historical Society, New York City and the Genealogical Society, Salt Lake City, Utah.

XVII.
Burren and Clooncallabeg

Early records found in the Public Record Office in Dublin show that a John Bourne, or perhaps two men of the same name, received grants of land in Co Cork. Grants made during the Act of Settlement in the reign of Charles II include the following to John Bourne, Gent of Carbury, Co Cork,[1] dated 19 June 1667 "In ye North East part of the plowland of Burrin 234 3 33, Cloyncallaghbeg ½ plowland, 143 0 22."[2] The total land awarded was 612 acres, 1 rod, 32 perches statue measure [3]

Land was again awarded under the Act of Settlement during the reign of William and Mary, to a John Bourne of Cork Unfortunately this particular document does not identify the grantee's place of residence, there is no description of the type or location of the land, and the exact date of the grant is not recorded We do find, however, that the amount of land granted was 178 acres, 8 rods and 6 perches [4] As William and Mary reigned from 1688 to 1702,[5] we know that the conveyance

---

[1] Carbery, Co Cork

[2] The Topographical Index of Ireland (1901) identifies Burren and Clooncallabeg as being in the Parish of Rathclarin, District of Bandon

[3] P R O Dublin Lodge's Record of the Rolls Act of Settlement (1667-1669), Vol XII, p 340

[4] Lodge, op cit Act of Settlement (William and Mary), Vol XIII, p 490

[5] Actually William and Mary reigned together only until her death in 1699 William ruled alone from 1699 to 1702

occurred within this fourteen year period and it is therefore chronologically possible that "John Bourne, Gent of Carbury, Co Cork" and "John Bourne of Cork" were the same person

The Registry of Deeds in Dublin has numerous land transactions involving the Bournes of Co Cork John Bourne of Burren and Clooncallabeg is prominent among the names of grantors and grantees. The Memorials of Deeds preserved in this repository have been invaluable in compiling the records of this family and have been used extensively, along with other sources, in establishing the pedigree presented below

I. John Bourne of Burren and Clooncallabeg was sworn a Freeman of Kinsale, Co Cork, 30 October 1685, became a Burgess, 9 November 1685,[6] and High Sheriff of Cork in 1704. He married in 1677 (M.L B Cork and Ross) Rachel, daughter of John Suxbury of Kinsale[7] by Margaret_____. Margaret Suxbury's Will, dated 24 July 1711, was proved in the Diocese of Cork by her daughter, Rachel, the sole executor.[8] They had issue.

   i Richard Bourne q v
   ii. John Bourne
   iii William Bourne
   iv Elizabeth Bourne.
   v Martha Bourne.
   vi Rachel Bourne who married James Cowan in 1719.[9]

II Richard Bourne of Burren and Clooncallabeg, the eldest son, was referred to as Colonel Bourne He married 1 March 1719,[10] Martha, daughter of Thomas Daunt of Owlpen and Gortigrenane, Co. Cork by Elizabeth, daughter of the Rever-

---

[6] Albert E Casey, *O'Kief, Coshe Mang, Sleve Lougher and Upper Blackwater in Ireland* (Birmingham, Alabama 1965), Vol 7, p 1847

[7] *Ibid*, p 1777 Will of John Suxbury, 1 July 1685

[8] P R O Belfast Equity Exchequer Bill #T 1021/7, p 21

[9] Casey, op cit, Vol 6, p 10

[10] Registry of Deeds #151 38 100275

end George Synge [11] Richard Bourne's Will was proved in the
Diocese of Cork 1747,[12] and his widow was still living in 1751 [13]
They had issue.

  i   John Bourne q v

  ii   Thomas Bourne who may possibly be the same Thomas Bourne
        whose death is given in the *Cork Advertiser* as 19 Nov 1803, aged
        74 [14]

 iii   Martha Bourne who married in 1759 the Reverend William
        Meade, Rector of Rincurran, Co Cork, son of William Meade,
        Dean of Cork, by Helena, daughter of Bryan Townsend of Castle
        Townsend [15]

III. John Bourne of Burren and Clooncallabeg[16] married in
1747 (M L B Cork and Ross) Anne, daughter of Robert
Sandford, Esq M P of Castlerea (Castlereagh), Co. Roscommon, Knight of the Shire of the county, by Henrietta, daughter
of William O'Brien, 3rd Earl of Inchiquin by Mary, youngest
daughter of Sir Edward Villiers and sister of Edward, Earl of
Jersey [17] John Bourne's Will was dated 2 January 1758 and

---

[11] Burke's *Landed Gentry* (1904 ed) See Daunt pedigree, Burke s *Peerage* for Synge
pedigree Different sources call Thomas Daunt's wife (Rev Synge's daughter), Elizabeth
or Martha It would appear that "Elizabeth" is correct See Eustace's *Abstracts of
Wills*, Vol II, p 40 in which Thomas Daunt's Will, dated 14 Feb 1745, appears

[12] Casey, op cit , Vol 8, p 1128

[13] Registry of Deeds #151 38 100275

[14] P R O Belfast Extracts from Newspapers, #T 1021/1, pp 13-23

[15] Rosemary ffolliott, *The Pooles of Mayfield*, (Dublin, 1958), p 144, Canon J Leslie's
Clogher Clergy and Parishes (under Derryvullan), p 159 Record of Martha Bourne's
marriage to William Meade in which her father is called Col Richard Bourne

[16] Registry of Deeds #110 94 93057, #167 91 111111

[17] Burke's *Extinct Peerage* (1962 ed), p 470, Lodge's *Peerage*, Vol I, pp 277-278,
P R O Belfast, Prerogative Wills, T 559, Vol 33, pp 356-357 The information contained within these sources is of special interest to the author because the gradual
amassing and sifting of separate pieces of evidence, supplemented by a certain amount
of intuition, has led to the conjecture that the Bourne family of Cork may have been
the first of this family in Ireland John Bourne of Cork was granted land in this county
during the Acts of Settlement and Explanation It is not unreasonable to assume that
some of his descendants migrated to western and to eastern Ireland The families we
have recorded as the Bournes of Connaught and those of Taney Hill and Terenure may
thus have been derived from those of Cork If the reader will refer to the early chapters
in this book devoted to the history and genealogy of the Connaught Bournes, he will
note that certain families, i e Crofton, Nicholson, Lloyd and O'Brien played a part in
forming the tapestry of the Bournes story These same names, also found in the Sandford pedigree, were of importance to the Cork Bourne family Is this purely coincidence?
Perhaps, but it seemed worth italicizing the fact for some future researcher who may be
able to find the proof (if indeed there is proof) which so far has eluded the author

proved 15 June 1774 in the Diocese of Cork The administration was granted to his son, Richard, in 1774 They had issue.

  i Richard Bourne q v

  ii Robert Bourne of Burren was born in 1755 and died 10 July 1826
     on the Island of Guernsey where he had lived for forty five
     years [18] He married Ann Le Marchant They presumably had no
     issue as only a niece and nephews were named in his Will, dated
     7 July 1826 [19]

  iii Margaret Bourne

IV. Richard Bourne was born in 1752. He was educated by
Dr Andrew Buck D D., Dublin and at Trinity College where
he matriculated as a Pensioner 9 July 1767. In 1772 he obtained his B A. and, in 1777 his M A [20] Richard Bourne had a
distinguished career in the service of the Church He was
ordained a Deacon in St. Munchin's, Cork, 1772, Rector of St
Werburgh's Dublin and Chancellor of St. Patrick's, 1781-1810,
Dean of Tuam, 1810-1813 and Chancellor of Armagh, 1813-
1817 He married in December of 1774 at Ballymartle, near
Kinsale, Lucy, daughter of Edmund Shuldham of Dunman-
way by Judith, daughter of Beverly Ussher M P of Cappagh,
Co Waterford [21] He died 16 July 1817, aged 65, at the Glebe
House, Kilmore [22] His widow died 31 January 1825, aged 73,
at Holles St , Dublin,[23] and her Will was proved in 1826

In a deed of settlement dated 4 October 1803, the Reverend
Richard Bourne was recorded as a trustee to lands in Co
Limerick [24] The deed was witnessed by Walter and John
Bourne who were members of the Taney Hill family This
mutual concern was our first indication that there may have

[18] P R O Belfast Extracts from Newspapers, op cit , p 22, Memorial inscription in
the Parish Church of St Peter Port

[19] Ecclesiastical Court of the Dean of Guernsey, St Peter Port, Channel Islands

[20] *Alumni Dublinenses* op cit

[21] Burke's *Landed Gentry* (1904 ed) For Shuldham pedigree see p 549 and for Ussher
see p 612

[22] Memorial Inscriptions to Reverend Bourne and to his sons Edmund, Richard and
Robert are in the North Gallery, St Werburgh's

[23] *Belfast Newsletter*, issue of 8 Feb 1825, in which she was called "Lucinda, relict of
the late Rev Richard Bourne "

[24] Registry of Deeds #568 220 380626

been some relationship between the family of Burren and Clooncallabeg and the Bourne family of Taney Hill

Richard and Lucy Bourne had issue.

    i William Bourne q v

    ii Edmund Bourne was born 1781 in Dublin and was an Ensign 32nd Foot in 1795 He was a Captain in the 81st Foot when he died unmarried and intestate, 15 July 1797, aged 17, at San Domingo The administration was granted to his father

    iii Richard Bourne was born 1784 in Dublin and died unmarried 15 May 1803, aged 19, at Colombo, Ceylon He was a writer on the Civil Establishment of that island

    iv Robert Bourne was born 1785 in Dublin and was educated by Mr White and at Trinity College where he matriculated as a Pensioner 6 July 1801, aged 16 [25] He died unmarried 18 June 1809, aged 24, at Kildress, Co Tyrone

    v Henry Bourne was baptised Feb 1787 at St Werburgh's, Dublin and resided at 10 Holles St, in that city He was a Captain in the Royal Navy and in 1810 was a Lieutenant on the "Spartan" when she defeated an entire French fleet in the Bay of Naples [26] In 1845 he resided at 41 Lower Leeson St, Dublin[27] and died 23 June 1854, aged 66, at 10 Holles St, Dublin [28]

    vi Sandford Bourne was born 1791 in Cork and educated by Dr Carpendale at the Royal School, Armagh and at Trinity College where he matriculated as a Pensioner 2 Nov 1812, aged 18 [29] In 1817, he received his B A, was ordained and Curate of Drumglass in the Diocese of Armagh in 1819 He died unmarried and intestate 21 May 1825 at Boyo, St Domino, Italy, while on the way from Rome to Geneva [30]

V William Bourne was born ca. 1780 in Dublin and educated by Dr Murrary and at Trinity College in Dublin where he matriculated as a Pensioner 13 August 1795, aged 15 He received his B A. in 1800 and his M A in 1832 [31] After he was ordained, he was Prebendary of Rathangan, Co Kildare, 1803-1862 and the Rector of St. Andrew's, Dublin, 1804-1862.

---

[25] *Alumni Dublinenses*, op cit

[26] For a full account of Henry Bourne's service record see O'Byrnes' *Naval Biography Dictionary*, p 102

[27] *Irish Almanac, Registry and Directory,* 1845

[28] *Connaught Watchman*, issue of 28 June 1854

[29] *Alumni Dublinenses*, op cit

[30] *Belfast Newsletter*, issue of 14 June 1825, Register of the Royal School, Armagh (1667-1919)

[31] *Alumni Dublinenses*, op cit

In 1816, he married Catherine, born ca. 1780, the eldest daughter of Kilner Brasier of Rivers, Co Limerick by Mary, daughter and co-heiress of John Creagh M D of Castle Creagh, Co Cork [32] She was the widow of Major John Mathias of Llangwarien, Pembrokeshire and Captain of the Pembroke Militia who died 15 December 1808. William Bourne resided at 10 Holles St, Dublin in 1852 and died 5 March 1862 at 41 Lower Leeson St, Dublin.[33] He was buried in the family vault at Rathangan His Will was dated 3 August 1854; Codicils dated 3 December 1857, 7 June 1859 and 5 September 1860 Will and Codicils proved, 5 April 1862.[34] They had issue

   i Richard Bourne q v

   ii Mary Bourne, who married 5 June 1837 Henry Brasier Mitchell of Mitchellsfort, Co Cork, the second son of Brooke Brasier of Ballyellis, Co Cork by Ellen, daughter and co-heiress of Henry Mitchell of Mitchellsfort [35] Henry Brasier Mitchell assumed the additional name of Mitchell He and his wife lived at Llennog Castle, Wales and had a son and heir born 30 April 1838 [36]

VI Richard Bourne, the only son, was attached to the 12th Foot and an Ensign, 1 September 1839 He married 29 January 1843 at Cove, Co Cork,[37] Catherine, only daughter of Attiwell Wood, Barrister at Law, of Leeds, Co. Cork by Mary, fourth daughter of Kilner Brasier of Rivers, Co Limerick Richard Bourne died 28 August 1852 at 10 Holles St, Dublin, during his father's lifetime [38] His widow died in 1883 and they had issue

   i William Henry Bourne, born ca 1845, married (by licence) 28 July 1866, Ansonia Anne, daughter of George John Rogers at the Mallow Parish Church, Co Cork He was described as a Gentleman of Mallow of full age She as a minor Witnesses were W R

[32] *Burke's Landed Gentry* (1958 ed) Creagh of Creagh Castle, p 188, Burke's (1912 ed) Brasier of Ballyellis, pp 69-70

[33] P R O Dublin Will Index

[34] Somerset House, London

[35] Registry of Deeds #1837 11 106.

[36] From Basil O'Connell's records, Newtown, Penn , U S A

[37] Now Cobh, Co Cork

[38] *Sligo Chronicle*, issue of 4 Sept 1852

Boulton and S W Russell [39] Formerly of 2 Castle St , Beaumaris, Co Anglesea, he died 1 March 1883 aged 38, at 26 Lower Baggot St , Dublin The administration of his estate was granted to his widow of Beaumaris [40]

11 Attiwell Richard Bourne, born ca 1851, was of Burren and Landscape, Doneraile, Co Cork and married 16 Dec 1902, Augusta Constance, daughter of John Henry Ellis Ridley, Col of the Queen's Bays by Anna Maria, daughter of the Rev John Michael Brook of Longfield, Co Cavan, Rector of Ahenagh Co Cork She was the widow of John Nicholas Nugent, Lieut R N who died without issue, 12 Sept 1901, leaving Landscape to his wife Attiwell R Bourne died 1 Nov 1924, aged 73, at Berry Hill. His Will was dated 22 Dec 1902 and proved 2 June 1925 [41] He was buried in Doneraile Cemetery [42] They had no issue

111 Lucy Bourne [43]

[39] Register of the Mallow Parish Church, Co Cork

[40] P R O Dublin, Custom House Register

[41] P R O Dublin Augusta Constance Bourne was residing at Berry Hill, Castle-lyons, Co Cork in 1925 and was said to be a widow, "aged 30 years and upwards "

[42] Casey, op cit , Vol 11, p 1086

[43] In the Will of Rev William Bourne of Rathangan, Co Kildare, previously cited, Lucy was called "the daughter of my deceased son, Richard "

XVIII. Taney Hill

Thomas Cowley Bourne was the immediate ancestor of the family of Taney Hill [1] Little is known about his background except that he had two brothers, Christopher and Daniel Bourne. Christopher, in turn, is identifiable only through the will of Daniel Bourne [2] Daniel, it would seem, was the most prominent of the three brothers because his name appears more broadly in various records Before beginning the pedigree of the Bourne family of Taney Hill, a short account of Daniel Bourne's family is presented

Daniel Bourne of St Patrick's South Close, Dublin was born in 1722 He was an attorney in 1747, admitted free of the Guild of Barber Surgeons by right of birth 12 October 1748, and he married Elizabeth_____ Among the lands that he held, the most interesting, genealogically speaking, were those in the Parish of Palmerstown, Co Dublin which were held by lease from Robert Bourne,[3] but nothing further is found to identify the latter Daniel Bourne retired to County Wicklow in 1792 and died 28 November 1795, aged 73 He was buried with his wife, who died 16 October 1785, aged 63, in the

[1] Frances Elrington Ball and Everard Hamilton, *The Parish of Taney, a History of Dundrum near Dublin and its Neighborhood* (Dublin 1895) In addition to Dr Lorton Wilson's records, this book also gives quite a complete account of the Bourne family of Taney Hill

[2] P R O Belfast, Prerogative Will #T 1021/5, p 25

[3] *Ibid* As the christian name of "Robert" is found in the pedigree of Bourne of Burren and Clooncallabeg and not in the pedigree of Taney Hill, we have a justifiable suspicion that there may have been some connection between the two families

Green Churchyard, St Patrick's, Dublin [4] They had issue of
one daughter, Frances, who married in May 1766, Walter
Peter, Attorney of Edgecourt, Dublin and Silver Court, Castle
St. To this marriage several children were born, the eldest
daughter, Eliza Peter, became the first wife of Walter Bourne
of Harcourt St , Dublin and Taney Hill.[5]

The pedigree of the Bourne family of Taney Hill follows

I Thomas Cowley Bourne married Mary Dunn Both were
living in 1795, as they were named, not only in Daniel Bourne's
Will, dated 26 July 1792, but also in a Codicil, dated 27 November 1795 They had issue.

   i   Walter Bourne q v

   ii Stephen Bourne named as nephew of Daniel Bourne and brother
of John Bourne [6]

   iii John Bourne of 55 William St , Dublin and of Priorland, Co
Louth,[7] was born in 1770 He was apprenticed to his uncle, Daniel
Bourne; sworn a Clerk of the Guild of Barber Surgeons, 20 Jan
1794, Clerk of the Peace, Co Louth and Deputy Clerk of the
Crown, Co Wicklow, Wexford and Kilkenny He married (he
Dublin) in 1791, Elizabeth Harriet Pigot and died intestate 21
April 1829, aged 59 She died 11 April 1831, aged 61, at Priorland
and both were buried in St Nicholas' Churchyard, Dundalk
They had issue

     (1) William Kemmis Bourne, the eldest son, was on the Committee of the Guild of Barber Surgeons 1815-1817, Warden
in 1816 and 1817 He died 23 May 1818 at William St [8]

     (2) Thomas Bourne of Killencoole, Co Louth, was born in 1807,
apprentice to William Curtis, Attorney of 3 Harcourt St ,
Dublin,[9] voted free of the Guild of Barber Surgeons as "son
of John Bourne our respected Clerk" and married Jane, only
daughter of the late Henry Brabazon, Esq of Seafield, Co

---

[4] Parish Register Society, *The Registers of Baptisms, Marriages, and Burials in the
Collegiate and Cathedral Church of St Patrick, Dublin, 1677-1800* (Dublin 1907) Under
Byrne we find several entries of the Bourne family and one of the few times the name is
identifiably misspelled in this manner ' Daniel Byrne or Bourne Atty (Attorney) of
the Little Close was inter'd in the Vicar's Bawn, headstone, November 29, 1795 " The
"Vicar's Bawn" was a section of the grave yard reserved for the Vicar's Choral

[5] See Dr Wilson's pedigree for details of the Peter family

[6] P R O Belfast, Chancery Bill #T 1021/8, p 76

[7] Priorland is near Dundalk town in the barony of Balrothery East

[8] *Saunders Newsletter*, issue of 23 May 1818

[9] Registry of Deeds #1831 874 58067, #1831 874 580721

Louth, 16 April 1836 [10] He died 23 Dec 1893, aged 86, she died 14 July 1877, aged 71 Both were buried in St Nicholas' Churchyard, Dundalk They had issue

    a Henry Bourne who died 2 June 1811, aged 9, and is buried with his brothers, Frederick and William, in St Nicholas' Churchyard, Dundalk The memorial inscription calls him the eldest son [14]

    b Frederick Bourne who died 18 June 1842, aged 8 years and 10 months [12] Called the second son [13]

    c Daughter born at Dundalk in Sept 1840

    d William Bourne who died 11 Nov 1844, aged 14 months Called the third son [14]

(3) Frances Bourne, eldest daughter, married 25 Aug 1825 in the parish church of St Nicholas, Dundalk, by the Rev John Hamilton Stubbs, George Elliott, Esq of Seafield, Co Louth [15]

(4) Harriet Bourne who married 21 Oct 1815, William Curtis, Esq Attorney at law [16] They resided at 3 Harcourt St, Dublin

(5) Charlotte Bourne, the youngest daughter, married 2 Oct 1827 in the parish church of St Nicholas, Dundalk, by the Rev John Hamilton Stubbs, George Lambert Boate, Esq, eldest son of George Boate of Duckspool, Co Waterford [17]

II Walter Bourne of Harcourt St, Dublin,[18] previously of Owenstown, and of Taney Hill, Dundrum, Co Dublin, was born in 1766 He was an attorney; free of the Guild of Barber Surgeons in 1794, First Lieutenant Attorney's Corps, November 1796; Freeman of the City of Dublin; Churchwarden of Taney 1807-1808 and 1818, Clerk of the Crown, Queen's

[10] Dr Wilson states that Canon Carmichael said she was a step-sister of George Elliott (perhaps the George Elliott of Seafield?) and of the same family as Anthony Beaufort Brabazon of Bath *Belfast Newsletter*, issue of 20 April 1836

[11] *Journal of the Association for the Preservation of Memorials of the Dead in Ireland*, Vol V, p 124

[12] The christian name "Frederick" is not common, insofar as we know, to either Bourne family, i e Burren and Clooncallabeg or Taney Hill It is, however, found in the pedigree of the Bourne family of Teremure, which follows

[13] *Memorials of the Dead*, op cit

[14] *Ibid*

[15] *Belfast Newsletter*, issue of 2 Sept 1825 in which Frances Bourne is called daughter of John Bourne of Priorland, Clerk of the Peace for Co Louth

[16] *Saunder's Newsletter*, issue of 25 Oct 1815

[17] *Belfast Newsletter*, issue of 5 Oct 1827 in which Charlotte Bourne is called daughter of John Bourne of Priorland, Co Louth, Esq

[18] Walter Bourne appears in various records as of 15, of 16 and of 17 Harcourt St, Dublin

Bench for fifty two years[19] and Deputy Clerk of the Crown for the northeast circuit. Walter Bourne married first (he. Dublin) 5 June 1788, Elizabeth (Eliza), daughter of Walter Peter, Attorney of Edgecourt, by Frances, daughter of Daniel Bourne of St Patrick's Close, Dublin. She died in March 1790[20] They had issue

1 Peter Bourne of 30 York St , Dublin and Fieldstown, Co Dublin, was born ca 1789 in Dublin He was educated by Mr McKenna and at Trinity College, Dublin, where he matriculated as a Pensioner 3 Oct 1803 aged 15, and obtained his B A in 1808 [21] Peter Bourne was a Freeman of the City of Dublin, a solicitor,[22] Clerk of the Crown, Co Dublin and married (he Dublin) 7 May 1820, at St Peter's Dublin, Ellen daughter of George Gibbs of York St , Deputy Clerk of the Crown, Home Circuit, by Jane, daughter of Andrew Carmichael, Clerk of the Crown for Leinster [23] He died intestate, 7 Oct 1844, at his York St residence,[24] and his wife died on or about 18 Sept 1882 at York St and was buried in Mt Jerome Cemetery, Dublin Her Will was proved 14 Nov 1882 in Dublin [25] They had issue

(1) Walter Bourne of Monkstown, Co Dublin was born ca 1826 in Dublin, a civil engineer, educated privately and at Trinity College, Dublin, where he matriculated as a Pensioner 3 July 1843, aged 17, and obtained his B A in 1848, his M A and M Eng in 1870 [26] He married Dec 1853, Anne (born 5 Jan 1827), daughter of the Ven William Ryder, Archdeacon of Cloyne, by Anna (married 1821), daughter of Rev William Ross of Ballinterry Co Cork [27] They had issue of two daughters, Ellen Jane and Annie Elizabeth

---

[19] *Dublin Evening Post*, issue of 21 Nov 1848 When Walter Bourne died in 1848, his son Walter was sworn in pro tem

[20] *Registers of St Patrick's*, op cit , "Mrs Byrn wife of Mr Watt Byrn Atty was inter'd March 20 1790 in the Vicar's Bawn"

[21] *Alumni Dublinenses*, op cit

[22] *Dublin City Directory* 1826-1900 Peter Bourne and his father, Walter were practicing attorneys in Dublin

[23] *Saunder's Newsletter*, issue of 8 May 1820 The ceremony was performed by Rev Mr Hobson

[24] *The Nation*, issue of 12 Oct 1844

[25] Somerset House, London, Index to Wills "Ellen Bourne, late of 30 York St , Dublin, widow, died on or about 18 Sept 1882 probate granted on 14 Nov 1882 at Dublin to the Rev John Grogan of Bahothen, Bilbuggan, Co Dublin, Clerk and Charles Farrell of Castle Kevin, Annamoe, Co Wicklow Esq, surviving executors Effects in England ", Mt Jerome Cemetery Records "Right of burial granted to Mrs Ellen Bourne of 30 York St , Dublin 2 Aug 1865 " A notation follows, "bodies brought from St Patrick's Churchyard to vault"

[25] *Alumni Dublinenses*, op cit

[27] Albert E Casey, *O'Kief, Coshe Mang, Slieve Lougher and Upper Blackwater in Ireland* (Birmingham, Alabama 1963), Vol 6, p 838

Walter Bourne's wife died in 1859 and he married secondly, Dorcas Kate Nason,[28] but by this marriage had no issue He died on or about 16 March 1882, aged 56, at Clifton Lodge, Seafield Ave , Monkstown, Co Dublin When his Will was dated, 5 May 1879, he resided at 12 Belgrave Square, North Monkstown Probate granted to his widow and William Henry Nason of Middleton, Co Cork 22 April 1882, Executors [29] Dorcas Kate Bourne died on or about 9 Jan 1887, aged 45, at the Rathcormack Glebe, Co Cork [30] They were both buried in Mt Jerome Cemetery, Dublin [31]

(2) Jane Bourne who married (lic Dublin) 1849, Charles Frizell of Castle Kevin, Annamoe, Co Wicklow

(3) Elizabeth Bourne was born 2 March 1829 and married 2 Oct 1850, at St Peter's Dublin, Rev John Grogan of Vesey Place Monkstown, son of John Grogan of Harcourt St , Barrister at Law, by Sarah, daughter of Charles Dowling Medlicott of Youngstown, Co Kildare Rev Grogan was born 2 Sept 1816 and died 28 Dec 1899 He was a nephew of Sir Edward Grogan First Baronet and was Vicar of Balrothery [32] Elizabeth Bourne Grogan died 24 July 1921 and had issue [33]

Walter Bourne of Harcourt St , Dublin and of Taney Hill married secondly (lic. Dublin 1791) 1 Jan 1792 at St Bride's Dublin, Elinor (Eleanor),[34] second daughter of Andrew Carmichael, Clerk of the Crown for Leinster by Jane, daughter of John Moore She died in 1838 and he died 18 November 1848, aged 82[35], at his residence Taney Hill, Dundrum, Co Dublin They had issue

    ii Walter Bourne q v

[28] Dr Wilson's pedigree does not indicate that Walter Bourne married for a second time However, a copy of Walter Bourne s Will is at the P R O Dublin, ref #12589, Principle Registry 1882 In the Will he refers to his wife, Dorcas Kate Bourne, otherwise Nason, her brother, William Henry Nason, solicitor, refers to his mother, Ellen Bourne, refers to his daughters Ellen Jane and Annie Elizabeth, both unmarried, refers to sisters Jane Frizell and Lizzie Grogan and to property at 30 York St , 27 Upper Dorset St and 6 Molesworth St , all in Dublin

[29] Ibid , Somerset House, London Will Index

[30] Somerset House Will Index Administration granted to William Henry Nason of Middleton and Annie Elizabeth Bournes(sic) of 5 Belgrave Square West, spinster

[31] Mt Jerome Cemetery records

[32] Foster's Baronetage (1882 ed), Lodge's Peerage (1907 ed)

[33] See Wilson s pedigree for details of the Grogan family

[34] Parish Register Society Marriage Entries from the Registers of the Parish of St Andrew, St Anne, St Audoen and St Bride 1632-1800 (London 1913)

[35] Dublin Evening Post, issue of 21 Nov 1848, P R O , Belfast Prerogative Will #T 1021/5, pp 26-27

iii Ellen (Eleanor) Bourne was born ca 1796 and died unmarried 16 July 1876, aged 80, at Grosvenor Square, Monkstown, Co Dublin [36] She formerly lived at Rutland Square, Dublin and at 25 Cresthwaite Park, Kingstown, Co Dublin [37]

iv Thomas Daniel Bourne of 16 Harcourt St and of Montview, Glenageary, Kingstown, Co Dublin was born ca 1799 He was Clerk of the Crown, Co Monaghan and Clerk of the Peace, Co Louth in 1871 [38] He died without issue 31 Jan 1877 at Montview, aged 78 [39]

v William Bourne, born in Dublin 1800, was educated privately and at Trinity College, Dublin where he was admitted as a Pensioner 7 Oct 1816, aged 17, obtained his B A in 1821 and his M A in 1832 [40] He was ordained, Clerk of Killiney in 1827 and Rector of Rathcormack, 1833-1851 He married (lic Dublin) 22 May 1833, Elizabeth, the eldest daughter of Charles Frizell of Castle Kevin, Co Wicklow[41] and he died without issue 5 April 1851

vi Andrew Bourne born in Dublin 1801, was educated by Mr Phillips and at Trinity College, Dublin where he was admitted as a Pensioner 3 Nov 1817 aged 16, obtained his B A in 1822,[42] admitted to Gray's Inn 2 May 1822 and called to the Bar, King's Inn, in 1824 In 1828 he became a Barrister at Law and resided at 25 Harcourt St, Dublin On the 17th of Dec 1829 he married at Endenderry, Queen's Co, Charlotte, the third daughter of Lyndon Bolton of Monkstown Castle by Jane, daughter of Richard Carpenter, Apothecary of Dublin [43] The ceremony was performed by Rev Lyndon H Bolton, brother of Charlotte Bolton [44] Andrew Bourne was living in Paris, France in 1855[45] and resided there in 1878, still a landowner of considerable property in Co Wicklow [46] He died without issue

vii Marianne Bourne was born ca 1801 and died unmarried 20 April 1878, aged 77 [47]

viii Emily Bourne was born 23 Sept 1811 and married (lic Dublin 17 Aug) 23 Aug 1831, at Taney, Keith Claringbold Hamilton

---

[36] Custom House Registers

[37] P R O Dublin, Index to Wills

[38] *Dublin Almanac* 1871

[39] Custom House Register, P R O, Dublin Will Index

[40] *Alumni Dublinenses,* op cit

[41] Casey, op cit, p 2142

[42] *Alumni Dublinenses,* op cit

[43] *Sligo Journal,* issue of 24 Dec 1829

[44] *Saunder's Newsletter,* issue of 21 Dec 1829

[45] Registry of Deeds, #1855 6 83 Dr Wilson wondered if the Andrew Bourne that he found living in France in 1855 was this same man, i e son of Walter Bourne According to the Memorial of 1855, it would seem likely that the "two" Andrews were indeed the same person

[46] *De Burg's Landowners of Ireland 1878*

[47] Custom House Registers

Hallowes, Solicitor of Dublin [48] She died 17 April 1899 at Arklow Rectory and was buried in Mt Jerome Cemetery, Dublin They had issue [49]

ix Richard Thomas Bourne of Taney Hill and 17 Harcourt St , Dublin was born 1817 in Dublin He was educated by Mr McCaul and at Trinity College, Dublin, admitted as a Pensioner 1 July 1834, aged 17 , obtained his B A in 1843, Irish Bar 1848 [50] and was Churchwarden of Taney Hill in 1850 On the 24th of Feb 1846, he married (lic Dublin) at Taney Hill Mary Sophia, daughter of John Hill Lindé of Drummartin House, Taney by Charlotte Maria, daughter of Sir Henry Jebb Witnesses to this marriage were Thomas Bourne and John Hill Lindé In 1877, Richard Thomas Bourne was residing at Glenageary, Montview, Kingstown, Co Dublin [51] and died without issue 27 Dec 1890

x Jane Bourne married (lic Dublin) 1812, Richard Carmichael M D and President of the Medical Association of Ireland, the fourth son of Hugh Carmichael, Deputy Clerk of the Crown for Ulster, by Sarah, daughter of Richard Rogers of Balgoon, Co Meath [52] Richard Carmichael died in 1849 and the Carmichael School of Medicine in Dublin was named after him [53] She died 21 Nov 1864 without issue

xi Eliza Bourne married (lic Dublin) April 1828 at St Peter's Dublin, Thomas Belton M D of North Frederick St , Dublin The ceremony was performed by the Rev William Bourne, her brother [54] She died 18 Jan 1880 and left issue [55]

xii Frances Margaret Bourne married (lic Dublin) 5 July 1827, at Taney, Bridges John Hooke, 34th Foot and a Captain 18 Dec 1828 They had issue [56]

xiii Anna Maria Bourne married (lic Dublin) 26 Jan 1826 at St Peter's Dublin, Rev Lyndon Henry Bolton, born 16 March 1801, of Burren and Cooleague, Co Cavan and Carrickmines, Co Dublin son of Lyndon Bolton of Monkstown Castle by Jane

[48] *Saunder's Newsletter*, issue of 3 Sept 1831 Called "the youngest daughter of Walter Bourne Esq of Harcourt St and Taney Hill "

[49] See Wilson's pedigree for details of the Hallowes family P R O Belfast #T 1021/25-32

[50] *Alumni Dublinenses*, op cit

[51] Richard Thomas Bourne was the sole executor of the estate of his brother, Thomas Daniel Bourne, and was residing at Montview when he died P R O Dublin Index to Wills

[52] Sir Charles A Cameron, *History of the Royal College of Surgeons in Ireland* (1886), p 365 See Dr Wilson s pedigree for additional biographical material

[53] *Sunday Independent*, issue of 13 Feb 1966

[54] *Saunder's Newsletter*, issue of 26 April 1828

[55] See Wilson's pedigree for details of the Belton family

[56] See Wilson's pedigree for details of the Hooke family

Carpenter of Dublin [57] Rev Bolton died 20 Nov 1869 and his wife died 14 May 1886 They had issue [58]

III Walter Bourne, eldest son of Walter Bourne by Elinor Carmichael, of 16 Harcourt St. and in 1854 of 17 Fitzwilliam Square, Dublin, was born 1794 in Dublin He was educated by Mr Martin and matriculated at Trinity College Dublin S C (Socius Comitatus), 8 November 1815, aged 21 [59] He was Clerk of the Crown, Co Antrim, Deputy Clerk of the Crown, Queen's Bench and a Freeman of the City of Dublin Walter Bourne was married by the Rev William Forde Vance, 6 August 1821 at Taney Church, to Louisa Arabella, daughter of Humphrey Minchin, Esq of Roebuck Lodge, J P. of Co Dublin, by his first wife, Frances Catherine, daughter of Major Joseph Sir Town Major of Dublin, 1762-1767 [60] He died 19 November 1881 and his wife died 2 January 1882, aged 82 [61] They had issue

  i   Walter Bourne was born 22 Aug 1822 in Harcourt St , and died there 3 Sept 1822

  ii Richard Carmichael Bourne was born 10 Nov 1823 in Dublin educated by Mr Brough and matriculated at Trinity College, Dublin as a Pensioner 2 July 1841, aged 18,[62] Royal College of Surgeons in Ireland 1847, Assistant Surgeon 3rd Dragoon Guards 13 July 1847, Reserve, 29 Nov 1850, Lic Society of Apothecaries, London 1853 [63] He died 15 April 1871

  iii Humphrey Minchin Bourne was born 1824 in Dublin, educated by Mr Brough and matriculated at Trinity College, Dublin as a Pensioner 2 July 1841, aged 17, obtained his B A in 1846,[64] admitted to Gray's Inn 5 May 1845 and called to the Bar, King's Inn, 1846 He resided at 16 Harcourt St , Dublin and at Esker Lodge, Lucan, a J P , and resided there from 1869 to 1875 He moved to Ballyowan House, Enniskerry and was there in 1877 Humphrey M Bourne died without issue

[57] Charles Knowles Bolton, *Bolton Families in Ireland* (Boston 1937) *Saunder's Newsletter* issue of 27 Jan 1826 The ceremony was performed by Rev William Bourne
[58] See Wilson's pedigree for details of the Bolton family
[59] *Alumni Dublinenses*, op cit
[60] *Burke's Landed Gentry* (1958 ed), p 636
[61] Custom House register
[62] *Alumni Dublinenses*, op cit
[63] Medical Register 1860 (1st ed) Roll of Army Medical Service
[64] *Alumni Dublinenses*, op cit

iv Elizabeth Eleanor Bourne was born 26 Jan 1827 at Taney Hill
and baptised there 7 Feb 1827 She married (he Dublin) 4 Sept
1849, Anthony Beauford Brabazon of Bath M D, born 1 Aug
1821 at Clonard, Co Meath,[65] son of Rev George Brabazon,
Rector of Painstown, by Leonore Jane, daughter of Rev Robert
Heyland He died in 1896, and she died 4 July 1912 and left
issue [66]

v Walter Bourne q v

vi Andrew Bourne of 16 Harcourt St was baptised 15 Aug 1830
at Taney Hill, admitted to King's Inn and a Barrister at Law in
1828 [67] He married _____Clarke and was probably the A M
Bourne who resided at Esker Lodge in 1859 He died without
issue in Dec 1893

vii William Henry Bourne M D was born 1833 in Dublin and
educated by Mr Flynn He matriculated at Trinity College,
Dublin as a Pensioner 3 June 1850 and died without issue [65]

viii Frances Bourne

ix Louisa Bourne was born 16 April 1835 at Whitehall, Dublin

x John Bourne, born 19 Oct 1836, was baptised 30 Jan 1848[69]
at Taney

xi Charles Henry Bourne was born in 1837 and admitted to Kilkenny College in 1854 [70]

xii June Adelaide Bourne, born 6 Nov 1840 was baptised 18 April
1841 at Taney

IV. Walter Bourne, son of Walter Bourne by Louisa Arabella Minchin, was born 24 May 1828 in Harcourt St, Dublin
He was educated by Mr Delamere and matriculated at
Trinity College, Dublin as a Pensioner 1 July 1845,[71] Carmichael School of Medicine M R.C S 1850, L M (Dublin)
1850, M D (Glasgow) 1851, Honorable Physician Bradford
Infirmary, Calcutta [72] He married 18 May 1870, Geraldine

---

[65] Cameron, op cit, p 554

[66] See Wilson's pedigree for details of the Brabazon family, *Burke's Peerage* (Earls of Meath), *Lodge's Peerage* (1908 ed)

[67] King's Inn, Dublin

[68] A William Henry Bourne was admitted Licentiate 9 Dec 1855 at the Royal College of Surgeons and Physicians in Ireland No further details given

[69] Parents were then "of Kilgobbin"

[70] P R O Belfast #T 1021/25-32, Newspaper extract (name of paper unknown) "died at No 59 S Richmond St, Walter Bourne infant son of Charles Henry Bourne, age 3 weeks" Buried at Mt Jerome Cemetery, Dublin 17 May 1870

[71] *Alumni Dublinenses* op cit

[72] *Lodge's Peerage* (1908 ed) shows him late of Calcutta

Caroline, only daughter of Sir John Judkin Fitzgerald, 2nd Baronet, of Lisheen, Co Tipperary by his second wife, Geraldine, daughter of Preston Fitzgerald of Dublin [73] Walter Bourne died 7 February 1897 at 5 Pittville Crescent, Cheltenham, England His wife died 26 August 1916 They had issue

1   Walter Fitzgerald Bourne of Weston House, Pittville, Cheltenham was born 20 May 1872 He was educated at Clifton and R M C Sandhurst: Royal Munster Fusiliers, 2nd Lieutenant, 29 Oct 1890, Lieutenant Indian Army 21 June 1893, Captain, Major, Lieutenant Colonel 10th Jats, served in the Chitral Expedition World War I, O B E He married Hilda, daughter of Major General Moore in 1905

ii   James Herbert Simpson Bourne was born in 1874 and a Midshipman of the Royal Navy in 1889 He died prior to 1907

iii   Arthur Umacke Bourne was born 23 Aug 1875 and educated at Clifton He was a Captain R A S C during World War I and married Margaret Ann, daughter of Robert Richardson in 1900 They settled in New Zealand

iv.   William Henry Philpot Bourne was born in 1879 He was a Royal Navy Lieutenant 15 Feb 1901, Lt Commander 15 Feb 1909 and died 23 March 1953 at Gloucester, England

v   Geraldine Louisa Bourne married George Washington Chadwick in 1905

vi   Edith Mary Bourne married in 1901, Sydney Charles Ivens, N Z C S of Carterton, Wairarapa

---

[73] *Burke's Peerage* (1898 ed) Fitzgerald of Lisheen, pp 572-573

XIX.   Terenure

The ancestry of the Bourne family of Terenure appears to be hidden in Ireland's seventeenth century history No pertinent land grants or other records have been located for this period and surprisingly the earliest clue to the family is found under an entirely different name, the Edwards family of Old Court, Co Wicklow.[1]

Richard Edwards, who came to Ireland from Wales, married Elizabeth, daughter and heiress of Colonel John Kynaston in 1655.[2] They had issue of six children, four of whom were named in Richard Edwards' Will, dated 27 January 1692/93 [3] These four children were Richard Edwards, Thomas Edwards, John Edwards and Mary Edwards Bourne

The eldest son and heir, Richard, was born in 1659 He married Mary, daughter of Sir Charles Wolseley, in 1682 and died in 1722 without surviving issue. His brother John, born in 1665, inherited Old Court after Richard's death In 1698, John married Jane, eldest daughter of James Butler of Rathelline, Co Carlow, and he died in 1728 His Will was dated 5

[1] Burke's *Landed Gentry* (1858 ed), p 310

[2] Colonel Kynaston received Old Court as part of a grant of land in consideration of military pay under the Acts of Settlement and Explanation, 1666-1684 This land was subsequently confirmed by patent, during the reign of Charles II, to Elizabeth, his daughter, and to her husband Richard Edwards (Roll 18th Charles II, third part, 15 Aug 1666, no 52)

[3] Dublin Grant Book, p 26 Richard Edwards' Will, proved 27 Sept 1693, also named his wife Elizabeth, his second wife, Penelope, and his sister, Mary Woolehouse(sic)

February 1724. Codicil dated 5 September 1728 In the Will he refers to his sister, Mary, as the widow of Richard Bourne [4]

Mary Edwards, daughter of Richard Edwards by Elizabeth Kynaston, married Richard Bourne prior to 1692/93, or when her father had dated his Will Unfortunately, Richard Bourne's ancestry is not known, but it is interesting to note that a John Bourne, Gentleman, resided in Co Wicklow at Tomie-land, Derralossery, 1662-1663 [5] We do not know if Mary and Richard Bourne had issue but it is likely that they did, for in the latter part of the eighteenth century, one finds the name of Edwards reappearing in records pertaining to five brothers and three sisters, hereafter identified as the Bourne family of Terenure

Terenure House, on the land of Terenure, is located in the Parish of Rathfarnham, Co Dublin and dates back to the Restoration Eventually the house and land, consisting of approximately 50 acres (English), was acquired by Robert Shaw, father of Sir Robert, 1st Baronet and representative of the City of Dublin in the Imperial Parliament for twenty-five years Terenure House was sold to Frederick Bourne of Dublin in the very early part of the nineteenth century and for over fifty years thereafter, the Bournes were owners of this magnificent estate Lewis' *Topographical Dictionary* gives a very complete description of this property. [6]

Unfortunately, it has not been possible to establish the parentage of these five brothers and three sisters. Their approximate birth dates do suggest, however, that the father may have married more than once

John Edwards Bourne of Dunkerrin, King's Co., [7] formerly of Nenagh, Co Tipperary, probably was the eldest of the five brothers He died intestate and the Administration was

---

[4] P R O Dublin Prerogative Will Book, 1726-1729

[5] Dublin Diocesan Administrations before 1800

[6] Samuel Lewis, *A Topographical Dictionary of Ireland*, (London, 1827), Vol II, p 540

[7] Since 1922 King's Co has been known as Co Offaly

Terenure House, Co. Dublin. From an original drawing by George Petrie Esq. *Ireland Illustrated*, published by Petrie, Bartlett and Bayes. (London, 1832).

granted to his widow, Martha Bourne, 14 January 1799 [8]
They had issue

   ı William Henry Bourne of Moorfield, Co Kildare who married
and had issue of at least two children [9]

   ıı Anne Bourne who married (lic Dublin) John Kinshela in 1807 [10]

   ııı Frances Matilda Bourne who married Lieutenant Matthew Will-
cock, 103rd Foot, in Dec 1810 [11]

Henry Hawker Bourne, born ca 1740, of Springmount,
Queen's Co , probably was the second eldest brother. He held
lands situated in the barony of Maryborough, Queen s Co [12]
by lease. dated 3 August 1737, from Ephraim Dawson ot Dawson's Court and Henry Fisher of Killery, both of Queen's Co [13]
These lands described as "Killiny, called Rahalass, Knock-
anspigoe, Classenisha, Shandhae, or Shanahoe" were subsequently willed to his younger brother, Richard Edwards
Bourne [14] He also acquired by conveyance, 27 January 1808,
from Robert Shaw of Dublin, the premises in Dublin City
known as the Royal Hibernian Hotel, Mail Coach Offices and
yards [15]

Henry Hawker Bourne was of Montasterevan, Co Kildare,
when he married (lic. Dublin) 18 June 1794 in the Parish of St
Catherine, Lucinda Darling, born ca 1773, of Grand Canal
Harbor [16] He died at Springmount, Queen's Co and was buried
14 April 1819, aged 79, in the Parish of Abbeyleix,[17] later to

[8] Genealogical Index to Administrations Intestate, G O #257 P R O Belfast,
#T 1021/32

[9] In the Will of Frederick Bourne, to be cited, he is called ' son of my late brother
John Edwards Bourne " In the 3rd Codicil, Will of Richard Edwards Bourne, also to be
cited, a legacy is left to "each of the two children, now in being of my nephew William H
Bourne of Moorfield "

[10] In the 3rd Codicil to Richard Edwards Bourne's Will she is called "daughter of my
eldest brother, John Bourne, deceased "

[11] *Walker's Hibernian Magazine,* Irish Marriages, 1771-1812, in which she is called
the second daughter of John Edwards Bourne, late of Dunkerrin, King's Co

[12] Since 1922, Queen's Co has been known as Co Leix

[13] Registry of Deeds #741 170 504705

[14] According to Richard Edwards Bourne's Will, to be cited

[15] National Library, Dublin, #M 5411

[16] *Faulkner's Journal,* issue of 3 July 1794

[17] Register of the Parish of Abbeyleix, Queen's Co

be re-interred in the family vault at Mt Jerome Cemetery, Dublin [18] His Will was dated 15 January 1819 and proved 27 April of this same year [19] Lucinda Darling Bourne's Will was dated 10 July 1852 [20] She died in 1852 at 31 Brunswick Square, Bloomsbury, Middlesex, England and buried 16 July in Mt Jerome Cemetery, Dublin, aged 79 [21] They had no issue

William Hawker Bourne, born ca 1757, probably was the third brother. Very little is known about him other than that his residence was Terenure House, and, on 22 September 1837, he died at Piccadilly, London [22] He was buried in the family vault, Mt Jerome Cemetery, Dublin, 30 September 1837, aged 80 [23]

Richard Edwards Bourne, born 1769 in Dublin, probably was the fourth brother He entered the Navy, a Plymouth Volunteer, aged 18, 30 September 1787, as a Captain's servant aboard the "Druid" By 30 November 1787, he was an able bodied seaman, becoming a midshipman in 1789 He applied for a lieutenant's rating, receiving his commission in the Royal Navy, 4 August 1797 Severely wounded during the attacks on the town of Hea, on the coast of Spain, in 1805 and 1806, he was unable to procure employment and accepted (under Order of Council 1816) the rank of Retired Commander, 10 December 1840 [24]

He married 21 December 1816, Louisa Helena, born ca 1797, second daughter of Ignatius Charles Blake by his wife, Helen, eldest daughter of William Cashel of Berwick-on-Tweed [25] The marriage settlement, dated this same day, was

---

[18] Mt Jerome Cemetery records The vault was acquired by his brother, Frederick Bourne of Terenure, 28 Sept 1837

[19] National Library, #M 5411 Various references refer to him as Henry Bourne, Hawkers Bourne and as H H Bourne but in most instances his complete and correct name of Henry Hawker Bourne is given

[20] *Ibid*

[21] Mt Jerome Cemetery records

[22] National Library, #M 5411

[23] Mt Jerome Cemetery records A Susan Bourne was buried in the family vault, 20 March 1858, aged 78 She was of Hamstead House and, according to the records, "brought from the Parish of Glasnevin, Co Dublin" Her relationship to the Terenure family is not known

[24] O'Byrne's *Naval Biography* (1849) Commissioned Sea Officers, R N

[25] Martin Blake, *Blake Family Records* See Blake of Ardfry

made between "Richard Edwards Bourne of Meadville, Co
Westmeath[26] of the first part, Louisa Helena Blake, spinster,
sister of the late Joseph Henry, Lord Baron Wallscourt, de-
ceased, of the second part, Henry Hawker Bourne of Spring-
mount, Queen's Co , Esq , oldest brother of the said Richard
Edwards Bourne of the third part, the Right Honorable Luke
Lord Clonbrock, the Honorable William LePoer Trench[27] and
Dominick Daly, Esq of Galway, of the fourth part "[28]

When he signed his Will, 27 June 1844, Richard Edwards
Bourne was residing at 7 Montpelier Parade, Monkstown, Co
Dublin His Will expressed the desire to be "buried beside my
late brothers Henry Hawker Bourne, Henry Hawker Bourne
(sic) and Frederick Bourne . "[29] He also named five children,
issue of his marriage with Louisa Helena Blake, and a son,
John, presumably a child by a former marriage [30] His property
consisted of the lands of Killiny called Rahalass, Knock-
anspigoe, Classenisha and Shandhae, all in Queen's Co ,
acquired from his brother Henry Hawker Bourne, deceased
The remainder of his property consisted of Nenagh, Toomavara (Toomavara) and Roscrea in Co Tipperary and a share
in the turnpike tolls of the Limerick Road the hotel stores
and stables, etc , in Limerick, Co Limerick Subsequently four
Codicils were made to his Will and dated 30 August 1847, 15
April 1848, 14 May 1849 and 23 December 1850 When the last
Codicil was signed, he resided at 81 Blackheath Park, Kent,

[26] Blake, op cit Blake's records indicate that Richard E Bourne was of Lynnbury,
Co Westmeath Leet's *Directory of Ireland* (1814) gives a Richard Bourne, Esq of
Clonard House, Clonard, Co Meath, whereas, Lewis' *Topographical Directory* (1837)
shows that a Richard Bourne, Esq resided at Lynnbury It is questionable if Richard
of Clonard House is the same as Richard E Bourne What is important, however, is
that in most records the middle name of Edwards is dropped, thus making identification more difficult

[27] Admiral Trench was named as a "friend" in Richard E Bourne's Will Lord Clonbrock was a descendant of Susanna Shaen, widow of Sir Arthur, by her second husband,
Robert Dillon

[28] Registry of Deeds #141 170 504705

[29] Insofar as is known, Richard Edwards Bourne had only one brother named Henry
Hawker Bourne

[30] A daughter, Margaret, was named in Frederick G Bourne's Will

England His Will and Codicils were proved 20 December 1851 [31]

Richard Edwards Bourne died in October 1851, aged 81, and was buried 18 October in Mt Jerome Cemetery, Dublin [32] His wife, Louisa Helena, died 15 February 1863 [33]

He had issue of at least two children by his first wife.

    i   John Bourne, born ca 1812, was residing at Upper Woburn Place, Dublin when his father made his Will He died in Dec 1894, aged 82, at 56 Waterloo Road, Donnybrook, Dublin and was buried in Mt Jerome Cemetery 22 Dec 1894 [34]

    ii   Margaret Bourne who was named in her uncle Frederick Bourne's Will as the daughter of Richard Edwards Bourne. She married (lic Dublin) 24 June 1844, Henry Hawker, son of Frederick Bourne of Terenure, Co Dublin

Richard Edwards Bourne by Louisa Helena Blake had issue [35]

    iii   Henry Blake Bourne of 37 Great Portland St , Middlesex, England, married Bethiah Frances_____ He died 31 Jan 1855 at Wyke House, Brentford, Middlesex His Will, dated 28 Oct 1852, was proved 9 Feb 1855 [36]

    iv   Frederick Dickinson Bourne who was under 21 years of age when his father made his Will in 1844 In 1855, he resided at Greenock, Scotland [37]

    v   Richard Hartley Wallscourt Bourne who was under 21 years of age when his father made his Will in 1844

    vi   Louisa Blake Bourne who married Maurice Hartland Mahon Esq Royal County Down Regiment of Foot, 7 Dec 1841 [38] They had issue

        (1) Amy Louisa Mahon, born in 1845, was residing at 81 Black-

---

[31] Somerset House, London It is interesting that George Smith Bournes of Rossport, Co Mayo resided at Blackheath, Kent later in this same century

[32] Mt Jerome Cemetery records

[33] Blake, op cit At the time the 1851 Census was taken, Louisa Helena Blake Bourne was residing at 81 Blackheath Park, Kent Her age was given as 54

[34] Mt Jerome Cemetery records

[35] A baptismal record was found in the Register of the Parish of Abbeyleix, Queen's Co of a child born to Richard and Louisa Bourne of Dublin The child s name is illegible, the baptismal date, 21 Nov 1819

[36] Somerset House, London

[37] National Library, #M 5411

[38] O'Byrne's *Naval Biography* (1849), Army lists for 86th Regiment Maurice H Mahon was an Ensign 22 July 1836, but not in the Officer's list the following year.

heath Park Kent with her grandparents in 1851 when the census was taken [39]

(2) Lucy Amelia Mahon was named as "my grand daughter" in the Will of Richard E Bourne

(3) Son, not baptised when Richard E Bourne made the first Codicil to his Will, 30 Aug 1847

vii. Frances Matilda Bourne, born in Ireland ca 1824, was residing at 81 Blackheath Park, Kent with her parents in 1851 when the census was taken She was unmarried [40]

Frederick George Bourne, probably the youngest of the five brothers, was, at one time, of Mount Mellick, Queen's Co, but later was of Terenure He was born ca 1775, was a Lieutenant in the Dublin City, Rotunda Division in 1796, and served on the Dublin Grand Jury in 1800. He, and his brothers, were directors of the Dublin and London Steam Marine Company [41]

His residence was Castle St, Dublin when, on 13 January 1792, he married Jane Shaw of Essex Bridge, in the Parish of St John's, Dublin [42]

Frederick G. Bourne made his Will, 13 August 1841, and named his five children as beneficiaries Also named were Margaret, daughter of Richard Edwards Bourne; a sister, Mrs Frances Rensher; William H Bourne, son of his late brother, John Edwards Bourne, Richard E Bourne, his brother of Monkstown, Co. Dublin, and Richard's two sons, Frederick Dickinson Bourne and Richard Hartley Wallscourt Bourne In a Codicil, dated 3 September of this same year, Frederick G Bourne refers to a marriage settlement made prior to the marriage of Edward Bulkeley Westropp Swift and his daugh-

---

[39] P R O Chancery Lane, London, in which her age was given as 6 years

[40] *Ibid,* in which her age was given as 27 years

[41] *Faulkner's Journal,* issues of 24 Nov 1796, 20 May 1800 Registry of Deeds #1836 17 177

[42] Sir William Betham, Vol II, p 146, Marriage Licences Prerogative Marriage Licences calls him 'Frederick George Bourne, Merchant' as does *Faulkner's Journal,* issue of 19 Jan 1792 Most records omit the middle name of "George" To add to the genealogical confusion, there was another Frederick George Bourne who also had a wife "Jane" This latter Frederick George was Governor of Newgate at the time of his death, 1 Nov 1829

ter, Louisa Emma The Will and Codicil were proved 9 March 1843 [43]

He died 31 January 1843 at Terenure House, aged 68, and was buried in the family vault at Mt Jerome Cemetery, Dublin [44] Nothing further is known about his wife, Jane They had issue

i   William Hawker Bourne of Bountree Lodge, Celbridge, Co Kildare the eldest son, was born ca 1807 He was residing at Terenure in 1841 and married (he Dublin) 11 Aug 1844, Sophia Jardine She was born ca 1808 and died March 1900, aged 92 at Naas, Co Kildare He died 11 Aug 1889, aged 82, at Naas [45] They both were buried in Mt Jerome Cemetery [46] and had issue

(1) Harriet Bourne who was of Bountree Lodge and unmarried in 1889 [47]

ii   Richard Edwards Bourne of Ashbourne, Co Meath, born ca 1809 in Dublin, was educated by Mr Martin and at Trinity College, Dublin where he matriculated as a Pensioner 18 Oct 1824, aged 15 He received his B A in 1831, his M A in 1834 and was admitted to the Irish Bar in 1840 [48] When his father died in 1841, Richard E Bourne was living at Terenure, and he married (he Dublin) Isabella Mangan in 1858 At the time of his death he was of Ashbourne, where he was a Justice of the Peace He was buried 29 March 1880, aged 55, in Mt Jerome Cemetery [49] They had issue

(1) Thomas Mangan Richard Bourne of Ashbourne, born ca 1858, was educated at King's Inn, where he received his B A and was admitted to the Middle Temple, 21 Jan 1881 [50] He married and had issue of at least one child

a   Richard Edwards Bourne who was buried 18 May 1889, aged 8, in Mt Jerome Cemetery He had been residing with his parents at 26 Nelson Square, Dublin [51]

[43] P R O Dublin Will Index
[44] Mt Jerome Cemetery records
[46] Custom House Register
[45] Mt Jerome Cemetery records
[47] Custom House Register, in which she was called daughter of William Hawker Bourne
[48] *Alumni Dublinenses*, op cit
[49] Mt Jerome Cemetery records
[50] Sir H F MacCreagh and H A C Sturgess, *Register of Admissions to the Honorable Society of the Middle Temple*
[51] Mt Jerome Cemetery records

(2) Frederick Bourne of 46 Mount St , Dublin who was buried
    15 Nov 1877, aged 19, in Mt Jerome Cemetery [52]

iii Henry Hawker Bourne of Molesworth St , Dublin, born ca 1814,
     was residing at Terenure in 1841 He married (lic Dublin) 24
     June 1844, Margaret, daughter of Richard Edwards Bourne,[53]
     and he died 20 July 1859, aged 45, at his Molesworth St residence,
     buried in Mt Jerome Cemetery [54] His Will was proved 14 Nov.
     1859 [55] They had no issue

iv Edward Sidney Townsend Bourne of Terenure was married 29
    July 1846 in the Presbyterian Church, Great Strand St , Dublin,
    by the Rev W H Drummond D D , to Hannah, eldest daughter
    of Peter Eckersley, Esq of Hollybrook Park, Co Dublin [56] He
    died in 1855 at Sandymount, Co. Dublin, at which time he was
    said to be "late of Belvidere, Sandymount and Constantinople "[57]
    In 1860, his widow was residing at Park Hill, near Manchester,
    Lancaster, England [58] They had issue

    (1) Son born in April 1847 [59]

v Louisa Emma Bourne was married (lic Dublin) in 1841 to
   Edward Bulkeley Westropp Swift of Clondalkin, Co Dublin,
   4th son of Godwin Swift by Jane Sophia, daughter of Richard
   Swift He died in 1888 and left issue of two sons and two daughters [60]

Frances Bourne, probably the eldest of the three sisters,
was born ca 1774 and married Mr. Rensher (or Rencher) [61]
She had been residing at Lakeview, Co. Roscommon prior to
her death and was buried 1 May 1844, aged 70, in Mt Jerome
Cemetery [62]

Jane Bourne, of Donnybrook, Co Dublin married (lic.
Dublin) in 1799, as his second wife, John Hartley of Tamgar
and Leamore, Co Wexford, son of the Reverend Humphrey
Hartley by Honor_____ They had issue [63]

[52] Mt Jerome Cemetery records
[53] National Library, Dublin, #M 5411
[54] Mt Jerome Cemetery records
[55] National Library, Dublin, #M 5411
[56] *The Northern Whig,* issue of 1 Aug 1846
[57] Dublin Diocesan Wills, 1800-1858
[58] Registry of Deeds #1861 26 253
[59] *Cork Constitution,* issue of 29 April 1847
[60] Burke's *Landed Gentry* (1912 ed) See Swifte of Swiftsheath and Lionsden,
pp 677-678
[61] In Frederick G Bourne's Will, dated 13 Aug 1841, she was named as "my sister "
[62] Mt Jerome Cemetery records
[63] Burke's *Landed Gentry* (1912 ed) See Hartley of Beech Park, p 299 in which Jane
Bourne is called the "sister of Frederick Bourne of Terenure "

    i. James Hartley who was born 15 March 1800 and died 12 Nov 1800

    ii James Hartley of Fairy Hall, Kent was married in 1828 to Martha Semple and had issue

        (1) Harry Hartley who married _____Paton

        (2) James Hartley who married _____McGready and had issue

        (3) Mary Anne Hartley who married H Carson and had issue

Harriet Bourne, probably the youngest of the three sisters, was married 6 February 1812 in the Parish of St. Anne, Dublin to Arthur Achmuty M D. of Kilmore, Co. Roscommon.[64] Her husband died prior to April 1848, at which time she was residing with the H. Lawder family of Aughmore, Co Roscommon.[65]

---

[64] P R O Belfast, #T 1021/32

[65] Will of Richard Edwards Bourne, 2nd Codicil, dated 15 April 1848, in which she is called "my sister"

Appendices

Appendix A

Extracts from Parish Registers

Diocese of Killala and Achonry

Register of the Parish of Killala, Co. Mayo

Baptisms

			Maiden Name
6 Aug	1810	Elizabeth daughter of Anthony and Elizabeth Hughes	Bourns
4 Sept	1814	Robert son of Anthony and Jane Hughes	Bourns
17 Sept	1815	Henry son of Andrew and Margaret Bourns	Fody
10 Jan	1816	Maria daughter of Anthony and Jane Hughes	Bourns
4 March	1818	Catherine Davis daughter of Robert and Jane Bourns	——
15 Oct	1818	Margaret daughter of Andrew and Margaret Bourns	Fody
29 Dec	1818	Michael son of Patrick and Elizabeth Monelly	Bourns
17 Oct	1819	Jane Celia daughter of Robert and Jane Celia Bourns	Bourns
1 Nov	1819	Margaret daughter of Joseph and Alicia Hughes	Bourns
26 Jan	1820	Anne daughter of Patrick and Elizabeth Monelly	Bourns
25 Feb	1821	Eleanor daughter of Robert and Jane Celia Bourns	Bourns
2 June	1822	Bridget daughter of Andrew and Margaret Bourns	Fody
9 Aug	1823	Alicia daughter of Robert and Jane Celia Bourns	Bourns
14 Sept	1823	Mary daughter of Andrew and Margaret Bourns	Fody

7 July	1825	Anne daughter of Robert and Alicia Faucett	Bourns
10 Dec	1828	George son of Samuel and Maria Bourns	Watts
10 March	1829	Anne daughter of Andrew and Margaret Bourns	Fody
15 June	1829	John son of Patrick and Elizabeth Monelly	Bourns
19 Sept	1830	Anne daughter of Samuel and Maria Bourns	Watts
23 June	1842	Richard Corvan Green son of William Bourns and his wife, Jane (Corvan is Cowan misspelled)	——

Marriages

11 June	1816	Patrick Monelly and Elizabeth Bourns, both of Killala
29 June	1819	Robert Faucett of Ballinglen and Alicia Bourns of Erris
15 Dec	1827	Francis Chambers of Ballina and Susan Bourns

Burials

24 May	1818	Samuel Bourns of Killala, aged 68
11 March	1826	Robert Bourns of Killala, aged 38
2 April	1829	Anne Bourns of Killala, aged 83
11 Jan	1845	Jane Loyde Burnes, aged 98

Register of the Parish of Ballysakeery, Co. Mayo*

Baptisms

8 March	1804	John son of Thomas and Jane B , Newtownwhite
3 July	1805	Thomas son of John and Jane B , Newtownwhite
25 Oct	1807	Martha daughter of Thomas and Jane B , Newtownwhite
29 March	1809	Robert son of Thomas and Mary B , Mullafarry
2 July	1812	Alice daughter of Thomas and Mary B
19 Nov	1815	Anne Maria daughter of John and Jane B
9 Nov	1823	Alicia Barbara daughter of John and Eleanor B , Rosserk
17 July	1829	Hannah daughter of Henry and Mary Coulter, of Rosserk
5 Sept	1830	Anne daughter of Matthew and Elinor B , Rosserk
11 Sept	1830	Mary daughter of Thomas and Elizabeth B , Rosserk
21 Nov	1831	Elinor daughter of William B and _____, Portacloy
17 June	1832	Craig son of Hugh and Margaret B , Rosserk
16 Dec	1832	Robert son of Matthew and Anne B , Rosserk
14 March	1833	Martha daughter of Matthew and Ellen B , Newtownwhite
18 June	1833	Matthew son of Matthew and Jane B , Newtowncrummer
13 Oct	1833	Margaret daughter of Hugh and Margaret B , Rosserk.
Jan	1835	Matthew Phibbs son of Matthew and Anne B , Rosserk
16 Jan	1835	John son of Thomas and Elizabeth B , Rosserk.
3 Sept	1835	Elenor daughter of Hugh and Margaret B., Rosserk

* These parish registers were copied originally with "B ' indicating the surname of Bournes, or Bourns They are recorded on this sheet exactly as they were obtained A later study of these same registers enabled us, in a few instances, to give the spelling as given in the register

27 Dec	1835	Jane daughter of Thomas and Alicia B , Newtownwhite
16 Feb	1836	Margaret daughter of Matthew and Eleanor B , Newtownwhite
28 Jan	1837	Hannah daughter of William and Hannah Bourns of Rosserk Father a police officer
7 June	1838	William son of Matthew and Catherine B , Newtowncrummer
10 Jan	1839	Matthew son of Thomas and Ally B , Newtownwhite
30 Jan	1839	Eliza daughter of Thomas and Bessy B , Ballysakeery
12 May	1839	Thomas son of Matthew and Eleanor B , Newtownwhite
11 Sept	1839	Eliza daughter of Hugh and Margaret B , Rosserk
14 May	1840	John son of Matthew and Catherine B , Newtowncrummer
10 Oct	1841	Hugh son of Hugh and Margaret B , Rosserk
14 Oct	1841	Jane daughter of Thomas and Eliza B , Ballysakeery
27 Nov	1842	Margery daughter of Matthew and Catherine B Rosserk
30 Oct	1843	Thomas Craig son of Hugh and Margaret B , Rosserk
6 March	1844	Thomas son of Thomas and Eliza B , Ballysakeery
1 March	1845	Eleanor daughter of Thomas Burns and Catherine Moran
4 Jan	1846	John son of Hugh and Margaret B , Rosserk
21 March	1846	Elizabeth daughter of Matthew and Catherine Bourns of Rosserk
28 June	1846	Thomas Coyan Green Bourns son of Thomas C Green Bournes of Rosserk, Gentleman farmer, and Margaret Born 3 April 1846 (A notation by this entry indicates that this child was dead by 3 Jan 1847 The correct name of this child should be Thomas Cowan Green Bourns)
6 June	1847	William Thomas Coyan Bourns son of Thomas C Green Bourns of Rosserk and Margaret Born 22 May (This child's name should be William Thomas Cowan Bourns)
16 July	1848	Mary Anne daughter of Hugh and Margaret B , Rosserk
15 May	1849	John son of Thomas and Margaret B , Rosserk
11 June	1851	Matthew son of Thomas and Margaret B , Rosserk
16 March	1853	William son of Thomas and Margaret B , Rosserk
13 Feb	1859	Francis son of Thomas and Margaret B , Magherabrack
5 Oct	1860	Jane daughter of Matthew and Matilda B Newtownwhite
18 Jan	1863	_____ daughter of Matthew and Matilda B , Newtownwhite
15 April	1864	Elizabeth daughter of Thomas and Margaret Bourns, Magherabrack
24 Jan.	1865	Matthew Bourns son of Thomas and Jane Bourns of Newtownwhite Born 15 Jan 1865
3 Sept	1865	Robert son of Thomas and Margaret B , Magherabrack
2 Dec	1866	Mary Anne daughter of Thomas and Jane B , Newtownwhite

6 Oct   1867   Samuel son of Thomas and Margaret B , Magherablack
1 Nov   1868   Margaret daughter of Thomas and Jane B , Newtown-white
14 Sept 1873   Eliza daughter of Thomas and Jane B , Newtownwhite
9 April 1876   Jane daughter of Thomas and Jane B , Newtownwhite
15 Jan   1877   Robert Bourns son of Thomas and Jane Bourns of New-townwhite
30 July 1882   James son of Thomas and Jane B , Newtownwhite
11 April 1885   Isabella daughter of Thomas and Jane B , Newtown-white

Marriages

16 March 1802   William Tollett of Enis, Parish of Kilmore, and Esther Rogers of Creeves
4 April 1809   John Boyd of Rosserk and Mary B , Carrowkelly
1 Nov   1812   George Gardiner and Jane B
31 Jan   1819   Henry Coulter of Skreen and Mary Boyd, alias Bournes, Ballysakeery
13 Jan   1820   John Bourns of Ballysakeery and Rebecca(?) Munns
24 Aug   1822   Matthew B and Elinor Mulvagh
3 March 1829   Thomas Bourns of Ballysakeery and Elizabeth Boyd of Ballysakeery Witnesses. William L Bourns and Alexander Boyd
22 Oct   1829   Hugh Bourns of Rosserk and Margaret Murphy Wit-ness Matthew Bourns
23 March 1830   Samuel McKinley, Newtownwhite and Frances B
2 Nov   1830   William McAndrew, School Master, and Elizabeth B.
2 Jan   1834   John Gardiner of Rosserk and Margaret B
6 Feb   1836   Matthew B of Ballysakeery and Catherine Timony
21 Feb   1842   Thomas Goodwin and Jane B
2 Nov   1852   Richard Faucett age 22, and Ellen B , age 22, daughter of Matthew B , Newtownwhite
15 June 1853   Richard Green and Mary Anne B , daughter of John B , Rosserk
28 Sept 1856   James Watson, age 25, and Anne B , age 23, daughter of Matthew B , Newtownwhite
5 Feb   1857   Arthur Gardiner, age 21, and Jane B , age 20, daughter of Thomas B , Newtownwhite
22 Dec   1859   Matthew B , age 21, Newtownwhite and Matilda B , Newtownwhite Matthew son of Thomas Bourns, Matilda daughter of Matthew Bourns
26 Feb   1863   William Eakins, age 25, and Margaret B , daughter of Matthew, Newtownwhite
17 Feb   1870   George Robinson and Matilda of Newtownwhite, widow, and daughter of Matthew B
9 March 1871   Matthew Goodwin and Maria B , daughter of Thomas B , Rosserk
18 Oct   1893   Matthew Henry B of Smithstown and Annie Polke
8 Sept   1894   Andrew Williamson Tod of Bootle and Mary Anne B , daughter of Thomas B , Newtownwhite

17 June   1895   Charles Higgins, age 35, and Elizabeth B , of Smiths-
                 town daughter of Thomas B

Burials

22 Dec   1802   John son of Thomas and Jane Bourns of Newtownwhite,
                 age 6
26 Feb   1803   Thomas B of Mullafarry, age 74
15 March 1804   John son of Thomas and Jane B , an infant
26 Feb   1805   Margaret relict of Matthew B , age 76, Rosserk
12 July   1821   Robert B of Rosserk, age 65
14 Jan   1829   Craig Bourns of Rosserk No age given
21 May   1835   Dolly, wife of Robert B , of Rosserk, age 84
29 Jan   1837   William B of Rosserk, age 33
19 March 1842   Craig B of Rosserk, age 13
12 Nov   1845   Thomas Bourns of Rosserk, age 41 years
 2 Aug   1860   Rev James Meehan, Rector of Ballysakeery for 30
                 years Buried at Crosspatrick
25 Sept   1867   Thomas B of Newtownwhite, age 70
24 June   1868   Matthew B of Newtownwhite, age 30
29 April 1873   Catherine B of Newtownwhite, age 80
30 March 1877   Matthew B of Newtownwhite, age 77
20 July   1887   Alice B of Newtownwhite, age 86 (This entry was
                 originally copied as shown A subsequent search re-
                 vealed her date of death to be 20 July 1890)
26 Feb   1892   Thomas G Bourns of Smithstown. No age given

Registers of the Parishes of Crossmolina, Adergoole, Kilfian and Moygannagh, Co. Mayo

Baptisms

12 March 1769   Elizabeth daughter of Francis Knox of Rappa
26 April 1777   William Henry son of Francis Knox Esq of Rappa and
                 Mary, his wife, Parish of Crossmolina
 2 Oct   1802   Margaret daughter of Thomas and Eleanor (Eleanor
                 crossed out and Helen inserted) Knox of Ballynacloy
10 Oct   1802   Sarah daughter of George and Anne Burns of Knockbane
28 Feb.   1804   Ellen daughter of Thomas and Mary Burns of Ballin-
                 kinletteragh
 1 Feb   1805   Thomas son of William and Susanna Bourns of
                 Knockeskehane
 1 Dec.   1805   George son of George and Anne Burns of Knockbane
22 Dec   1806   Alice daughter of Thomas and Mary Burns of Ballin-
                 kinletteragh
11 March 1810   Francis son of Thomas and Helen Knox of Rockfield
15 Oct   1812   Mary daughter of Robert and Anne Burns of Rathmore
22 June   1815   Anne daughter of Robert and Anne Burns of Rathmore
22 June   1817   Margaret daughter of Robert and Anne Burns of Rath-
                 more
16 April 1819   Sarah daughter of Robert and Anne Burns of Rathmore
                 Born 12 April 1819

2 June	1822	Elizabeth daughter of Robert and Anne Bourns of Rathmore Born 30 May 1822
28 Nov	1824	George son of Robert and Anne Bourns of Rathmore
Feb	1825	Anne daughter of Henry and Frances Bourns
21 May	1826	John son of Edward and Elizabeth Bourns of Ballinagur Born 14 May 1826
12 April	1829	Helen daughter of Robert and Margaret Bourns of Rathmore Born 7 April 1829
26 April	1829	Maria daughter of Henry and Elizabeth Bourns of Crossmolina Born 17 March 1829
12 June	1831	Samuel son of Edward and Elizabeth Bourns of Ballinagur Born 6 June 1831
6 Oct	1833	William son of Edward and Mary Bourns of Ballinagur Born 2 Oct 1833
15 Dec	1833	Maria daughter of William and Dorothea Maxwell of Rathduff Born 7 Dec 1833
31 Aug	1834	Jane daughter of Edward and Mary Bourns of Ballinagui Born 29 Aug 1834
12 July	1835	Henrietta Anne daughter of Henry and Eliza Bournes of Crossmolina Born 12 July 1835.
8 Sept	1839	John son of William and Dorothea Maxwell of Crossmolina
19 June	1840	William Andrew son of David and Elizabeth Ruttledge, Parish of Crossmolina

Marriages

15 Oct	1806	William Robinson of Castletown in the Parish of Lacken, Co Mayo and Barbara Smith, Parish of Rathmore, by licence
18 Feb	1808	Thomas O'Donel of Cloonagh and Anne Morrison of Crossmolina, spinster, by licence
8 Dec	1808	Robert Wills of Ballinagur and Anne Burn of the same, widow by licence
6 May	1810	Richard Faussett of the Parish of Kilglass, Co Sligo and Alicia Rogers of Glanedagh, Parish of Kilfian, spinster, by licence
9 Aug	1812	Lloyd Johnston of Crossmolina and Marianne Bourke of the same place, spinster, by licence
15 March	1815	Oliver Jackson of Rathmore, Parish of Crossmolina and Elizabeth Bourns of Knockbane, spinster, Banns
20 Sept	1815	Dudley Joynt of Ballyglan, Parish of Dunfeeny and Margaret Ready of Rathcreevy, Parish of Crossmolina, spinster, by licence
18 Feb	1817	John Bourns of the Parish of Kilcommon-Erris and Mary Ready of Rathcreevy, Parish of Crossmolina spinster, by licence
28 May	1818	Francis Knox and Margaret O'Donel alias Knox, both of Millpark Lodge, Parish of Kilfian, by licence (Note in register this couple were married some thirty years before by a Roman Catholic Priest)

23 May 1821 Robert Wills and Elanor Rogers alias Bourns, widow, both of Ballinagur, by licence

6 May 1823 John Faussett of Mount Glyn, Parish of Dunfeeny and Matilda Knox, widow of Stonehall, Parish of Crossmolina, by licence

17 March 1828 Callwell Joynt of the Waterguards and Frances Bourns of the Parish of Kilcommon-Erris, spinster, by licence

25 June 1830 William Nixon of Newport, widower and Frances Rutledge of Moylaw, spinster, by licence

7 March 1832 William Clarke of Crossmolina and Mary Bourns of Rathmore, spinster, Banns

23 Oct 1832 William Maxwell of Rathduff and Dorothea Joynt of Kinnard, spinster, by licence

11 Jan 1834 John Patterson of Rathmore and Anne Bourns of Crossmolina, spinster, by licence

18 March 1835 Thomas Bourns of Newtownwhite in the Parish of Ballysakeery and Alicia Craig of the Parish of Kilscaseby, by licence

3 June 1836 Robert Neely and Margaret Bourns, by licence

12 Sept 1838 John Wallace, Parish of Easkey, Co Sligo, to Mary Joynt of Crossmolina, by licence

16 Aug. 1842 Michael Barr to Maria Cormick, both of this parish, by licence.

Burials

4 June 1775 William son of Samuel and Jane Smith of the Parish of Kilfian

25 Feb 1776 Michael Cormick Esq of the Parish of Crossmolina

24 March 1777 Richard Cormick of Mullinmore, Parish of Crossmolina.

5 Jan 1812 William Smith of Rockfield, Parish of Moygannagh, Surgeon, aged 24

9 March 1816 Francis Cormick of Castlehill, Parish of Adergoole, Esq at Adergoole

16 Jan 1821 Eliza Knox of Stonehall, aged 6

27 May 1826 Thomas Knox of Stonehall, aged 19 Died 25 May

30 Nov 1826 Anne Bourns of Rathmore, aged 34

18 May 1832 Francis Cormick of Castlehill, at Adergoole Died 16 May

25 June 1833 James Maxwell of Rathduff, aged 95 Died 23 June

8 Sept 1834 Jane Bourns of Ballinagur, aged 9 days

11 Sept 1834 Matthew Maxwell of Rathduff, aged 65 Died 9 Sept

4 July 1839 Annesley George Knox, late of Rappa Castle, aged 71

21 Feb 1840 Mary Maxwell of Crossmolina

21 Feb 1841 Thomas Knox of the Parish of Crossmolina

18 Jan 1848 Mary Leandrum alias Bourns of Ballinagur, aged 104

9 Feb 1848 James A Knox, Crosspatrick, Parish of Killala, aged 46

6 March 1848 Jane Knox of Crossmolina, aged 42

24 April 1848 St George Knox, Fahy, aged 8

13 Dec. 1864 Rev St George Knox, Dsomerd(?), aged 64

9 Aug 1869 Samuel Handy Knox, Greenwood, aged 23

3 Dec   1870   Thomas Rutledge, Rathduff, aged 60
2 July   1873   Emily Frances Knox, Gortner Abbey, aged 12 hours
31 July   1875   John Henry Knox, Greenwood, aged 32
31 March 1877   Francis St George Knox, Gortner Abbey, Crossmolina,
                 aged 13½ weeks
9 May   1882   William Knox of Fairfield, no age given
23 May   1884   Willa Louisa Knox, Gortner Abbey, aged 14 days
25 May   1884   Harriette Elizabeth Knox, Gortner Abbey, aged 38
22 Aug   1894   Jane Adelaide Knox, Greenwood Park, aged 87

Confirmation Lists

1804
    Sarah Bourns

17 Sept   1817
    James Ready
    Mary Ready
    William Ready

29 Sept   1821
    Henry Bourns
    Edward Bourns
    Anne and Sarah Bourns

Registers of the Parishes of Straid, Castleconnor and Kilmoremoy.

Parish of Straid, Co. Mayo

Burials

16 June   1882   Walter Rutledge of Leckee, Foxford, aged 2 years and
                   2 months

Parish of Castleconnor. Co. Sligo

Baptisms

3 May   1802   Elinor Anne daughter of Thomas and Esther Bourns of
                 Castleconnor
13 Nov   1802   Thomas son of Darby and Honor Bourns of Castleconnor
1 July   1803   William son of James Burns of Castleconnor Baptised
                 by Rev Robert Scarlett
13 May   1806   Thomas son of Andrew and Bridget Bournes of Dooneen
18 May   1806   Alicia daughter of Thomas and Esther his wife of Castle-
                 connor
6 June   1806   Margaret daughter of Darby and Honor Bourns of
                 Castleconnor
4 Feb   1808   Julia daughter of Darby and Honor Bournes of Runroe
16 Oct.   1808   Henry son of Andrew and Bridget Bournes of Runroe
24 Dec   1809   Mary daughter of James and Elizabeth Bournes of Park
4 Feb   1810   Jane daughter of James and Margery Bourns of Scur-
                 more
6 May   1810   James son of Darby and Honor Bournes of Runroe

16 May   1810   Eleanor daughter of James and Marianne Bourns of Ballintean

12 May   1811   William son of James and Elizabeth Bourns of Park

2 April   1812   Henry son of James and Elizabeth Bourns of Park

15 April   1812   Marienne daughter of James Bournes Esq of Kilglass and Marienne, his wife

20 July   1812   Mary and Jane, twin daughters of Darby and Honor Bournes of Runroe

1813   Thomas son of Thomas and Elizabeth Bourns of Lackmaslave

28 March 1813   Mary daughter of Andrew and Bridget Bournes of Runroe

21 March 1814   Margaret Fleanor daughter of John and Ellen Bourns of Ballina

5 June   1814   Jane daughter of Thomas and Elizabeth Bourns of Lackinslave

21 Aug   1814   John son of Darby and Honor Bourns of Runroe

18 Sept   1814   Arthur son of James and Elizabeth Bourns of Park

5 Nov   1815   Mary daughter of Thomas and Elizabeth Bourns of Lackinaslave

8 June   1817   John son of Andrew and Margaret Bourns of Scurmore

1819   Bridget daughter of Andrew Bournes of Dooneen and Mary Atkinson

8 Aug   1819   Margaret daughter of Matthew and Winifred Bourns Born 6 July 1819

23 Sept   1820   James son of James and Mary Bourns of Farrengarode

29 Dec   1820   Henry son of Henry and Mary Bourns of Lackmaslave

28 Feb   1822   Elizabeth Jane daughter of James and Barbara Bourns Born 22 Feb 1822

26 Feb   1842   Mary Jane daughter of William and Mary Bournes of Farrengerode, mason Born 18 Feb 1842

8 April   1845   James son of Thomas Bourns and Elizabeth Kilroy, Knockroe, Gentleman Born 29 Dec 1844

15 Aug   1847   Elizabeth Anne daughter of John and Caroline Bourns, Knockroe Cottage, Gentleman. Born 27 July 1847

8 Oct   1848   Alicia daughter of John and Eleanor Bournes, farmer of Bangor Erris Born 26 Oct 1848 (Note baptismal date probably should be 28 Oct)

10 Aug   1850   Thomas son of John Bournes and Elizabeth of Dooneen, farmer Born 4 Aug 1850

24 July   1853   Jane Anne daughter of John and Elizabeth Bournes of Dooneen, farmer Born 10 July 1853.

10 April   1858   William son of John and Eliza Bournes, farmer

Marriages

17 Feb   1805   John Watts of Learnavegh, Castleconnor, weaver and Ann Burns of the same place

25 Feb   1805   Thomas Rolton of Ballyflynn and Mary Burns of Lacken, Kilglass Rev James Burrowes, vicar. (Rolton is probably Roulston, see M L B Killala and Achonry)

6 March 1806   Robert Weir and Diana Bourns of Castleconnor Rev Robert Scarlett, vicar

18 May   1806   James Bournes of Castleconnor and Mary Anne Bournes of Ballina

10 Feb   1807   David Weir of Skreen and Mary Bournes of Attycree

10 Dec.   1807   Patrick Crawford and Eleanor Bournes

5 Feb   1809   James Bournes of Park and Elizabeth Bournes of Leaffaney, Kilglass

6 March 1810   Robert Morris of Easkey and Elizabeth Bournes of Kilglass

17 Oct   1810   Thomas Bournes of Leaffaney, Kilglass and Elizabeth Strong of Ardwoody

14 June   1811   Anthony Hughes of Killala and Jane Bournes of Attycree

21 Aug   1814   Andrew Bournes and Margaret Foody

19 Jan   1815   John Wilkins of Skreen and Jane Bournes of Kilglass

26 April   1815   Joseph Hughes of Killala and Alicia Bournes of Castleconnor.

29 Jan   1818   Henry Bournes of Leaffaney and Margaret Strong of Ardwoody.

24 July   1818   James Bar of Ballysakeery and Elizabeth Bournes widow of Thomas Bournes of Kilglass

13 Nov.   1837   Henry Bournes of Attyclare, Parish of Castleconnor and Jane Alicia Bournes of Ardglass Witnesses John Bourns brother of the bride and William Bourne father of the bride

11 Sept   1838   Henry Watts of Castleconnor and Catherine Rutledge of Quignalecka, Parish of Kilmoremoy Witnesses: Charles Smythe and Andrew Watts

17 July   1840   James Rutledge of Carrowcollar Lodge, Kilglass and Maria Boland of Tully She being 23 and he 34 Witnesses William Boland and M Wilson

10 Feb   1842   James Rollston of Lacken, Parish of Kilglass and Mary Bournes of Carrowcarden, Castleconnor Witnesses Henry Simpson and Henry Simpson Sr

Burials

7 Jan   1807   Matthew Bournes of Scurmore

29 Nov   1807   Mrs Bourns wife of Thomas Bourns of Castleconnor, aged 27

4 June   1812   Margaret Bourns wife of William Bourns of Park

23 March 1815   Thomas Bournes of Knockane

5 July   1815   Henry Bourns of Leaffaney

30 Nov   1817   Hilary Bourns of Scurmore

15 Jan   1819   Andrew Bourns of Scurmore

2 Nov   1834   Elizabeth widow of Henry Bournes of Lackinaslave, aged 78

14 Nov   1841   Thomas Bournes of Carrowcarden (No age given)

17 May   1845   Thomas Bournes of Knoclere aged 35

25 Feb   1847   Widow Bournes of Dooneen aged 65

3 Sept   1849   Darby Bournes of Dooneen aged 83 Died 1 Sept

5 Sept   1859   Mary Anne Bournes of Castleconnor aged 68
14 Jan   1862   James Bournes of Castleconnor Cottage, aged 94
19 July   1862   John Bournes of Scurmore aged 38

Parish of Kilmoremoy, Co. Mayo

Baptisms

16 Jan   1818   Robert son of John and Anne Ormsby Born 15 Jan 1818
14 June   1818   James son of Andrew and Sarah Gardner Born 7 June
                    1818
12 July   1818   Mary Ann daughter of John and Elinor Bourns Born
                    9 July 1818
25 Oct   1818   Ormsby son of Ormsby and Mary Ann Rutledge Born 22
                    Oct 1818
15 Nov.   1818   William son of William and Sarah Bourns Born 12 Nov
                    1818
17 March 1819   Elizabeth daughter of Thomas and Eliza Ruttledge
                    (No birth date)
14 May   1819   John son of James and Frances Higgins (No birth date)
4 July   1819   James son of James and Eliza Bourns (No birth date)
8 Aug   1819   Margrett daughter of Matthew and Winified Bourns
                    Born 6 July 1819
2 Sept   1819   Robert son of Henry and Bridget Smith (No birth date)
28 Nov   1819   William son of William R Smith and Catherine Born
                    21 Nov 1819
6 Dec   1819   Margaret daughter of Richard and Anne Faussett (No
                    birth date)
            1820   John son of George and Anne Ormsby (Baptised between
                    1 March and 7 May 1820)
11 June   1820   Mary daughter of Andrew and Sarah Gardner Born 10
                    June 1820
18 June   1820   Mary Anne daughter of William and Elizabeth Ormsby
                    Born 16 June 1820
28 Sept   1820   Thomas son of Thomas and Eliza Rutledge Born 18
                    Sept 1820
7 Jan   1821   Eleanor daughter of William and Barbara Higgins Born
                    28 Dec 1820
7 March 1821   Jane daughter of William and Sally Burns Born 6 March
                    1821
1 April   1821   George son of John and Catherine Burn (No birth date)
29 Aug   1821   George son of James and Frances Higgins Born 25
                    Aug 1821
1 Nov.   1821   Elinor daughter of Anthony and Mary Ormsby Born 18
                    Oct 1821
18 Nov.   1821   John son of Matthew and Winified Bourns Born 3
                    Nov 1821
25 Nov   1821   James son of Richard and Anne Faussett Born 16 Nov
                    1821
22 Jan   1822   Susanna daughter of John and Ann Ormsby Born 18
                    Jan 1822

28 Feb   1822   Elizabeth Jane daughter of James Burns and Barbara Burns Born 22 Feb 1822

6 June   1822   Frederick Edgar son of John Frederick and Anne Knox Born 29 April 1822

8 Aug   1822   Barbara daughter of Thomas and Eliza Rutledge Born 5 Aug 1822

26 Dec   1822   James son of Philip Ormsby Smyth and Mary Feeny. Born 19 Dec 1822

16 Feb   1823   Richard son of Francis Knox and Biddy Cane Born 2 Feb 1823

19 May   1823   Susanna daughter of William Gardner and Jane Ormsby Born 11 May 1823

3 Aug   1823   William son of James Gardner and Sally Burns(?) Born 24 July 1823

3 April   1824   William son of Thomas Burns and Sarah Sims Born 24 March 1824

9 May   1824   George son of Matthew and Winny Bourns Born 7 March 1824

9 May   1824   Uchtre Augustus, son of Frederick Knox and Anne Gore Born 7 April 1824

23 Aug   1824   Jane daughter of Patrick Foley and Catherine Burns Born 4 Aug 1824

24 Dec   1824   Jane Sarah daughter of Annesley Knox and Eliza Hodgens Born 14 Dec 1824

14 April 1825   Jane daughter of Annesley Knox and Eliza Hodgens(sic)

15 May   1825   Utred Augustus son of John Frederick Knox and Anne Gore Born 19 April 1825

17 July   1825   of Bourns

17 July   1825   Thomas son of James Bourns and Elizabeth Bourns Born 11 July 1825

14 Dec   1825   John son of William and Sarah Bourns Born 11 Nov 1825

12 July   1826   Anne daughter of Matthew and Winny Bourns Born 6 July 1826

27 Aug   1826   Thomas son of Elias and Mary Bourns Born 23 Aug 1826

21 Jan   1827   Charles son of James and Ellen O'Brien Born 17 Jan 1827

15 April 1827   Matthew son of Matthew and Winny Bourns Born 2 April 1827 (Out of place in the register)

22 Aug   1827   Caldwell son of William Gardner and Jane Ormsby Born 2 Aug 1827

14 Oct   1827   Mary Anne daughter of Philip O Smith and Mary Feeny Born 30 Sept 1827

14 Oct   1827   Thomas son of Thomas Moran and Mary Ruttledge (No birth date)

27 Jan   1828   Anne daughter of James and Ellinor Burn Born 22 Jan 1828

29 Feb   1828   Catherine daughter of James Burns and Sarah Burns Born 28 Jan. 1828 (Leap year)

Feb 1828   Maria Julia daughter of Annesley Knox and Eliza Hodgens Born 21 Feb 1828 (No day of baptism)

15 June   1828   Eliza daughter of William and Sarah Burns Born 4 June 1828

16 Feb   1829   William son of James Higgins and Frances Atkinson Born 14 Jan 1829

17 Feb   1829   Robert George son of John Higgins and Agnes Poke Born 10 Feb 1829

16 April   1829   John Henry son of John Burns and Mary Burns Born 9 April 1829

3 May   1829   Elizabeth daughter of William Burns and Sarah Colher(?) Born 19 April 1829

21 May   1829   Sarah daughter of William Gardner and Jane Ormsby Born 19 May 1829

17 June   1829   Alfred William son of John Frederick and Anna Maria Knox Born 5 May 1829

19 April   1830   Jane Louisa daughter of Arthur Gore Knox and Sarah Knox Born 8 April 1830

6 Aug   1830   James William son of Annesley and Eliza Knox Born 16 July 1830

19 Aug   1830   Julia Anne daughter of James and Frances Higgins Born 25 July 1830

1 Feb   1831   Margaret daughter of Alexander Galbraith and Maria Rutledge Born 24 Jan 1831

4 Feb   1831   Thomas son of Symon Breaden and Jane Knox Born 4 Feb 1831

4 Feb   1831   Thomas son of Thomas Grundleter(?) and Catherine Smith Born 3 Jan 1831

13 Feb   1831   Mary daughter of Patrick O'Donnell and Mary Gardner Born 9 Feb 1831

10 June   1831   William son of Duke Ormsby and Mary Anne Charlton Born 1 June 1831

5 Oct   1831   Charles James son of Arthur Knox Gore and Sarah, his wife Born 20 Sept 1831

12 Oct   1831   Alberic Edward son of John Frederick and Maria Knox (No birth date)

2 Jan   1832   Anne Jane daughter of John Bourns and Margaret Knox Born April 1832 (Suggest birth date should be April 1831 as following entry is also a Jan baptism)

29 March 1832   William son of William Gardner and Jane Ormsby Born 28 March 1832

19 April   1832   Robert son of Anthony Ormsby and Mary Faussett Born 9 April 1832

17 June   1832   Sarah daughter of William and Sarah Bourns Born 6 June 1832 (An "X" above and below name "Sarah" and the name Whiteside referring to her maiden name)

8 July   1832   George son of William Bourns by Judith Cavanagh Born 30 June 1832

6 Jan   1833   Jane daughter of John Ormsby and Anne Gardner.
                  Born 1 Jan 1833

19 Feb   1833   John son of Andrew Joint and Margaret Gardner. Born
                  10 Feb 1833

13 Sept   1833   Susannah daughter of James Bourns and Jane Farquer.
                  (No birth date)

13 Sept   1833   Matilda daughter of Lt Col Knox Gore and Sarah his
                  wife (No birth date)

10 April 1834   Charles son of James Higgins and Frances Atkinson
                  (No birth date)

11 April 1834   James Ormsby son of James Knox Gore and Harriet
                  Knox Born 7 March 1834

3 Aug   1834   Elizabeth daughter of Philip O Smith and Mary Feeny
                  Born 12 July 1834

15 Oct   1834   Margaret daughter of Anthony Ormsby and Mary
                  Faussett Born 4 Oct 1834

29 Jan   1835   Mary daughter of Andrew and Margaret Joint Born
                  15 Dec 1834

20 June   1835   Marie daughter of Alexander Galbraith and Maria Rut-
                  ledge Born 30 May 1835

28 Dec.   1835   Elizabeth daughter of James and Jane Bourns (No
                  birth date)

4 April   1836   Margaret Jane daughter of William and Jane Bourns
                  Born 26 March 1836

13 April 1836   John Ethelred son of John Frederick and _____Knox
                  Born 7 March 1836

14 Jan   1837   Letitia daughter of Andrew and Margaret Joint Born
                  6 Jan 1837.

5 Feb   1837   Ellinor daughter of Matthew Bourns and Anne Matthews
                  Born 2 Feb 1837.

2 April   1837   George son of Robert Jones and Margaret Bourns Born
                  15 March 1837

2 April   1837   James son of James Morton and Mary Bourns. Born 25
                  March 1837

14 April 1837   Elizabeth Eleanor daughter of John Bourns and Margaret
                  his wife Born 10 Feb 1837

11 June   1837   Robert son of William Bourns and Sarah his wife Born
                  14 May 1837

2 April   1838   Andrew son of David and Bess Ruttledge of Toomore
                  parish Born 5 March 1838

12 Feb   1839   Matilda daughter of Andrew and Margaret Joint Born
                  26 Jan 1839

10 May   1839   Eleanor Louisa daughter of John F Knox and Anna
                  Knox Born 5 April 1839

22 Sept   1839   William son of Robert Jones by his wife Margaret
                  Bourns Born 16 Sept 1839

24 May   1842   Mary daughter of William and Sarah Bourns of Ballina,
                  Hatter. Born 9 May 1842

15 May   1843   Robert son of Andrew and Margaret Joynt The
                  Backs   Born 15 May 1843 (Same day as baptism)

6 Nov   1843   William Edward son of John and Maria Fair of Ardnaree
                 Born 7 Oct 1843

28 Nov   1844   George Charles Fair son of John Fair and his wife Maria,
                 merchant Born 29 Oct 1844

11 March 1845   Sarah daughter of William Bourns and Sarah Bourns,
                 hatter Born 18 Feb 1845

26 Feb   1846   Agnes daughter of Andrew Joynt and his wife Margaret,
                 farmer Born 24 Jan 1846

12 Aug   1847   Jane and Matthew children of William and Dorothy
                 Maxwell of Ardnaree, carpenter Born 4 April 1847

25 March 1849   Albert James son of John and Maria Fair of Ballina,
                 merchant Born 26 Feb 1849

13 Aug   1854   Richard son of Thomas and Margaret Bournes of Castle
                 Road, farmer Born 2 July 1854

12 May   1855   Louisa daughter of John and Jane Bourns of Ballina,
                 printer Born 17 April 1855

16 May   1857   John son of Joh and Jane Bourns of Ballina, printer
                 Born 25 April 1857

7 Aug   1859   Anne daughter of John and Jane Bourns, printer of
                 Ballina Born 9 July 1859

29 Dec   1861   Sarah daughter of John and Jane Bourns, printer of
                 Ballina Born 1 Nov 1861

13 Jan   1864   Mary Jane daughter of John and Jane Bourns of Ballina,
                 printer Born 3 Nov 1863

18 April 1866   Kate daughter of John and Jane Bourns of Ballina,
                 printer Born 10 March 1866

16 June 1866   William Thomas son of Robert and Jane Burns of
                 Ballina, cabinet maker Born 30 May 1866
                 (Gap in register from 1868-1874)

8 April 1876   Arthur Robert son of John and Jane Bourns of King St,
                 Ballina, printer Born 19 Jan 1876

Marriages

21 March 1802   John Shannon of Kilmoremoy and Bridget Burns
25 Feb   1818   Joseph Clark and Elizabeth Ormsby Witness   John
                 Layng
29 March 1818   Elias Burns of the Parish of Castleconnor and Maria
                 McKenzie of Ardnaree Witnesses Dr Hines, William
                 Rogers and Alexander McKenzie
21 Jan   1819   William Gardner of Killala and Jane Ormsby of the
                 Parish of Killufad Witnesses Andrew Ormsby and
                 John Layng
24 Jan   1819   An T Knox of Kilmoremoy and Eliza Hodgins Wit-
                 nesses John Layng and G Hutton
13 Jan   1822   Patrick O'Donnell of Cloonagh and Maria Gardner
                 Witnesses John Layng and Henry Masterton
14 Dec   1822   Philip Ormsby Smith of Kilmoremoy and Mary Feeny of
                 Kilmoremoy Witnesses John Atkinson and John
                 Layng
27 Dec   1822   Henry Bourns of the Parish of Crossmolina and Frances

Watts of the Parish of Kilmoremoy Witnesses. Richard Faussett and Henry Edgar

19 Dec 1824 John Bourns of Kilmoremoy and Margaret O'Donnell Witnesses Samuel Bourns and Benjamin Wilson

13 Feb 1827 Thomas Christie of Castlebar and Jane Bourns of Kilmoremoy Witnesses John Bourns and John Layng

7 July 1828 James Bourns and Jane Faurquer Witnesses George Buchanan and Thomas Forker (The bride signed her name as "Fourker")

4 Dec 1828 John Lee and Anne Knox Witnesses John Craig, Matthew _____ney

17 March 1829 Alexander Galbraith of Argyleshire, Scotland and Maria Rutledge Witnesses Archibald Gillis and William Johnston

10 Aug 1829 George Fenton of Kilglass and Elizabeth Ormsby of Killufad Witnesses John Layng and John_____

9 April 1830 George Smith and Hannah Feeny Witnesses John Atkinson and Patt. Feeney.

22 June 1830 John Bourns of Ballysakeery and Margaret Knox of Kilmoremoy Witnesses William Bourns and William West

26 July 1830 Duke Ormsby of Killufad and Mary Anne Charlton of Attymas Witnesses James Higgins and George Ormsby

26 Feb 1832 Matthew Bourns of the Parish of Ballysakeery and Anne Matthews of the Parish of Kilmoremoy Witnesses William Bourns and Thomas Matthews

26 Feb 1832 Andrew Joynt of Ballynehay and Margaret Gardner of Kilmoremoy Witnesses John Layng and John Gardner

22 Aug 1832 William Marsden of Kilmoremoy and Jane Smith Witnesses. William Burns and John Layng

5 Nov 1832 William Bourns of Kilmoremoy and Judith Cavanagh of Kilmoremoy Witnesses John Craig and John Cavanagh

23 April 1833 Charles Hillier of the 27th Regt and Margaret Farrel of Kilmoremoy Witnesses Thomas Gordon and ?

12 June 1833 Thomas Wills of the Parish of Kilmoremoy, North Mayo Staff and Agnes Higgins alias Poke Witnesses. D Masterton and William Rickett

14 Feb 1840 Thomas Mathews of Kilmoremoy and Agnes Gardner of Ballynahaghsh Witnesses John Gardner and William Joynt

22 Oct 1841 William Knox of Ardagh and Jane Roe of Crossmolina Witnesses James ? ?

7 Nov 1844 George Higgins of Kilmoremoy and Elizabeth Ready of Kilmoremoy Witnesses Robert Mostyn and James Higgins.

27 Dec   1852 William Bourns of Kilmoremoy, a policeman, and Jane
                 Brennan alias Smith of Ballinacalla Witnesses John
                 Bourns and Sarah Bourns

Burials

28 Aug   1818 Charles O'Brien, Kilmoremoy (No age given)
 4 Sept   1818 Charles O'Brien, Kilmoremoy, aged 64
 2 Nov   1818 Maria Knox, Kilmoremoy, aged 73
 7 Nov   1818 Diana Gardner, Ardagh, aged 76.
 3 Dec   1818 Anthony Ormsby Killufad, aged 74
15 March   1819 ___ ___Knox, a constable, Erris aged 40 in Ardnaree
14 July   1820 Charles O'Brien, Kilmoremoy, aged 25
30 Oct   1820 Anne Faussett, Kilmoremoy, aged 82
25 Nov   1821 James Knox, Kilmoremoy (No age given)
 8 March   1822 M Bourns, Kilmoremoy (No age given)
 8 July   1822 Charles Ormsby, Kilmoremoy, aged 83.
12 Jan   1823 William Smith, Castleconnor, aged 50
 6 March   1824 Paul Ormsby, Killufad, aged 64
14 Oct   1824 George Ormsby, Killufad, aged 40
30 May   1825 Jane Smyth, Kilmoremoy, aged 69
21 June   1825 Dr Caldwell Ormsby, Kilmoremoy, aged 29
 6 Nov   1825 George Bourns, Erris, aged 59
18 April   1828 Dr William Knox, Kilmoremoy (No age given)
30 April   1828 Henry Smith, Kilmoremoy (No age given)
15 Sept   1829 William Higgins, Ardnaree, aged 9/12 months.
25 Nov   1829 Andrew Ormsby, Kilmoremoy, aged 45
27 Nov   1830 Thomas Smith, Kilmoremoy, aged 80
 5 Jan   1831 Charles Gardener, Kilmoremoy, aged 27
 2 Nov.   1831 Catherine Ruttledge, Kilmoremoy, aged 60
 3 Sept.   1832 John Smith, Kilmoremoy, aged 19
18 Sept   1833 William Bourns, Kilmoremoy, aged 44
26 Sept   1833 Anne Faussett, Kilmoremoy, aged 48
14 March   1834 John Bourns, Kilmoremoy, aged 60
30 July   1834 Mary, Mrs. Dr Gardiner, Kilmoremoy, aged 40.
 6 Sept   1834 Jane Knox, Kilmoremoy, aged 9
13 Jan   1837 James Knox, Surgeon, Kilmoremoy, aged 78
 7 June   1837 Son of William Bourns,* Kilmoremoy, aged 5
13 Sept   1837 John Bourns, Kilmoremoy, aged 40
 7 May   1839 Susy Bourns, Kilmoremoy, aged 76
27 Sept   1839 Elinor Bourns, Kilmoremoy, aged 56
 3 May   1840 William Ruttledge, Moy Quay, aged 25
 9 May   1840 Alicia Bourns, Ballina, aged 13
26 Sept   1840 Philip O Bourns, Behey, aged 83
12 Dec.   1840 Margaret Bourns, Roserdu,** aged 24
28 April   1842 James Smyth, Behey, aged 17
 6 Aug   1842 Margaret Bourns, Dublin, aged 30
15 Nov.   1842 Sarah Bourns, Ballina, aged 23

* The christian name appears as Bullmer or Bullman
** Roserdu is Rosserk incorrectly spelled

29 Jan	1843	Margaret O'Brien, Ballina, aged 67
5 April	1843	Anne Gardner, Ardnaree, aged 29
23 May	1843	John Bourns, Ballina, aged 37
7 Jan.	1844	Frances Higgins, Ballina, aged 91
13 Nov	1844	Mary Knox, Ballina, aged 83
30 Dec	1844	Frances Higgins, Ballina, aged 52
25 Feb	1845	Sally Gardiner, Ardnaree, aged 53
16 June	1845	Winifred Bourns, Ballina, aged 50
22 Sept	1845	Charles Gardiner, Cloonagh, aged 69
14 Jan	1846	Margaret Knox, Ballina, aged 70
27 Aug	1846	Anne Bourns, Ballina, aged 19
14 Nov	1846	Edward Gardiner, Rathlee, buried at Ballynahaglesh, aged 40
8 Dec	1846	William Bourns, Ardnaree, aged 96
12 Dec	1846	David Ruttledge, Foxford, aged 45
12 Jan	1847	John Bourns, Ballina, aged 22
6 Feb	1847	John Rutledge, Ballina, aged 49
3 May	1847	William Knox, Netley, aged 33
9 Feb	1849	James Annesley Knox, Crosspatrick, aged 46.
23 May	1849	John Gardner, Ballina, aged 7
11 Aug	1849	Eliza Knox, Garden St , Ballina, aged 55
15 June	1852	Frances Higgins, Ballina aged 79
27 Sept	1852	James Gardiner, North House, Ballina, aged 69
22 Aug	1853	Thomas Bourns, Ballina, aged 8
30 Jan	1854	Sarah Bourns, Ardnaree, aged 60
16 Feb	1855	John Ruttledge, Quignamanger, aged 83
13 July	1857	James Higgins, Ballina, aged 65
8 June	1859	Hannah Knox, Ardnaree, aged 88
29 Sept	1859	Capt Henry William Knox, Netley Park, aged 51
11 Jan	1860	John Knox, Ballina, aged 74
9 Dec	1860	Andrew Joynt, Ballina, aged 72
25 Jan	1861	Lieut Francis Knox, 1st Regt., Ballina, aged 74
22 Nov	1861	Elizabeth Bourns, Ardnaree, aged 84
20 April	1862	William Bourns, Ballina, aged 66
13 Oct	1863	Mary Anne Gardiner, Ballina, aged 24
30 Oct	1863	Annesley Gore Knox, Netley, aged 48
20 Jan	1864	Richard Faussett M D , Ballina, aged 86.
4 April	1882	James Bournes, Ardnaree, aged 63
11 June	1882	Jane Bournes (Mis), Ardnaree, aged 70
12 Dec	1883	Mis Margaret Bourns, Parish of Ballysakeery, Smithstown, aged 47
28 Dec	1883	William Bourns, Ardnaree, aged 65
27 Feb	1892	Thomas C G Bournes, Smithstown, aged 64

St. Michael's Church, Ardnaree, Ballina, Co. Mayo
Vestry Book*

Baptisms

3 Feb   1770   William Burns son of John and Mary

* The Vestry Book cover indicates that the entries are from 1768 through 1792 Actually the entries are up to 13 July 1815

4 Nov   1770   John Cormick son of Michael and Diana
23   Edward O'Donnel son of Edward and Mary (No month
                   or year given Previous entry 4 Dec 1770, next entry
                   17 Feb 1771)
28 Oct   1771   Alice Burns daughter of John and Elizabeth (There is
                   some doubt about this baptismal date but both the
                   previous and subsequent dates are in this month and
                   year)
1 Feb.   1772   William O'Donnell son of Edward and Mary
4 May   1773   Matthew son to Matthew and Elizabeth Bourns
15 Aug   1773   Mary daughter of John and Elizabeth Byrne
5 Sept   1773   Neal son of Edward and Mary O'Donnell
26 Dec   1773   Thomas son of John and Eleanor O'Donnald
9 Feb   1774   John son of Samuel and Ann Bourns
17 Sept   1775   Robert son of Robert and Bridget Smith
13 July   1802   Fanny daughter of Matthew and Elizabeth Bourns
24 Oct   1802   Baptised by me Arthur Knox, son to Rev. Arthur Knox
                   and Hannah Wilson, his wife, both of Ardnaree, Co.
                   Sligo Signed, John King, Vicar of the Union of Kil-
                   moremoy in the Diocese of Killala
8 Sept   1803   Thomas son of Thomas and Ann O'Donnell of Cloonagh
24 March   1804   Margaret Eleanor daughter of John and Eleanor Bournes
                   of Ballina

Marriages

17 Aug   1772   Henry Smith and Bridget Murphy of Ballina, by licence
24 Jan   1803   David Ruttledge of Tanganamore in the Parish of
                   Kilbilfad was married to Bridget Howly of said place
                   and parish by the Rev Mr Bell, Curate of Foxford

Burials

2 Aug   1772   William Burns of the Parish of Kilmoremoy

Signatures—

    Anes (Annesley) Gore signed as churchwarden in 1769 and in 1770
    Michael Cormick signed in 1770
    John Burns signed at the vestry meeting held 5 June 1770
    Anes Gore signed the vestry book 14 April 1773, 14 June 1773,
        5 April 1774 and 17 April 1775
    John O'Donnell signed 20 Dec 1775
    James Faussett was churchwarden in 1779 and in 1780
    Phill Smith signed 6 April 1780
    Matt Bourns signed 6 April 1780 and Monday 16 April 1781
    James Knox signed 6 April 1790
    George Fawcett signed 6 April 1795
    Joynt Smith signed 29 March 1796
    James Faussett signed 5 April 1796
    Ans (Annesley) Knox signed 10 April (No year, probably 1797)
    Anes Knox signed Tuesday 10 April 1798
    James Knox and Anes Knox signed 27 May 1800 and 20 April 1802

James Knox was churchwarden in 1804 and signed the vestry book
   26 April 1806
James Knox signed 1808
John Bourns signed the vestry book Tuesday 4 April 1809
James Knox, Richard Faussett and John Bourns signed 24 April 1810
James Knox and Richard Lloyd signed in 1812
James Knox and William Byrne signed 28 March 1815

Register of the Parish of Easkey, Co. Sligo

Births

23 Nov	1827	Thomas Shiell at Easkey Glebe son of Thomas Burne and Olivia Catherine Shiell Rev Shiell, vicar
31 March	1838	Sarah daughter of William Morrison and Elizabeth
2 Dec	1838	James son of John Ruttledge and Anne
15 May	1847	Henry son of Robert Burns of Cloonagleevagh and Catherine
5 May	1849	Jane daughter of Robert Burns of Cloonagleevagh and Catherine

Burials

4 March	1824	Elizabeth Bournes at Clooneen
4 June	1832	John Burns Jr at Cloonagleevagh, aged 16 years
14 Nov	1832	James Burns Sr at Cloonagleevagh, aged 89
6 Nov	1866	Mary Burns at Dunowla
20 Oct	1871	William Burns at Roslee

Diocese of Tuam

Registers of the Parish of Kilcommon, Co. Mayo

Hollymount Church marriages

| 30 Nov | 1864 | Francis Ruttledge of full age, a bachelor and Gentleman, of Athy Road, Calgar, son of Rev Francis Ruttledge, clergyman, married Hester Elizabeth Frances Lindsey of Hollymount House, spinster, of full age, daughter of Thomas Spencer Lindsey, Gent Witnesses: D E Browne, T Spencer Lindsey (Signature of D E Browne is questionable, might be D E Bourne) |
| 30 Sept | 1877 | William Henry Field of full age, a bachelor, Capt of H M Hussars of Aldershot, son of Col William Field, married Margaret Harriet Ruttledge, a spinster of full age, of Bloomfield, daughter of Col Robert Ruttledge Witnesses W Field, Robert Ruttledge |

Claremorris baptisms

| 7 Feb | 1878 | William Ormsby son of William and Elizabeth Ruttledge (Born 30 Sept 1866) |
| 7 Feb | 1878 | Thomas Ormsby son of William and Elizabeth Ruttledge (Born 13 Jan 1871) |

21 Feb 1878 Isabella Lynda daughter of William and Elizabeth Ruttledge (Born 27 April 1859)

21 Feb 1878 Emeline Abivina(sic) daughter of William and Elizabeth Ruttledge (Born 23 April 1861)
The parents, William and Elizabeth Ruttledge, were described as being of Ballyhooley, Knock

Claremorris marriages

2 June 1851 William Ruttledge of full age, a bachelor, Gentleman of Ballyhooley, son of Thomas Ruttledge, Gentleman, married Elizabeth Gray of full age, spinster of Claremorris, daughter of John Gray, a retired excise officer. Witnesses _____Ruttledge, Andrew French

Register of the Parish of Kilmaine, Co. Mayo

Baptisms

9 Aug 1823 Robert son of Margaret and the Rev Francis Rutledge, Rector of Kilmaine.

13 Oct 1879 Henrietta Bedelia, daughter of Jenny Young and George R Fair, a farmer of Clonbur Born 23 Sept 1879

5 Sept 1880 Sarah Frances, daughter of George and Jane Fair of Clonbur Born 20 Aug 1880

7 May 1882 Mary Elizabeth daughter of George and Jane Fair of Clonbur Born 24 March 1882

27 March 1884 James Abbott son of George and Jane Fair of Clonbur Born 8 Feb 1884

29 June 1885 Isabella Jane daughter of George and Jane Fair of Clonbur Born 13 May 1885

9 Sept 1888 John son of George and Jane Fair of Clonbur (Born in 1888, date illegible)

Marriages

6 Feb 1747 Morgan Burn and Mary Carthy

13 July 1825 John Fair Esq of Kilmaine Parish and Maria Rutledge of Hollymount Parish Witnesses E Rutledge, Robert Fair Jr, George Bourns (This surname is doubtful—between the first and last name of the witness is what appears to be a capital "W" with a small "d" after it Two lines through both letters)

12 April 1837 James Fair of Fair Hill, Parish of Ross, and Bedelia Keyes daughter of Henry Keyes and niece of George Rutledge of Togher

Register of the Parish of Castlebar, Co. Mayo

Burials

7 June 1848 Thomas Ruttledge of Breaffy, age 70

17 May 1851 Mary Maxwell of Castlebar, age 76

Register of the Parish of Turlough, Co. Mayo

Baptisms

4 April   1845   George son of Margaret and Owen Clynes of Cluankesh

Marriages

14 May   1828   At Turlough Church Henry Bourns of Crossmolina and
                Eliza Young of Aghs, alias Castlebar   Witnesses
                Henry Ayres and William Young

Register of the Parish of Ballinrobe, Co. Mayo

Baptisms

6 July   1817   Mary daughter of David Rutledge and Elinor Courtney
                (Born May 25th)
                Joseph Lambert son of David Rutledge and Ellen
                Courtney was born on Aug 2nd 1834 (Inserted on
                page ending 1823)
14 Nov   1824   John Rutledge son of Peter and Maria Rutledge (Born
                Oct 13th)
9 Feb   1826   Robert Rutledge son of Peter and Maria Rutledge
                (Born Jan 19th)
5 Feb   1834   Anne daughter of William and Frances Ruttledge
                (Born Jan 20th)
21 Nov   1835   Letitia daughter of William and Frances Ruttledge
                (Born Nov 8th)
22 April 1845   Peter George son of Peter and Sophia Ruttledge, Bal-
                linrobe, Gentleman (Born March 31st.)

Marriages

21 Dec   1820   Peter Ruttledge, Corporal in the 4th Dragoon Guards to
                Maria Hamilton, both of Ballinrobe, by licence
24 Jan   1821   William Ruttledge of the Parish of Kilbronan and Frances
                Maria Ruttledge of Ballinrobe, by licence

Burials

17 Feb   1824   Elizabeth Rutledge, age 70
29 Sept 1824   Elizabeth Rutledge, no age given
14 Sept 1831   Catherine Ruttledge, age 79 (Died Sept 7th)
26 Dec   1834   William Ruttledge, age 62 of the Parish of Ballinrobe.
                (Died Dec 24th)
2 Nov   1854   Isabella Ruttledge, Bushfield, Hollymount, age 56
19 May   1855   Jane Ruttledge, Bushfield, Hollymount, age 19
14 Jan   1857   John Ruttledge, Cariavilla, age 14 days
23 May   1858   Maria Ruttledge, Castle Villa, Hollymount, age 41
6 Aug   1858   Elizabeth Ruttledge, Bushfield, Hollymount, age 17
29 July 1863   Thomas Ruttledge, Bushfield, Hollymount, age 57
31 July 1875   James Ruttledge, age 30

8 Oct 1880 Barbara Ruttledge, Castle Villa, Parish of Kilcommon, age 32

22 July 1887 James Ruttledge, Castle Villa, Parish of Kilcommon, age 77

Register of the Parish of Westport, Co. Mayo

Baptisms

30 Nov 1842 James Webb son of Peter and Charlotte Sophia Ruttledge, Rosbeg, Gent

21 Sept. 1864 David Aubry son of George Oliver and Jane Olivia Ruttledge, Murrish, Gent

12 July 1888 Ella Emilie Jane daughter of Thomas Francis and Harriet Emilie Ruttledge of Turlough Park, Castlebar, land agent (Born 19 April 1883)

28 Sept 1893 May Winifred daughter of Thomas Farr and Harriet Emily Ruttledge, Rosmally, Gent (Born 30 Aug 1893)

Marriages

8 Dec 1881 Thomas Fair Ruttledge, of full age, a bachelor, Gent of Westport, son of Thomas Ruttledge, Gent married Harriet Emilie Cather, of full age, a spinster of Westport, daughter of John Cather, Archdeacon of Tuam Witnesses Robert Ruttledge Farr. Ada Robinson and Geoffrey Cather

Register of the Parish of Aughagower, Co. Mayo

Marriages

5 May 1829 Richard Maxwell, Sergt of Police, stationed at Foxford and Margaret Scott of Aughagower, by licence Witnesses. Richard Scott, James Bale

Register of the Parish of Burrishoole. Co. Mayo

Marriages

4 July 1888 John Clinton of full age, a bachelor of Lisduff, Newport, son of Alexander Clinton, farmer, married Kate Bournes of full age a spinster. daughter of John Bournes, printer Witnesses Thomas Greene. John Bourns

Diocese of Ardagh

Register of the Parish of Kiltoghart, Co. Leitrim

Baptisms

19 Sept. 1830 Anne Elize daughter of Henry and Margaret Burns, Carrick-on-Shannon, Royal Sappers and Miners

27 March 1836 Mary Catherine daughter of Arthur and Jane Bourns, Carrick-on-Shannon, Gentleman

28 Sept   1836   Elizabeth Henderson daughter of Robert and Frances Bourns, Summerhill, Gentleman

20 Oct   1837   John Houston Thomas son of Arthur and Jane Bournes, Carrick-on-Shannon, post-master

14 Sept   1838   Robert Whitelaw son of Robert and Frances Bournes, Summerhill, Esq

18 Feb   1839   David Browne son of Arthur and Jane Bournes of Carrick-on-Shannon, post-master

17 Nov   1840   Frances Eliza daughter of Robert and Frances Bourns, Summerhill, farmer

19 Jan   1843   Elizabeth Henderson daughter of Arthur and Jane Bournes, Carrick-on-Shannon, post-master

13 April   1843   Daniel Charles Grose son of Robert and Frances Bournes, Drumagh, Gentleman, (twin)

13 April   1843   John Houston son of Robert and Frances Bournes, Drumagh, Gentleman, (twin)

Dec   1844   Susanna Adelaide daughter of Arthur and Jane Bournes, Carrick-on-Shannon, post-master

2 July   1845   Arthur Henderson son of Robert and Frances Bournes, Summerhill, Gentleman

2 Aug   1847   Charles Wilson son of Robert Wilson and Frances Margaret Bourns Summerhill, Esq (Born July 2nd)

28 July   1848   Jane Alicia daughter of Arthur and Jane Bournes, Carrick-on-Shannon, post-master

3 June   1850   Evans son of Robert W and Frances Bournes, Summerhill, farmer

20 Dec   1852   Newcomen Whitelaw son of Robert Wilson and Frances Margaret Bournes, Hatley, Gentleman, farmer

20 Sept   1877   Lydia Mary daughter of Robert Whitelaw and Marian Bournes, Hatley Gentleman (Born Aug 13th)

29 June   1883   Marion May daughter of Robert Whitelaw and Marion Bourns, Hatley, Gentleman. (Born May 26th)

Marriages

26 May   1834   Robert Wilson Bournes of this parish and Frances Margaret Grose, by licence Witnesses A Grose, Arthur Brown

4 May   1835   Arthur Henderson Bourns of this parish and Jane Elizabeth Browne of this parish, by licence Witnesses D H Browne, Evans B Grose, R W Bourns

Burials

    1882   Jane Bournes of Carrick-on-Shannon (No date or age given)

16 Nov   1907   Robert Bourns of Carrick-on-Shannon, age 71

Register of the Parish of Tashinny and Abbeyshrule, Co. Longford

Baptisms

29 Oct   1843   Edward son of John Fry and Mary Burne of Killonbore

27 June   1846   Alicia daughter of John Fry and Mary Byrne(sic) of Killonbore Born 20 May

| 6 Aug | 1848 | Jane daughter of Francis Dimond and Anne Burns of Tully, parish of Kilglass, farmer Born 22 May |
| 2 Sept | 1866 | Sarah daughter of Robert Dimond and Margaret Burns, farmer of Sunfield Born 7 June |

Burials

27 Nov	1848	Elizabeth Burns of Dirming, Parish of Kilglass, aged 15
2 July	1854	Jane Burns of Newton Forbes, aged 17
20 Sept	1857	Hannah Burns of Clooncoose, Parish of Templemichael, aged 4½
28 Sept	1857	Joseph Burns of Clooncoose, Parish of Templemichael, aged 9
23 Oct	1861	Margaret Burns of Drumnacor, Parish of Shrule, aged 49

Diocese of Elphin

Register of the Parish of Kilbryan, Co. Roscommon

Baptisms

| 4 Feb | 1897 | Frances Kathleen Peyton daughter of John P F Burns and Esther of Largan, Gentleman (Born Oct 31st, 1896) |
| 23 Feb | 1898 | John Robert son of John P F Burns and Esther of Largan, Gentleman (Born Dec 15th, 1897) |

Register of the Parish of Boyle, Co. Roscommon

Baptisms

15 Nov	1793	Richard Lockhard son of Alexander and Margaret Burnes, (or Barnes)
6 Aug	1798	Jane daughter of Alexander and Margaret Burnes (or Barnes)
22 Sept	1816	Isohella daughter of Joseph and Susannah Burnes (or Barnes) Maiden name of mother, Black
17 Dec	1820	Frederick William son of John and Mary Burnes (or Barnes), of the 25th Regt Maiden name of mother, Young
10 Feb	1823	Andrew son of John and Catherine Sindall, of the 23rd Regt Maiden name of mother, Burne
31 Oct	1829	James son of Joseph and Susanna Burnes (Born Oct 17th)
2 April	1831	Ellinor daughter of Elias and Mary Burns (Born March 30th)
7 Aug	1831	Thomas son of John and Mary Burns (Born June 1st)
8 Dec	1834	Susanna daughter of Joseph and Susan Burns of Erris.
14 Sept	1836	Hermione daughter of Joseph and Margaret Burns of Erris
14 Sept	1836	Juliana daughter of Joseph and Margaret Burns of Erris.

20 March 1839   William Henry son of John and _____Burnes of Erris
                Maiden name of mother, Williams
19 March 1842   Augustus Hartney son of Joseph and Margaret Burnes of
                Drum

Marriages

13 Jan   1812   Robert Davis Burns of Carrick and Olivia Grattan of
                Boyle, by licence, in presence of William Grattan and
                Freeman and many others
30 Sept   1822   Matthew Burns, a pensioner, and Mary Sharkey, both
                of Boyle, being thrice called in church

Marriages

20 Oct   1836   William Cox of Killuken and Isabella Bournes of Boyle
                Parish, by licence
5 Nov   1844   Archibald Myles Lyons and Eliza Burns, by licence
19 Feb   1850   Arthur Burns age 30, a bachelor, trader of Mohill, son
                of William Burns, a farmer, and Mary Anne Hayes
                age 22, a spinster, daughter of James Hayes, a farmer
                Witnesses Joseph McCormick, T A McCornwall
27 Aug   1870   James Washington of full age, a bachelor, Private 56th
                Regt of the Barracks, Boyle, son of Richard Washing-
                ton, a farmer, and Mary Burns, a minor, a spinster of
                Boyle, daughter of Thomas Burns, a labouci Wit-
                nesses W Nash, Anne Burton

Burials

19 Dec   1845   William Burns of Erris, aged 32
9 Sept.   1847   William Burnes of Erris, aged 47
24 Dec   1852   John Burns of Erris, aged 26
10 Oct   1857   Joseph Burnes of Erris, near Boyle, aged 73
16 May   1861   Susan Burnes of Erris, aged 75
30 Dec   1861   Jane Burns of Boyle (Age not given)
13 Jan.   1890   Margaret Bournes of Carrick Road, Boyle, aged 86

Register of the Parish of Ardcarne, Co. Roscommon

Baptisms

26 Dec   1821   Sarah daughter of David and Eliza Bournes of this
                parish (Born Dec 23rd)
         1822   Elizabeth daughter of Joseph and Susan Bournes of
                Erris (Born March 18th)
15 June   1825   David Oldfield son of David and Elizabeth Bournes of
                this parish (Born June 1st)
24 Dec   1835   Eliza daughter of Henry and Eliza Bournes (Born
                Dec 19th)
18 April   1837   Catherine daughter of Francis and Sarah Berne of the
                Whiteparks (Born April 3rd)

24 Dec 1838 Eliza daughter of Henry and Jane Bournes (Born Dec 19th)

3 Jan 1856 Elias son of David and Mary Bouins of Ardglass, a farmer (Born Oct 17th, 1854)

3 Jan 1856 Eliza Barbara daughter of David and Mary Bouins of Ardglass, a farmer (Born Sept 17th, 1855)

19 April 1870 Robert son of David and Mary Bouins of Ardglass, Gentleman farmer (Born April 7th)

25 Aug 1899 Henry Edward son of John Peyton Frazer Burns and Esther of Aughnatum, landholder (Born July 25th)

Marriages

18 June 1818 Robert Davis Bournes of Carrick-on-Shannon and Celia Bourns of Ardglass

20 March 1821 Patrick Rock and Margaret Berne of this parish by licence

8 Oct 1849 David Burns of full age, a bachelor, a physician, son of Stephen Burns, a farmer of Granard married Katherine Peyton Frazer of full age, a spinster, of Aughnasurin, Parish of Kilbryan, daughter of John Peyton Frazer, a farmer Witnesses George Carleton, John Peyton Frasel

6 Feb 1862 Alexander Dickie of full age, a bachelor, land steward of Rockingham, Parish of Ardcairne, son of Alexander Dickie, land steward married Susan Burns of full age, a spinster of the Parish of Boyle, daughter of Joseph Burns a farmer Witnesses. James Burns, Joseph Anailo(sic)

Burials

29 Oct 1820 Mrs Cecelia Bournes (No age given)
13 Feb 1848 Bridget Burns, age 20, of Errona(sic)
6 Aug 1860 Eliza Bourns, age 75, of Ardglass
22 Dec 1865 David Bournes, age 84, of Ardglass
10 May 1867 Frances Bournes, age 33 of Ardglass
20 Dec 1884 Mary Bournes, age 60, of Ardglass, at Killuken
3 July 1900 Kate Peyton Burns, age 80, of Aughnasurin
2 May 1908 Mary Burns, age 50, of Faus
8 Feb 1910 David Bournes, age 84, of Faus, Ardcairne

Register of the Parish of Drumcliff, Co. Sligo

Baptisms

21 June 1816 Jane daughter of James and Mary Burns of Attyduff, by Rev John Yeats Born 9 April

16 Nov. 1817 Susanna daughter of James and Mrs Burns, by John Yeats, Rector Born 14 Nov

18 April 1819 Catherine daughter of William Thomas and Ann Burns, by Rev J Armstrong Born 6 April

17 Oct	1819	Mary daughter of James and Mary Burns, by Rev John Yeats Born 7 Oct
28 Jan	1825	Phenny daughter of James Burns by Rev Mr Yeats Born 27 Jan
9 Jan	1831	Margaret daughter of James and Mary Burns Born 8 Dec
26 Aug	1832	Ann daughter of James and Mary Burns of Ballygelgan, farmer

Marriages

14 Jan	1811	James Bornes of Clonclare Parish and Catherine Blair of this parish, by John Yeats, Rector Witnesses Samuel Shaw, Miles E Reynolds.
1 July	1813	James Bourns of this parish and Mary Young of same, by John Yeats, Rector Witnesses Booth P Wilson, William Wallace

Burials

1 March 1813	Twin children of James Burns of this parish
16 March 1813	Catherine Burns of this parish

Diocese of Leighlin
Register of the Parish of Abbeyleix, Co. Leix*

Baptisms

21 Nov	1819	Child of Richard and Louisa Bourne, at Dublin (Name of child illegible)

Burials

14 April	1819	Henry H Bourne Esq

Diocese of Cork
Registers of Cork City, Co. Cork

St Mary Shandon, Baptisms

16 July	1803	Ann daughter of James and Ellen Bourn of Mallow Land Sureties Edward Bourn, Catherine Davis, Elizabeth Keating
23 Dec	1807	Mary Anne daughter of James and Ellen Bourn of Mallow Land Sureties William Myles, Catherine Bourn, Anne Davis

St Mary Shandon, Marriages

24 June	1809	Godfrey Holmes Esq and Miss Susanna Lowe by licence Witnesses William Allen, B Maxwell

* Co Leix was formerly Queen's Co

26 Nov   1815   Joseph Gramsky and Mary Nowland, by banns
19 Feb   1835   William Maxwell Browne and Anne Nash by licence

St Anne Shandon, Baptisms

14 May   1786   Edward son of Edward Bourn Sureties John Buckerage,
                Richard Bowen, Mary Murphy, Mary Bourn
28 June 1786   Ann daughter of Isaac and Catherine Davies Sureties
                Edward Bourne, Elizabeth Bourne, Catherine Bourne
   Dec   1786   John son of ? Sureties Michael Donovan, Margaret
                McCarty, John Bourn.
20 March 1789   Thomas, Ann and John sons and daughter of Edward
                and Catherine Bowen Sureties David Cashman,
                Richard Bairett, Elizabeth McCormick, Eliza Bourn
3 Oct   1790   Sarah daughter of Thomas and Ann Legg Sureties
                Mary Bourne
24 Feb   1793   John son of John and Catherine Bourn Sureties James
                Bourn, William Sullivan Mary Bourn
12 Feb   1794   Mary daughter of John and Catherine Bourn Sureties
                Charles Dredge, Edward Walsh, Ann Barrett, Mary
                Bourn
12 Feb   1794   Jonathan son of Isaac and Catherine Davies Sureties
                Charles Dredge, Edward Walsh, Ann Barrett, Mary
                Bourn
19 March 1795   John son of William and Mary John(sic) Sureties
                Matthew Bourn
23 Jan   1803   Richard son of John and Catherine Bourn Sponsors.
                James Bourn, Isaac Harvey, Mary Murphy
11 Oct   1807   Francis son of William and Margaret Bourne Sponsors.
                James Moore, Margaret Bourne
25 Oct   1807   Alice daughter of Thomas and Alis Chute Sponsors
                Joshua Vent Redmond Walsh, Margaret Bourne
28 June 1809   William son of James and Ellen Bourne (This name ap-
                pears earlier as Burn and later as Byrne)
1 Dec   1822   John son of James and Judith Bourne, 6th Dragoon
                Guards Born 22 Nov 1822 Sponsors William Car-
                ron, Oates Sutliffe, Mary Carron
7 Dec   1823   Christopher son of William and Anne Maxwell, 1st
                Vet Bn Born 30 Nov 1823
24 Feb   1824   Peter son of Peter Maxwell, 70th Foot Born 8 inst

St Anne Shandon, Marriages

21 Dec   1807   Thomas Whelan and Anne Nowland, banns
1 March 1815   Francis Nowland and Honora Griffin, banns
3 Nov   1817   Robert Williams and Anne Nowlan, banns

St Anne Shandon, Burials

27 Aug   1780   John Maxwell's child
6 Oct.   1780   John Born's(sic) child
26 Nov   1780   Jonathan Born's(sic) child

16 Nov	1785	Benjamin Maxwell
20 Dec	1785	John Maxwell
11 Dec	1787	Mary Maxwell
12 Nov	1789	Edward Born's(sic) child
21 Nov	1789	William Nowlan
19 July	1790	Edward Buin's child
28 Aug	1790	Thomas Buin's child
1 Jan	1791	James Buin's child
7 Jan	1791	David Buin's child
12 June	1791	Thomas Buin's child
31 Jan	1792	Philip Nowlan's child
30 Aug	1792	Patrick Buin
19 Feb	1793	Maigaret Nowland
26 Feb	1793	Maiy Nolland
23 Nov	1793	James Burn's child
14 June	1794	John Burn's child
15 May	1795	Elm Buin
9 Sept	1795	Philip Nollan's child
28 May	1796	John Burn's child
30 Dec	1797	Michael Burn
1 July	1798	Thomas Burn's child
6 July	1798	William Buin
28 June	1799	Catheime Nowland
24 Jan	1800	Philip Nowland's child
25 April	1800	John Nowland's child
29 May	1803	Wenny Buin
30 June	1803	Catherine Noland (Theie are two apparently distinct names in the iegistei Moyland and Nowland This entiy might be eithei)
19 July	1803	Patiick Noland
8 May	1805	Mary Buin
13 June	1805	Maigaret Maxeswell(sic)
13 June	1805	William Buine
6 Feb	1808	John Buin's child
8 March	1808	James Buine's child
2 Sept.	1808	Hugh Buine's child
17 Jan	1809	Catheime Nowlan
7 Feb	1809	Maiy Nowlan
19 Feb	1810	Maiy Buin
17 Nov	1810	Cornis Nowlan
9 Feb	1813	Mary Buine
9 July	1813	Matthew Burne
31 Oct	1813	Catherine Nowlan
22 Maich	1814	Matthew Buine's child
11 June	1815	Batw Burne's child
3 Dec	1815	Catherine Burne
24 Dec	1817	Hatty Buin
25 Dec	1817	John Nowlan
26 Feb	1818	Richard Burn

St Fin Baire, Marriages

18 Aug 1768 John Myard, stationer, and Elizabeth Maxwell by licence (Licence calls him John Myers)

30 June 1785 Isaac Davies clothier, and Catherine Bourne, by licence (Licence calls him Isaac Davis)

16 Feb 1794 Cole Maxwell, writing clerk, and Sarah Bennett by licence

29 March 1795 Thomas Fitley, earthenware merchant, and Elizabeth Maxwell by licence (Licence calls him Thomas Tetley)

11 July 1802 James Bourne and Elinor Sullivan by licence

18 Oct 1823 Thomas Deane and Cherry Bourne by licence

St Finn Baire, Burials

1 Aug 1765 Infant son of Nowland

12 July 1776 Mrs Nowlan

23 Aug 1783 Eleanor Burne.

1 Dec 1783 John Burne.

14 Dec 1783 Pearce Burne.

St Nicholas, Marriages

15 Sept 1766 John Maxwell and Elizabeth Wiginge

Christ Church, Baptisms

8 Oct 1797 Joseph son of Cole and Frances Maxwell

Christ Church, Marriages

26 May 1770 Peter Nowland certifies Protestantism of John Hamilton, Master of the ship "Avis" of Dublin who marries Ann Irwine of this parish

22 Oct 1788 David Cairnge married Mary Maxwell by licence Certificate signed by James Maxwell and Peter Eason Jr

Christ Church, Burials

26 Dec 1793 Widow Nowlan

27 June 1830 Mr. William Maxwell

Princes Street, Unitarian Church, Baptisms

21 May 1767 Jane daughter of William and Mary Bourn

27 May 1771 John son of William and Isabell Burn, soldier 63rd Regt

16 Aug 1771 David son of William and Isabell Burn, soldier 63rd Regt

11 March 1775 William son of William and Isabell Burn, soldier 63rd Regt

4 July 1791 Elizabeth Ann daughter of Thomas and Jane Burn, soldier 61st Regt

Register of the Parish of Kinsdale, Co. Cork

Baptisms

24 Oct   1781   Miss Dorothy Ann Maxwell, sponsor to the child of Lt John Lambton Carter of the 32nd Regt

Marriages

10 June   1778   Peter Maxwell, invalid married Phebe Lilly, widow

Presbyterian Church Registers[*]

Sligo Co Sligo Baptismal Register

27 June   1824   Alexander son of Edward and Dorinda Maxwell, Castle St, Sligo Born 19 June 1824

21 April   1830   James Maxwell son to the Rev David Rodgers, Mullyfairy, Killala Born 23 March 1830

5 Jan   1862   Elizabeth (Lizzie), daughter of Thomas Maxwell and Mary Jane Wagner, residing at Old Market St, Sligo Born 9 Nov. 1861

Boyle Co Roscommon Baptismal Register

9 March 1863   George Edwin son of Alexander Dickie of Rockingham and Susan Burns, his wife Born 24 Dec 1862

27 April   1863   Emma daughter of Alexander Dickie (as above) Born 17 March 1863

10 Sept   1865   Alexander son of Alexander Dickie (as above) Born 28 July 1865

8 Aug   1869   Florence daughter of Alexander Dickie (as above) Born 28 May 1869

9 March 1873   Caroline daughter of Alexander Dickie (as above) Born 18 Jan 1873

20 Feb   1875   Edmund Burn son of Alexander Dickie (as above) Born 1 Jan 1875

25 June   1876   Susan daughter of Alexander Dickie (as above) Born 30 April 1876

Westport Co Mayo Baptismal Register

30 April   1859   James son of William Burns and his wife Margaret, Plumber Born 19 April 1859 at Westport

27 Nov   1860   William son of William Burns (as above) Born 4 Oct 1860

8 Jan   1863   George Angus son of William Burns and his wife, Margaret alias Stephens Born 31 Dec 1862

17 April   1863   Jessie daughter of Thomas Maxwell and his wife Mirron Maxwell alias McWhirter A shepherd Born 4 April 1863 Of Kylemore, Co Galway

---

[*] The Presbyterian Registers are in the custody of the Sligo and Ballina Presbyterian ministers

12 Nov 1867 Marian daughter of Thomas Maxwell and his wife
              Marion Maxwell alias McWhirter Born Oct 1867
              (n d) Of Kylemore, Co Galway

Westport Co Mayo Marriage Register

11 Aug 1896 David O'Brien of full age, a bachelor, of Westport
              (occupation illegible), son of David O'Brien a watch-
              man, married Henrietta Frances Cook of full age a
              spinster of Westport, daughter of Joseph Cooke a
              Police Sergeant Witnesses Henrietta Frances Cooke
              and Alfred J Cooke

13 July 1898 William Henry Faussett, a widower, of full age, farmer
              of Ballycastle, Co Mayo, son of Henry William
              Faussett a gentleman, married Anna Gibson Syming-
              ton of full age, a spinster, of Luffertown, Castlebar,
              daughter of James Symington a farmer Witnesses
              Jessie Mary Symington and Alfred E Cairns

Ballina Co. Mayo Baptismal Register

17 Aug 1893 William Bouins son of John Bouins, Inspector of tele-
              graphs, Ballina and his wife, Anne Biock Born 15
              July 1893

Diomore West Co Mayo Baptismal Register

13 June 1859 Robert John Burns son of Arthur and Mary Jane Burns
              Farmer of Kilmacshalgan Born 19 Dec 1858

13 June 1861 Thomas Burns son of Arthur Burns (as above) Born
              10 Oct 1860

19 April 1864 Arthur Burns son of Arthur Burns and Mary Jane
              McIntosh, farmer of Kilmacshalgan Born 1 July 1863

Killala Co Mayo Baptismal Register (Moywater or Mullafairy)

 4 Nov 1849 John son of William and Maria Gardiner Born 1 Jan.
              1849

Killala Co Mayo Marriage Register

10 Feb 1846 Thomas McNeice, age 24, a bachelor, married Jane
              Gardener age 24, a spinster of Maugherabrack, daugh-
              ter of James Gardener, farmer Witnesses James
              McNeice and Farmer McNeill Sr

21 Oct 1852 William Carson of full age, a bachelor, farmer of Bal-
              lintain, son of William Carson, married Catherine
              Burns, spinster, of full age of Newtownwhite, daughter
              of Matthew Burns, farmer Witnesses William Carson
              and Thomas Foster

 7 Sept 1871 Duke Ormsby, of full age, a widower, a Colporteur,
              of Ballinglan, son of William Ormsby, a farmer,
              married Eliza O'Brien of full age, a spinster of Fox-
              ford, daughter of Patrick O'Brien, member of coastal
              service Witnesses Charles Gardiner and Sara Blair

11 March 1875 William Gardiner, age 23, a bachelor, farmer of Ballinglan, son of Robert Gardener, farmer, married Anne
Joynt, of full age, spinster of Ballinglan, daughter of
Andrew Joynt, farmer Witnesses John Merron(?)
and Lizzie Shannon

20 Jan   1888 Duke Ormsby, widower, married Mary Jane McDonald,
widow of Ballina, daughter of. Andrew Gardiner,
farmer

Turlough Co Mayo Baptismal Register

11 Aug   1822 William son of David Campbell of Cloghodochan Born
11 July 1822

21 Sept 1823 Mary Olivia daughter of Mr William Maxwell of Castlebar Born 18 Sept 1823

3 Jan   1866 Margaret Louisa daughter of William Burns and his
wife, Sarah Ann Gracey Born 18 Dec 1865

13 July 1868 Hans Hamill son of Hugh Nelson and his wife Jenette
Higgins Born 13 May 1868

Turlough Co Mayo Marriage Register

5 Dec   1819 James Campbell to Mary McLean both of the Parish
of Turlough Present Capt William Rutledge, David
Campbell, John Riddle and others

26 June 1821 David Campbell to Mary Maxwell both of the Parish of
Turlough Present Alexander Keady John Riddle and
James Leither

Ballinglen Co Mayo Baptismal Register

16 Sept 1877 Catherine daughter of William Gardiner and Annie
Joynt of Ballyglen Born 20 May 1877

19 Oct   1879 William Gardiner son of William Gardiner and Annie
Joynt of Ballyglen Born 22 May 1879

20 May 1883 Belinda daughter of William Gardiner and his wife
Annie Joynt Born 31 Jan 1883

Ballinglen Co Mayo Members and Adherents List—1871

Members Duke Ormsby, Mary Jane Ormsby

Adherents Fannie Ormsby, Letitia Ormsby, Marcella Ormsby, Lizzie
Ormsby, Emma Ormsby, John Duke Ormsby, Mrs Duke
Ormsby, Matilda Ormsby

Ballinglen Co Mayo Communicants List—1876

William Gardiner

Presbyterian Marriage Notice Books

Genealogists seeking clues beyond those given in official records would
do well to consult the Marriage Notice Books which may be found at
some Presbyterian rectories The books "noted" the names of bridal
couples and often gave particulars regarding age and length of residency

For example, the marriage of William Carson and Catherine Burns which is recorded in the Diomore West register (see above) was also listed in the Marriage Notice Books The latter tells us that William Carson, the groom, was 30 years of age when married and that he had been a resident of Ballintam for one year it also states that the bride (no age given) had been a resident of Newtownwhite for one year

Methodist Church Registers[*]

Westport Co Mayo Marriages

17 Dec	1873	James Culbert of full age, bachelor, farmer of the Mall, Westport son of Jacob Culbert, farmer, married Henrietta Bournes of full age, spinster, of the Mall, Westport, daughter of Henry Bournes, merchant Witnesses Davis R Sand, Samuel C Bournes

Sligo Co Sligo Baptisms

2 Feb	1835	Margaret Jane daughter of William and Eliza Rutledge of the Town of Sligo Born Jan 1835
3 April	1840	Fanny daughter of above Born 14 March 1840
21 March	1843	Eliza Sarah daughter of above Born 27 Jan 1843
14 July	1847	William Leech son of above Born 29 Oct 1846
10 June	1849	Rebecca daughter of above Born 19 March 1849

Killala Co Mayo Baptisms

	1854	Christiana daughter of Thomas and Catherine Higgins, Ross, Co Mayo Aged 6 weeks

Erris Co Mayo Baptisms

11 May	1856	Anna Maria daughter of George Smith and Elizabeth Hartley Bournes, Rossport House Twelve days
10 Aug	1861	Annie Maria Carolina Wallace daughter of George Smith Bournes (as above) Six days Born 5 Aug 1861

Castlebar Co Mayo Baptisms

20 Aug.	1838	Jemima Farrell daughter of Isaac V and Jane Farrell of Westport Born 18 July 1838
17 Jan	1840	John son of Peter Rutledge and Jane Rutledge alias Matthews of the townland of Carravilla or Carrahusta, Parish of Kilcommon Born 6 Jan 1840
5 Feb	1843	Anna Maria, wife of William Smith Esq. of Westport baptised in the Wesleyan Chapel of that town
24 Dec	1844	Anna Maria daughter of William Smith Esq and his wife, Anna Maria, of Westport Born 23 Feb 1844
8 April	1877	Samueletta Davis Eliza daughter of the late Samuel Bournes and his wife Annie Born 7 Jan 1877

[*] All Methodist Registers are in the possession of the Methodist minister in Sligo

Ballina Co Mayo Circuit Baptisms

20 Aug   1837   Henrietta Bourns of Crossmolina, Co Mayo Born 20
                    July 1837
19 Aug   1838   George Claudius Bourns of Crossmolina Born 28 July
                    1838
10 May   1840   William Fletcher Bourns of Crossmolina Born 8 April
                    1840
23 May   1841   Edward Hardinge(?) Young Bourns of Crossmolina
                    Born 11 April 1841
 2 Oct   1842   Samuel Davis son of Henry and Eliza Bourns Born 25
                    Aug 1842
 9 March 1845   Henry Osborne son of Henry and Eliza J Bournes of
                    Crossmolina Born 26 Nov 1844.
29 Oct   1871   Thomas Henry Charles Wilson son of William Henry
                    and Lizzie Anne Bournes Born 17 Oct 1871
12 Oct   1873   Maria Elizabeth Watts daughter of Dr William Henry
                    and Elizabeth Anne Bournes Born 15 April 1873

Lists of Classes and Members in the Ballina Circuit

June   1840   no 1   William Bourns
                        Thomas Bourns (added later in pencil "died in the
                        Lord " Out of 1841 District, died in 1840?)
                no 4   Margaret Bourns
                no 5   Ellen Bournes (In 1841, add Jane Bourns)
         1841   no. 1 Henry Bourns, Leader
                no 2   Eliza J Bourns
                        Maria Bourns (to Castlebar)
         1851   no 1   Henry Bourns, Leader and Trustee of Crossmolina
                        Eliza J Bourns
                        Henrietta W Bourns
March 1864   no 1   Henrietta Bourns
         1873-1876   Margaret Bournes of Belmullet
                        Mary Bourns of Rossport

Lessees and Trustees of Belmullet and Rossport Wesleyan Chapels,
dated 9 May 1859 Note attached "All documents are in the conference
safe in Dublin " Samuel and George Smith Bourne, Trustees of Belmullet
and Rossport Wesleyan Chapels

Tombstone Inscriptions

Co. Mayo Cemeteries

Kilgalligan Cemetery, Erris.

                   Beneath this tomb are/deposited
                   the Memorial/Remains of Mary
                   Burns/Alias Redy who departed/
                   This life Feb 10 1829/Aged 35
                   years/Erected by order of John
                   Burns Bangor/

Rossport Cemetery, Erris

> Here lies the body of Andrew Bournes
> Who departed this life 1st July 1865
>
> Henry O Bournes died 12th May 1873
>
> William Bournes M D died 16th January
> 1875 (interred at Killala)
>
> Sacred to the honored memory/of
> Samuel Bournes who/Departed this
> life/30th April 1864/His devoted
> wife Maria/who died 14th Jan 1864/
> and/Their revered mothers/Mary
> Bournes and Anne Watts/who died
> 12 Nov 1855/And 16th May 1859/
>
> Blessed are the dead which/Die
> in the Lord from/Henceforth yea
> saith the/Spirit that they may
> rest/From their labours and their/
> Works do follow them/
> > > > Rev XIV 13
>
> Here lies the body of
> Anna Maria/Beloved wife
> of Rev T W Baker/And
> eldest child of Samuel
> and/Maria Bournes Died
> 15 March 1875/

Protestant Cemetery, Binghamstown, Erris

> Anne Jane Bournes died 6th Jan 1868.
>
> Maria Knox died 25th May 1869

Ballysakeery Cemetery, Tirawley

> Erected to the memory/of
> Marget Bourns who/Departed
> this life 25 Feb 1805/age
> 70 years Also her husband/
> Mathew Bourns who departed
> 19 Nov /1813 age 86 years/

Ardnaree Cemetery, Ballina, Tirawley.

> Rev Arthur Knox Huston/
> Rector of Kilmactigue, Co
> Sligo aged 67 years/Died
> on 6th Feb 1871/

This tomb is erected by Margaret Bourns
As_____and of her/husband
John Bourns_____/for life on
1st September A D 1837/
Aged 56_____In this life_____
And his end was peace/

This tomb has been erected in memory/
Of George Bourns Esq aged 58 years/
4th November 1826/By his devoted
son William Bourns/

This tomb was erected by Henry
Huston/of Ardnaree Esq on the 3rd
June 1821/and beneath which lies the
remains of/His mother in law Anne
Rogers alieas/Bourns Huston is_____/
Body of her sister Elizabeth Rogers
_____/Body of Henry Huston who
departed this/Life February 9th
1827 aged 68 years/

Hollymount Cemetery, Hollymount Town

To the memory/of/William Ruttledge Esq /of Caira
Villa/May 23rd 1856/aged 68 years/And of his wife
Frances/M Ruttledge/Born June 1808/Died Jan 14th
1878/

Here lyeth the body of/William Ruttledge of Holly/
mount, gent who departed/this life the_____7/_____
58th year of his age/and also his wife_____Rutt/
ledge who departed this life_____/_____/

Here lyeth the body of/Peter Ruttledge Esq of Bally/
_____la Castle who departed/this life the 30th day
of March/1805 aged 63 years/

_____/_____ _____ Peter/Ruttledge of Hollymount Esq /
_____ye hands of/his Creator May 9th 1793/age 59
years/

George Ruttledge Esq /late of Togher House/Co Mayo/
Castleconnor Co Sligo/died Nov 6th 1876/aged 74
years/

In memory of Thomas Ruttledge/of Cornfield D L./
who died on the 18th of May 1877/aged 51 years/
erected by his widow/in living memory/and in ever

loving memory of/Fiancis Ruttledge/late of Royal
Dragoons/who died on the 10th July 1898/aged 45
yeais/And in loving memoiy of Jane Ruttledge Fair
widow of the above Thomas Ruttledge/and only child
of Robert Fair Esq /of Bushfield/who died 31st
December 1905/aged 73 years/

Co. Sligo Cemeteries

Killanley Cemetery, Castleconnor

Heie is the body of Elenor Bouins
alias/Rutledge who departed this
life/_____1784 aged 47 yeais/
And also Hester O'Biien wife of/
Thomas Bouins Esq who departed/
this life Novembei 28 1808 aged
30 yeais/Also Thomas Bouines Esq
of Castleconnor/

Here lieth the body of Mary Bourns/
Who departed this life the 28th of/
Feb 1800 aged 42 yeais and ciected/
by her loving husband Wm Bourns/And
also Ah_____O'Biien Spinster/sister
of My Bouins Ju who depaited/this
life 12 January 1810 aged 56 years/

Sacred to the memoiy of
Thomas Burns/Exq who
depaited this life May 15th/
1845 aged 35 years. Eiected
by his/father James Burns Esq.

St Anne's Cemeteiy, Easkey

Geoige Ruttledge died June 21st 1813.

John Atkinson died March_____1800

William Morrison died July 7th 1821, 75 years

Robert Morrison died May 14th 1891, 68 years.

St. John the Baptist Cemetery, Sligo Town

In/Affectionate Remembrance/of/Elizabeth Grace
infant of/David and Elizabeth Rytledge/who
died July 4th 1869/aged 3 months and 18 days/

Journals of the Irish Memorials Association
Extracts

And the Spirit and the Bride
say Come/Sacred to the Memory
of Anne/the beloved wife of
Joseph Wallace/the deceased
who departed this life on Feb.
10th/1843 aged 63 years was
the direct descendant of the
Dillons Earls of Roscommon/
Also Theobald Wallace her son
who passed from/This scene
of trials to his Eternal rest
on the 3rd of November/1843
aged 25 years/ZACHARIA WALLACE/
Died on the 1st of February
1857/Also his son/John Martin
Wallace/Died 4th June 1887/
Trusting in Jesus

(Vol XI, p 424 Coolock Church Cemetery, Co Cavan The reading in
the *Journal* was emended slightly by Rev T Cunningham as a result of
personal inspection See *Breifne* (1966), pp 133-134)

Glory be to God on High/
Pray for the soul of/
Elizabeth Bourns alias Harte/
Who departed this life/May
16th 1812 aged 73 years/and
also James Bourns/who departed
this life/aged_____years/
May they rest in peace

(Vol. II Easkey Cemetery, Co Sligo)

Appendix B

The following letters written in 1866 and 1867 by James Henry Higgins, eldest son of Rev John and Anne (Bournes) Higgins, are among the Higgins Papers, indexed MS 1057, in the National Library, Canberra, Australia

James Henry was only 17 years of age when he left Ireland and journeyed to New York The account of his voyage and his brief stay in America presents a graphic description of life slightly over one hundred years ago

We felt these letters merited inclusion in the book for they are of some historical interest It also seemed a means of paying a small tribute to a boy who showed such promise but never lived to become a man.

> Commercial Hotel,
> Foyle Terrace,
> Londonderry
> 6th. Oct. 1866
> 5 5 P M

My dearest Mother,

You will be surprised to learn that I am not away yet After waiting on board the tender "Lion" till about 3 30—the emigration agent, Capt. Gough, came on board, and after the tickets were examined, he told us all that the vessel (tender) would not leave till six o'clock to-morrow (Sunday) morning

The steerage passengers got 1/6 each to provide them-selves till that time and my expenses will be paid There are very few cabin passengers but myself—indeed the only one I am sure about is the young man Father saw. This is a very busy place. Steamers arrive here very often

I parted with Father at one o'clock He will be with you before this reaches.

I hope you are very well, and not giving way to any grief. As I wrote you last night, I intend to keep fast to the good advice you and Father gave me

Father and I saw Dolph Meyer at McArthur's this morn-ing. He is grown very much, and is quite a young man now.

I hope Sammy continues well, and that Ina has got rid of her cough.

How is poor little Charlie? He said to me when I was bidding him good-bye yesterday morning "A you goin' Amoky, Dape?" and then gave me a nice hug Kiss him and all the rest of them for me. (There are a lot of people round me, and I find it hard to write in a connected manner)

I think this is the last letter I will be able to write in Ireland,—you may expect one from New York in three weeks or a month I have heard that this vessel the "Iowa" generally takes about 12 or 14 days to go across. Did any letters come from Cozs Anna or Mary, the morning I left? It is a pity that the Sabboth will have to be broken to-morrow, but it would be a great expense to keep the "Iowa" waiting. With love & kisses for all, and kind remembrance to Newry friends,

I remain,
Ever your fondly-attached
Son James

DIARY

Tuesday, 9th October, 1866. I have found it impossible to write any of the Diary I contemplated yet.

We got fairly under way at about 11 a.m on Sunday—at

1 o'clock we passed Inneskirk Island on the right, and shortly
after a very heavy squall came on and the sea washed over the
fore-castle several times The poor sailors were wet to the
skin—The first officer was up there one of these times, and
when he saw the wave coming he ran up the ropes like a cat,
but got well wet in spite of all About 2·15 p m we lost sight
of land—A very heavy breeze blowing all the time since passing the headland of the Foyle. 1 began to get sea-sick, and
when I went down to the cabin at dinner hour, I was not
able to take any, but, after retching I went upon deck, and
remained there some hours At 6 30 p m being tea hour, I
felt rather better, and went down stairs, but the close and
confined smell of the cabin and of the cooked meat quite over-
powered me, and I succumbed again to that dreadful sicking
I then remained upon deck for some time, and we passed a
sail on the larboard, and shortly after, another on the starboard bow, a stiff breeze blowing the whole time, and the
water pouring in at the scuppers (the hole at the side just
above the level of the lower deck). About 8 30 p m. I went to
bed, and positively enjoyed myself for a few hours, though I
could not go to sleep, but the re-action from that feeling was
terrible. I hardly slept any during the whole night, and rose
about 6 30 a m in the morning I forgot to mention that I
found it impossible, without help, to undress myself that
night, and after taking off my coat, I just turned in, with all
the rest of my clothes on!

At breakfast hour, yesterday morning, I was not able to
eat anything, but had a return of the sickness I, however, got
a piece of sea biscuit from the Steward, which I ate on deck
Several birds kept flying round the vessel all day, one of which
was caught three times, and escaped every time—it is however, now caught a fourth time, and not likely to escape again.
At dinner hour I was able to take a little soup, but when the
other dishes were uncovered, the smell of the cooked meat
again over-powered me, and I - - -. I felt much better at tea
hour and was able to take a little I felt very weak—not hav-

ing taken anything hardly, for nearly 48 hours The last meal I took was my tea on Saturday evening, as I had to be on board the tender at 6 a m on Sunday morning After tea, I went upon deck, well muffled, and walked for a few hours I like to keep as long as I can in the open air, and as little as possible in my almost smothering little berth There are four of us in the one little room, and I have to climb into my one as it is about 6 feet from the ground

There was great dancing and singing among the steerage passengers this evening Nearly everyone appears to have got over their sickness I heard some very good songs by both Irish and Scotch (There are a great many of the latter on board) There was an Irishman, who had his flute with him, and played some very good jigs

I spent a very pleasant night, compared with last night I have not, I think, completely got over the sickness I rose early this morning again and had a walk on the deck before breakfast There are a few birds like sparrows still about the vessel, besides a sea-hawk, and a starling After breakfast, the Captain and first mate climbed the masts after the hawk and starling, but neither are caught yet There are several Scotch-men in the second cabin, who sat up to a late hour last night, drinking toddy and singing I am really now beginning to enjoy the heaving and rolling of the vessel, though it is no easy job writing There are several old travellers between the new and old world on board, who say that they were never so sick on board any vessel as they have been on this The Cunard and Inman lines are very comfortable, and far more steady We have had a steady head wind ever since we started till this morning—there is now a three-quarter wind and we have out the main sails and the main top sails The sea is a good deal calmer this morning and the sails help to keep the ship steady There is a Belfast man, named Cluff, on board— he sleeps just underneath me—who is a great singer, though not a very nice one He is just now over-head with about a dozen more breathing "sounds symphonious" The Scotch-men here have already christened him "Professor"

The Captain (Craig), a Scotchman, has just come down here enquiring after the bird caught yesterday—he has caught the starling at last, and wants to have them both together He appears to be a very nice man, and likes some sport

A few minutes after writing above I went on deck just in time to see a sailor climb to the fore-mast yard and catch the hawk, when coming down he caught a little bird that waited quite quietly for him on the cross-trees After dinner we were delighted to hear a good brass band playing overhead. It appears that an American on board is bringing over these men to go about in America. There are four at present but the company formerly comprised eleven persons After playing for a while some of the second cabin and steerage passengers got him to play some quadrilles and polkas and danced for a couple of hours The steerage passengers then got the boards to themselves and danced till tea time After tea the chief musician brought out a fiddle, and some sailors danced American jigs They are very amusing At the time I now write there are three musical companys on board One, just overhead dancing to the violin—another just outside the cabin door, composed exclusively of Irish, and another at the Captain's cabin, under the superintendence of the "Professor." If there were any nervous persons here they could not bear the noise at all

Nearly all the sails are set now, and we are speeding along at the rate of about 10 or 12 knots an hour The purser says that if the present wind continues we will likely be in New York by next Friday week. This night was rather rougher than any since Sunday—however I slept very well

Wednesday 10th October All possible sail set and speeding along with a very fair wind A great crowd of passengers (principally steerage) just over-head who are trying to carry on singing class under the superintendence of the Professor. It is just 2 years since Grey's to-day. Shortly before dinner a dense fog descended and the fog whistle began to sound. The fog lasted till a late hour of the night

Shortly before dinner a man was brought up from the engine room and put in irons for striking another. He was put down in the Black Hole behind the wheel and kept there till 12 o'clock at night

Thursday 11th October A very fine day. We had the first real sight of the sun to-day The wind is very fair, blowing nearly due west I had a game of Scotch Skip on the deck in the evening At 8 p m the Professor began his grand concert etc.— there was a great many from the 1st cabin came to this one They kept piping, singing, and reciting to a late hour of the night.

Friday 12th. October. A little squally—There were a great many sea-gulls kept flying about the ship the whole day We are not far off Newfoundland now and expect to pass it on Saturday or Sunday It was a rather rough night, but I slept well

Saturday 13th. October. Rather rough The wind is very favorable—An increase to the number of sea-birds There are a great many now. It began to be very rough in the evening. The sea rose mountains high, as the saying is. A tremendous sea broke over the whole vessel—swept the deck and drenched the officer on the bridge But these are the least important things it did. It likewise smashed to atoms the small boat which is fastened about 8 feet above the level of the deck by davits, and is also very strongly strapped down It also rushed into the cabin as well as right over it, and wet everyone in it. We had then to keep the door and skylight closed which made the place very close The night was positively *awful*. The Captain says that it is very seldom ships ride through a worse night in safety. At one time the deck was covered with water to the gunwale and the men were nearly smothered. Everything was floating about· there were about 50 tons of water at one time on board. The water got into our berths and kept washing over the cabin floor from side to side according as the vessel

rolled. Everyone was very wet, but nobody suffered from it
There were no colds caught though we had nearly all to lie
down in wet beds!

I am sure you will think I am writing very carelessly but
if I were paid for it I could not write better Many others have
given up the idea of writing altogether It is really next to impossible. The vessel has a very uneasy motion

I was really afraid of being knocked out of my berth—
My feet were at one time far higher than my head, and at
other times I was almost standing.

Sunday, 14th October The seas are rather abated, but it
is not unusual for the sea to break over the whole ship drench-
ing everyone We had no regular service, but the Professor, a
Unitarian, read Matthew 5th Chap There were a couple of
Hymns sung also, but they were objected to There are a great
many religions on board and each one is very bigoted for his
or her own section We have Church of England, and of Scotland, Old and New Presbyterians, Unitarians, Coventanters,
Catholics. I think some who have no religion—and one Wesleyan (myself) all in this second cabin—There are also some
Jews on board, but those I have mentioned above are all in
my cabin

In the evening the Doctor (Morier) came in and we had
some old Presbyterian tunes accompanied by the harmonium.

Monday, 15th. October The wind is beginning to freshen I
think—it is blowing nearly due South. We are, however, going
along very fast.

The Captain has just been in—he says we are on the
"Banks" of Newfoundland. We may get a sight of the Island.
It is *very* cold It is nearly always so when passing it, as I hear.
Just after dinner word was brought that a vessel and Newfoundland were both in sight Everyone hurried on deck. The
vessel came on beautifully—it was a brig, and her white sails
shone in the sun, which was shining brightly The mate who

was on the watch, supposed she was timber laden, and bound
from Saint John, Nova Scotia (Perhaps she is bound for
Newry) As she disappeared (she was about a mile to the
starboard) Newfoundland first became visible to the naked
eye It appeared like a blue cloud only a very little above the
level of the sea, but after a little assumed a more natural
appearance It just looked like a blue painting above the level
of the sea It was bitterly cold, but the air was very bracing,
and the ship very calm This evening was the quietest since I
came on board There was very little motion perceivable in
the vessel

Tuesday, 16th October This is a beautiful sunshiny morning, but very cold The sea is very calm compared with a few
days ago I find it easier to write now—but there are always a
great many people around me. and I find it very hard to write
anything like a connected chronicle of events I am sure you
will think this scribble very unsatisfactory

It has continued very fine all day, and I played a game of
Scotch Skip after dinner We have Drafts and Dominoes in the
cabin and altogether the time is going round very pleasantly
There is never any gambling in connection with these games
It was a fine, bright, starlight night, and dancing was kept up
on deck to a late hour We have some noted characters on
board viz—for instance—a Federal and Confederate Officer
and a Quaker—Vegetarian About 11 p m the ship was stopped
and the load heaved We are passing by somewhere near
Seavil Island. The wind is straight ahead, and we are going
only at the rate of about 8 knots an hour

Wednesday, 17th October. Got up early this morning and
had a pleasant time on deck before breakfast It is very fine
weather—the sky clear, sun shining, and everybody appears
invigorated. About 10 o'clock a full rigged ship hoved in sight
and passed us on the starboard bow It was a British vessel
and bound for Europe It is really a beautiful sight to see the

white sails shining in the sun and is especially grateful to eyes so long accustomed to the wearisome monotony of the waste of waters. The wind is still ahead and we do not expect to be in New York before Saturday night A few minutes after writing the above, on going upon deck I saw a very large Yankie ship which came nearer than any one yet Flags were hoisted on both vessels, but we could not find out her name The night was beautifully clear and bright but cold

Thursday, 18th October Had several games of Shuffle Board to-day on deck The sea is very calm I have seen the waves at Warrenpoint[1] far higher Shortly before dinner a large steamer hove in sight and passed us on the starboard bow. Signals were exchanged between both vessels The Captain supposed she is a mail steamer, but can't be sure, as she was a long way off About 5 30 p m a small brig, beating up against the wind, passed us on the larboard It was very near—we could distinguish men on board quite plainly— also a dog whose bark we heard She was painted yellow, but could not discover her name This night the Captain sent up rockets and blue lights for a pilot to come and we expect him every minute (Friday 19th) We have not yet seen land, but expect it very soon. I think we will disembark early to-morrow

Friday, 19th. October The sea is just as calm now as ever I saw it at W point There is scarcely any perceptible motion in the vessel, and some old travellers say they never saw it so calm We are going along at the rate of $9\frac{1}{2}$ knots an hour The weather is just like summer only a little more chilly The sun is shining as brightly as ever I saw it 2 15 p m The pilot has just come on board The boat is a very pretty one,—rigged like a yacht. At the time he came on board there were 5 vessels in sight besides this one which is No 13 We will almost surely be in New York to-morrow As yet we have not seen land.

I shall have to close my Diary now as the mail will leave at 10 a m tomorrow morning. The Purser will get this posted for

---

[1] Warrenpoint, Co Down is approximately 6 miles from Newry

me I have enjoyed my voyage very much. The weather is
more sunshiny than the hottest summer I ever enjoyed in
Old Ireland though the air is rather colder The nights are
beautiful—the moon and stars always shining. I am sure you
will think this Diary very straggling and unconnected, but it is
really impossible to keep one's thoughts fixed on any subject
with a great many people around making noise

So now, dearest Father, good-bye for the present, I expect
I shall write next Saturday, giving a little account of my doings
in a great and strange City It makes me sometimes feel
rather queer to think that I have to go to such a place to make
a livelihood far from home and kindred, but I am more and
more convinced that it is for the best, when I hear people who
have been there before telling of the manifold opportunities for
advancement I often think of you all and earnestly pray for
your welfare I send my fondest love and kisses to you all I
hope you will soon send me likenesses of you all. If I do not
get the likenesses I shall always at any rate keep your images
in my mind's eye. Likenesses may err but I shall never forget
you. Kind remembrance to all Newry friends and to Cozs
Anna and Mary, George &c &c when writing. I hardly know
what I am writing there is so much noise and interruption I
hope none of you will fret for me, I have made up my mind
with the help of the Most High, never to give you cause.

> I remain,
>> As ever your devoted and very affectionate
>> Son—James.

Rev. John Higgins,
> Newry,
>> Ireland

> 86 Sixth Avenue,
>> New York, 1st. Nov. 1866.
>>> Thur. Evening

My beloved Father,

I wrote you last on board the "Iowa" which I trust you

are either just receiving, or are about to receive. I received Henry's and your welcome letters yesterday week (24th) I did not write last Saturday as I purposed as I had nothing very particular to communicate I got on shore shortly after 11 o'clock on Saturday (30th) and got safely to Mr Mc-Cormacks Mr McC was at Church Street I did not see him till the evening After taking an early dinner I, in company with Mrs McC. and some lady friends also some of her nephews, went to the Central Park, which is the most beautiful (artificial) place that ever I was in.

The day was oppressively hot, and there was a cloudless American sky I hardly know where to commence narrating the beauties of that place. Everything was there to charm the eye and the trees looked unusually beautiful (as I was told) in the Indian Summer the leaves begin to fade, at one part of a tree they may be an orange colour, another red, another green &c &c so that a group of trees at a distance looks more beautiful than any picture ever I saw There was a splendid band performing in a beautiful marque just like a Chinese Pagoda Seats were placed all round, and tents and cool grottoes invited you at every few paces to take advantage of their shade There were hills and valleys, and a great number of beautiful fountains, and picturesque lakes in which were sailing a great number of brightly painted boats crowded with people The charge is only a few cents for the circuit of the principal lake. There were magnificently furnished restaurants scattered over the park, and at the Arsenal (a grand looking old building occupied by the soldiers during the War) there was an Art Gallery and a number of wild animals such as can be seen in the Zoological Gardens in Dublin. At the carriage drive there were hundreds of vehicles of every shape and size, except the Irish Jaunting car They look down upon it. More shame for them, for there were far worse looking articles (I really don't know what to call them) in which New York fashionables were driving. After getting home that evening Mr. McC said that he was sorry he could not make room for

me to sleep in his house (before I had opportunity to ask him
to direct me to a suitable Boarding-House), and then brought
me here which is a very nice place and is kept by a Dr Richardson, who is a member of the Washington Sq M E Church,
where Mr McC attends He first told me that he would expect
me down to breakfast in the morning, and that I should take
my meals with him till I should get comfortably settled (the
Richardsons merely rent rooms, they do not board their
lodgers) Next day (Sunday) I attended the Washington
Square Church It is a most beautiful building, far surpassing
any place of worship I have ever seen There is a splendid
organ choir. The pews have all spring cushions at the back as
well as the seat, and the floor is carpeted all over The sermon
in the morning was preached by Rev Ridgway, it was a
very good sermon (addressed entirely to Sunday School
Teachers!) There was a Sunday School in the morning at 9
o'clock at which there were about 500 present It was held in
the lecture room underneath the Chapel. My teacher's name
is Mr Digges There was another Sunday School in the evening at 2 o'clock, a "Young Man's Prayer-Meeting" at 6 p.m .
the Morning Service commences at 11 and in the evening at
7 30 o'clock. In the evening (same place) the Rev Mr. Ezray
preached a sermon, the like of which I never heard before, and
I hope I never will again Nearly the whole time he was either
smiling or else laughing heartily and the congregation could
not help joining him! ! ! He began the sermon with a joke!
saying that Mr Ridgway had asked him to preach a sermon
to young men with regard to their part in the business of life,
but that that was beyond his power though he had no doubt
Mr Ridgway could as he was a far more clever man than himself, "However," he said, "I will do my best, and will commence by selecting a text that has nothing whatever to do
with the subject—this is often the case with sermons, though
the preachers won't own it sometimes!" He then began a most
stirring appeal to the young men to support the Union during
the coming elections! and he had no doubt they had all made

up their minds to vote on the side of right (conservative) He
kept to this theme all through, though he often got into a
rigmarole! I will tell you some of the things he said that occur
to me now, to give you an instance—"Humanity catches
something else besides the measles "—"Though I am a Conservative myself I see some good in the Radicals, but that
won't make me come on any closer quarters with the pack "
He also spoke against the Daily Papers (on the opposite side)
and their editors, and spoke of Rev Henry Ward Beecher as
an "old boy " He likewise said "Now I know there are people
who say that I am a very odd kind of fish, but I can't make
myself any better than I am Some ministers will be very
holy and sanctimonious before you, but to tell you the plain
truth I don't bother my head very much about it, a little
religion is very good, but too much of it is a regular bore "!
&c &c He is one of the M E ministers and has charge of a
church in the City

On Monday I went in company with Mr. McC to C C
North, who received me very kindly, and said he would let
me know if he heard of any suitable place Mr McC then
told me to make myself easy in his house and not to trouble
myself any more at present about getting a situation When I
said that was too kind and that I would feel obliged by his
getting me a Boarding House, he would not hear of it, and so
I remained with him for the next few days On Wednesday
evening I went to a meeting of the Freedmen's Union Commission at the Cooper Institute I heard Gen O O. Howard,
Rev Henry Ward Beecher, and T. J Durant, Esq (Southern
Loyalist) speak It was a great meeting and there were a
great many blacks at it. On Wednesday Mr McC went to a
Mr McKillop (a Belfast man) who has a very large Mercantile Agency in Park Place, but was unable to see him Next
day (Thursday) I went with him to the same place, but we
were disappointed On Friday, however, we saw him —he
told me to write him a letter to show my handwriting, and he
would do what he could for me I brought it to him on Satur-

day morning, and on Monday evening he sent for me to go on Tuesday morning, which I did, when he told me that he would engage me himself, that I could try how I would like it for a few days, and then he would arrange the terms He said he would like to make an engagement with me for two or three years at an increasing salary which could be arranged in a few days. Mr. McC. says this would do very well if I liked the place, and he gives enough This is my third day with him and I like it so far. He has about fifty clerks employed (as near as I can count) A great many of them are old men You need not be anxious about me having a good deal of writing to do as I am adopting your mode of sitting and John Hoey's of holding the pen.

On Tuesday evening I went to a grand Centenary Floral Exhibition of the children of the Sunday School, in connection with Washington Square. It was beautiful There was a temple of flowers erected in the place for the pulpit and there were beautiful birds singing in it. I heard Miss Florence Reynolds (a little girl) singing some beautiful songs. I send you a ribbon I got to wear at the Festival which will show you a little of the great taste with which it was all conducted I likewise got a medal to commemorate the event. There have been love feasts nearly every evening since I came. Of course these are special and are to commemorate the Centenary here.

The hours in McKillop, Sprague & Co. are from 8 a.m to 6 p.m I have to have my breakfast taken before I go there. It takes ½ an hour to walk there from here, so I get it in a restaurant very cheap. I can get a very comfortable breakfast for 15 cents (about 6d) I likewise have to take my dinner there too But this has only been for the last few days I hope before the end of the week to get into a Boarding House. The McCormacks (not McCormicks) have been *very* kind to me I spent a very pleasant Hallow-Eve there yesterday evening

I have a great deal more to say but I think I have said what was of most importance, and it is now getting late I forgot to mention, lest you should be anxious, that I am not going to engage till I let Mr McC know the terms, and then he will advise me in the matter

I very often think of you all, and though I may sometimes feel a little lonely I soon get over it by reading over yours and Henry's letters in which you tell of what I knew before (but still it is so comforting to have it in your writing to look at) that is that you all love and think of me as I do of you. Please remember me kindly to all the Newry &c friends and relatives. You might let Mr Langston know that I am still in the flesh, as he kindly asked me to let him know that. I am very tired, and 1 only hope you will not have much trouble making out this letter I hope Henry will get something to do shortly that will suit him. I will try and abide by the good advice you gave me. With fondest love and kisses for each and all,

> I remain, as ever,
> Your loving Son
> James.

Rev John Higgins,
Newry

P S Please direct to Mr McCormack till I let you know that I have obtained a permanent lodging

> 86 Sixth Avenue,
> New York, Thurs Evening,
> Nov 15th/66

My own darling Mother,

I wrote to Father just this evening fortnight, Thursday 1st November, and am now daily expecting a second letter from you I am still at McKillop, Sprague, & Co's Office at a salary of $5 (dollars) a week to commence with I expect a "rise" in a few weeks (2 or 3)

You will be glad to hear that I am now thoroughly "seasoned" to the American climate—I went through that

interesting process last week in the shape of a cold and some
twinges of neuralgia.—Just what every new arrival (in the
fall) must expect, as Dr Richardson (with whom I am stopping) said He is a very nice kind man, and I imagine, greatly
resembles Garibaldi Mrs Richardson is a very kind woman
also They have been very kind to me and you will be glad to
hear that I now board with them They are not in the habit
of keeping boarders, but merely "let" the rooms, but while I
was unwell she said to me that she had been thinking that it
was hard for me (as indeed it was) to have to go to restaurants
for my meals, as I had not been accustomed to them, and that
if I liked she would board me Of course I gladly accepted her
offer, as it is so much more pleasant to be with good, agreeable
people than to go to a regular Boarding House. I think I told
you in my last that they are Methodists (members of the 4th
St —Washington Sq —Church) They are all called churches
here—there are no chapels I called on Dr Scott (sometime
Rev Robinson) at 56 Wall St last Saturday He had just
been gone a short time when I called I got his private address
(147 East 15th St) but have not had time to call there since
I purpose doing so as soon as possible

I think I did not tell you that I have a "room-fellow"
here—a very nice, agreeable one—a "Vermont boy"—Mrs
Richardson advised me to take a share of the room with him
as it would come cheaper and he was a good, moral young
man He has been about 3 years at business (boots & shoes)
commenced at $6 and now gets $15 I made no agreement
whatever (nor did he ask me) with Mr McKillop, but just
intend stopping as long as it suits me. The house where his
office is in, is full of offices—five stories high house—and a
person would nearly lose oneself among them all. You will
doubtless be surprised to hear that there are railroad tracks
through most of the streets and cars running on them drawn
by horses It is very pleasant riding in them, they go so
smoothly What struck me first on entering the city was the
shops or stores as they are always called here. In a large 6

story house—the general size here—they will have one or two
stores on every landing A person would wonder that they all
got enough to do, very often they are all of the same business—but every one appears to thrive here There is none of
that sly, underhand, backbiting work for which, I am sorry
to say, Newry is remarkable They have a curious way of
advertising themselves by putting in marble flags on the path
outside their doors with their names &c cut on it They also
have the kerb stones covered with paper advertisements and
they erect awnings to shade their windows &c with their
names painted on them It came rather strange to me at first
to have all the money in paper except the single cents I send
Ina a new cent in the paper which I send along with this—to
let you see what they are like I also send a photograph of
Lincoln's death-bed, for which I only paid 3 cents, about a
penny I do not much care for the photographs of Henry and
self, you sent me I think it would have been nicer if the color
was not in the scarf, and the gold in the watch-chain did not
look well either I think Henry has a far better position than
I have—I appear awkward

I don't think I told you in my Diary that we saw some
porpoises the day the pilot boat came alongside. They appeared as if afraid of being jammed between the steamer and
the pilot boat and kept floundering about very curiously (I
mention this especially for George's edification, as I expect he
will forthwith "commit to canvas" the above-depicted scene)

The way I manage here about my meals is this—I have
breakfast at 7.15 a m. and bring a luncheon with me When I
get home in the evening at 6 p m , they have what is called
here "supper" it is dinner and tea all in one They take bread
and butter and tea at 12 o'clock, which does them instead of a
dinner They don't appear to know how to make tea in
America at all They make it weaker than you would give it to
douty little Chaumsey and without even as nice a taste as it
would have Some people here do not drink tea at all, but
take water On my way to the office I some time pass

"Lindsay, Chittick & Co's, at the corner of Duane Street.
It is a fine looking place but nothing at all to some of the other
"Dry Goods" stores —Henry will tell you everything else
about it I pass by "A. T. Stewart & Co's" two establishments
at Broadway They are splendid looking buildings but there
is no show about them—not even a name above the doors to
say who lives within I also pass by a lot of theatres—some
very grand looking—one of them the "N Y Theatre" was
once a church You will say that it is now sufficiently de-
moralised! I also pass "Barnum's Museum"—a fine looking
place with a lot of banners up and the walls covered with
pictures of the animals inside (I wish George were here
after a little practice he would make his fortune by his paint
brush, as the people here appear to care more for flare and
show than neatness!) I also wish he saw all the steamers and
vessels I saw on the morning of my arrival "I guess" I saw
about two or three hundred steamers at the least Some grand
large ferry-boats and some about as large as the "James" or
the "Peter Duffy" Think of either of these lighters rigged up
like a steamer, with the engine working above deck, and you
will have a very good idea of what a great many of them were
like. The wharfs, or what you call quays are all built of wood
The house rents here are very high For this house, or rather
three stories of it, as there are shops on the ground floor,
Dr R pays $1,500 a year rent! The rooms are just a little
larger than the ones in "42" and there are not as many of
them The R's live in three of the rooms They have two
children—Waldo & May—

There is a love-feast in some of the churches here nearly
every fortnight They are very well attended and the people
are far more earnest than they are in the old country Some of
them hold curious doctrines One old man said that he had
been a long time seeking for a new heart and at last he found
that he did not need one—that he had one already and that
he could not remember the time he had not one—in fact he
believed it was born with him. They have a curious habit of

picking at one anothers bread. They will take about the size of the head of a pin off and then hand theirs back in return for a nibble—At first I thought they were making fun, but I found out they did this in token of friendship—I do not, however, admire the custom They have beautiful tunes here and they are just as well sung Especially those in the Sunday School are *most* beautiful. I will try and get the music of some of them for you, as I never heard as nice They have a splendid harmonium just for the use of the Sunday School alone There is also a splendid library for the use of the schol- ars. They are going to have a great Christmas festival—they are talking of it already The scholars collected $1,200 for the Centenary fund and were presented with a splendid medallion of Rev John Wesley by C C North, in the name of the Central M E Church Committee

In McKillop's they published a directory of the United States on the 1st day of January every year, they are hard at work now at N Y They are selling the types & printing in the same room, as fast as the clerks write They have agents all over the States and can tell what each man who sets up in the business is worth and his general character They can tell as far back as 45 or so

I have got a piece of news for Margaret, that is that the people here have their clothes lines on the tops of the houses, which are built rather flat with balconies round the edges and dry all their clothes there Ask her for me how she would like spreading the clothes at a height of 6 or 7 stories above the ground!

I learn by the papers that John Bright is now in Dublin, I hope that he will get a lot of converts there and do some good for "ould Oureland " Would you please tell Mr. Pierce that I have been unable to get any information yet about his trade, but I have very little hesitation in saying that it is well paid Carpenters and stone-cutters here get between 5 & 6$ a day That would come to a very decent sum in the year.

I have got a good lot of unconnected bits of news that

sometimes occur to me and then are lost slight of while I am writing others—Writing is such a slow way to get rid of ones thoughts How I would enjoy a few hours converse with you all I know a few hours would not tire me at any rate The "Observer" which I send you with this is published in the same house as the office is in I also send Anna a little paper I got in the Sunday School. Though I write this letter this evening it will not go till Saturday morning (the 17th)

I must now conclude I very often think of you all and try and imagine what you are doing. I have to calculate about 5 hours forward of the time it is here—as the time here is about 5 hours slower than European time It is now 10 30 p m here, so I think you are now all fast asleep in your bed at 3 30 a m in the morning I have written closely to get in all the news I could I hope you will not have trouble reading it I send my fond love and kisses to each and all Please send my love to Cozs George, Thos Anna, Mary &c also my kind remembrance to the Kinnears, Andersons, Littles, Glennings, Davidsons, Mr Lingston, Rolton, Jas Sevann, Geo White &c and ask the latter to remember me to Mr Hansby, and all others of the men in Greys, Bradley &c &c—also to the Murrays, Mrs Hamilton, Mr Nichol, &c &c &c Please give all the loved circle the kisses for me and accept the same, my dearest Mother,

from,

Your ever devotedly-attached
Son James

86 Sixth Ave·
New York, Thur Eve
22nd. Nov 1866

My own loved Mother,

I received your very welcome letters last Friday evening (16th) which brought the very welcome news of my having got a new baby brother I felt quite strange when I read of it first—to think there was one in the family I had not seen, and that when I would see him (D V) he would be perhaps like my own little Chaumsey, or bigger, according to the time we may be separated; and that Chaumsey would be a fine big boy if spared Poor dear little Chaumsey! It is just what might be expected of him—his grieving after me—he was always so very much attached to us all real affectionate love—young as he was never appeared strange to him; it seemed to be in his very nature, as soon as he was able to understand anything I cannot soon forget how I bid him good-bye He and Anna had got to bed and were standing in our room near the window (regardless alike of coughs or colds) When I was kissing them, Anna smiled, but Chaumsey had a grave but wondering look as he said "A' you goin' to Moky, Dapey?" I said "yes," and he gave me one of his endearing little hugs, and began to look quite sorrowful He appeared to comprehend what parting meant in a wonderful degree for so young a child I think the little darling must have done a good deal in his own way towards comforting you all I have been thinking over about the second name for little "Bill," but I cannot fix upon one

I have been thinking a good deal over the "private" matter mentioned in your letter It is indeed a subject that demands very much thought —To turn one's back on the land of one's birth and seek health and a home at the other side of the world! However, I think that it is what is pointed out by Providence, and agree with you in thinking that you ought to see about going in July It will be the best weather (likely) and Father can have all arranged with the Conference It will no doubt be a very great pecuniary loss, apparently, but then it will be a gain of health, and I feel sure your children would try to do a little more than merely—as you say—"help us to get on." I feel, myself, at not being in a position to "help the work forward" (as the saying is) by some means or other I may be able to do something before that time—I hope I will. A thought occurred to me almost as soon as I read your letter—that Cousin Henry ought to accompany you He was ordered something of the sort by the Doctors, and he would be well cared for, I am sure, and he would run less risk about his health by going with you It is a great pity of him, he is suffering so much, and I certainly think that the change of climate, voyage, &c would do a great deal for him It is very kind of the Newry friends to speak so kindly and flatteringly of me—I am sure very little of it was merited on my part It was a curious thing for Mrs Wood to say of me that I was affable when (if I remember aright) I never spoke to her; and I was never any good in conversation I am sorry to hear that Rolston is sick again in his head, I hope he will be able to get clear of Grey quietly, but that is no easy job I am not sure, from what I have heard, that America would be the best place for him, as he has a weak chest, but I hope he will be guided aright I have had on my flannels now more than a fortnight The weather has been rather variable—some days there was a kind of sultry heat, with very little sunshine, but to-day we have had rain, and it is now feeling rather cold I think that is a very suitable book you are getting for Rolston, I hope he and Geo Kinnear will like their keepsakes In reply to your enquiry about my clothes &c , I did not lose anything, neither was anything spoiled, though some of the things felt damp, and I am glad to say that I did not catch cold The voyage, I think served me very much—I enjoyed what you would call rude health while I was on board—no blast, or draft, or exposure had the slightest effect on me, and the effects on my spirits was very exhilarating I hardly expected to hear of Dr Waddell and Miss Harrison's nuptials so soon I hope the morning and evening contrast augured nothing to the happy pair, though some people would say it depicted the morning and evening of their wedded life—though perhaps they have both commenced it in the evening of life—no hints about the lady's age of course I am sorry to hear that about Mr Donaldson's son—Wm and hope he will reform in his new country I am very glad to hear that Henry is learning French and German especially. I could not have imagined that America was so full of Germans as it is It seems to me that there are far more Germans in New York than speakers of the English tongue—no matter of what nation There are some German clerks in the office with me and a great many of those who speak English without hesitation are of German parentage, but have lived in America so long that the foreign accent has worn off, and they call themselves American citizens The clerk sitting beside me is called Van Nest

The names of a great many of the large firms here are very outlandish-sounding German, such as—"Sulzbacher, Gitterman, and Wedeler, and "Vorhies," &c &c

The American element of "pertness" shows itself in the children here while very young The other day at table, Di Richardson's little daughter, May, was asked by him—"May, will you have a little meat?" she replied "No, pa, I'll hardly mind any this evening, but if you've got any baked potatoes over there, I'll take some " She is not a bit bigger than Anna! The very children smoke and chew quite methodically I have seen little fellows about Sammy's size coming to Sunday School smoking a cigar (or as they spell it here "segar") with such an air of nonchalance that it was really laughable! Then when they get into Sunday School, they bring out their "chewing tobacco" and forthwith begin spitting about in a manner which is very dangerous to clean boots in proximity, or clean clothes either There are spittoons placed in each pew in the churches A good many of the ministers chew and smoke. Last Sunday evening week there was a disappointment in the church—The Pastor—Mr. Ridgeway was away and a substitute who was engaged, shirked the job After waiting about a quarter of an hour, I saw a young fellow, not much older than I, I think, walking up the aisle and into the pulpit quite unconcernedly He then began "addressing the audience" with a "naivite" that to me at least seemed wonderful. He said he was the only "man" that was present who was "available and willing to occupy the pastor's place," then after the customary apology, he went through a chapter, expounding it with as much assurance as an old and practised preacher and held the meeting right through! Now that was a *smart* thing of a person like him to do,—to address hundreds of a critical city audience, among them a good many old men— older &c. Last Sunday morning I went to hear a famous preacher called Corbett, who used to be a common laboring man in the city—He is certainly a beautiful preacher In the evening I heard Dr Newman in our own church, preach upon "Saul, Saul, why persecuted thou me?" It was—in my opinion—one of the most elaborate sermons ever I heard In the prayer meetings here all the prayer leaders go up into the Communion Rails (or as they call it here the "Altar") and one of them takes charge of the meeting, and they generally conclude by having a kind of love feast, that is speaking their experience

At the love-feasts here, each one is allowed about a minute to speak One man, in one of those I was at, was speaking rather long and an old member arose and told him to sit down, but he continued speaking the louder, whereupon the man who raised the singing that night (There is generally one man in charge of that department, whose business it is to strike up a verse or two every two or three minutes or so) began singing with all his might—the congregation joined him—but the man still attempting to speak a big man or two took him by the shoulders and held him down and peace was restored That is what they call "singing a man down " They would not have done it but this man had very often interrupted the meetings before Newry people might do better by going a little more on the short speaking system Mr McKillop's wife died last Sunday quite suddenly She had been for a long time ailing from an internal disease and had a return of it for some days before Mr McK was in Phil and was thinking of not coming home till Monday morning but he arrived home on Sunday morning She felt badly but not worse than usual About 3 minutes before she died she said suddenly to her husband—"I think I'm going to die" and then she began trying to sing "I'll praise.   but those were her last words—she was going to sing "I'll praise my Maker whilst I've breath" etc , but as the minister said of her "she finished it in Heaven!" Mr McK feels the loss very keenly—He is delicate—and by her nursing he is alive now I have not made any engagement with him—neither will I, since I have heard of your contemplated arrangements There is a very popular "Fenian" song here that nearly all the Hurdy Gurdys play called—"The Wearing of the Green " One of them I heard playing the other day played immediately after that tune—the famous tune George played on the flute, called "Johnny comes marching home " There is an old American in the office with me called *John Higgins*, we are sometimes confounded. I saw a most beautiful bunch of flowers today made out of carrots, turnips, parsnips, and beets and the leaves of the flowers were all made of parsley It was the most natural looking bunch of artificial flowers ever I saw. They have a very original way of advertising themselves here—At one eating house in Broadway they sometimes have a turtle outside the door in a vessel of water, and on the animals back is a notice that this turtle will be cooked for dinner on such a day At fur houses they have stuffed buffaloes and bears looking out of the door in such a natural-looking manner that a nervous person would get a start Suspended across the pavement a clothing house has in gigantic letters "Our Motto—The *world* with clothing to supply, And all our patrons satisfy!" As you will learn by my last letter (written this day week) I called on Dr Scott the Saturday before I received your letter, but did not see him Last Saturday evening I went with the letter to his private residence and learned that he had started that morning for Phil and would not return till a few days before embarking for Ireland I am going to write to him with your letter I got his address—I have not had time yet and ask him to drop me a line advising me when I can call upon him here &c In answer to Henry's kind enquiry (one would think he was afraid I fasted) I spent a very pleasant Hallow Eve at Mr. McCormack's They have invariably been most kind to me, and take a lively interest in all my concerns, so that I know where to go for kind advice—always freely given—when I require it. Mr McC is a very good man and takes a part in nearly all the meetings of the Church He appears to be quite a favorite among all the people Miss Martin, his sister-in-law carries on the head-dress and fancy ca.   . making business in a retired kind of way in the house.

Well, I am pretty well tired after having got over so much paper I have had to write closely and small—I hope you will be able to read it My thoughts are following you all now—how I hope you all are well and happy—there is no use fretting at all, we know that we all love one another dearly, and wish for every prosperity for one another. I send as ever my fond love and kisses to you all—give wee-Bill plenty of them but don't smother him—you say he is fat! My love to Cozs George, Anna, Mary, &c They may be expecting a letter from me, but please tell them I really have not time and when you are writing you can give them all the news contained in mine. I would be delighted to have a letter from any of them or the Newry friends—Geo Kinnear, &c Please remember me kindly to the Kinnears, Andersons (congratulate R J for me), Littles, Glennys, Davidsons, Mi Nichol Mrs Hamilton, The Murrays, Masseys, Flangans, Mi Langston, Rolston Gilliard, James Swan, Geo White (tell those both for me that if they think of going to America carpenters get between 5 and 6 dols a day at present,) George, Morton, Mr Hansby, Shaw, David Bradley, and the rest of the men There are so many to be remembered to I hope I have forgotten none

I remain, as ever,
Your very affectionate & loving son,
James H. Higgins

P S. I sent two papers &c. last week.

Rev J Higgins,
    42 Queen Street,
        Newry,
           Ireland

303 West 12th Street. (Abingdon Square)
New York, Thurs Evening,
4th. December 1866

My dearly beloved Father,

I received your packet of five welcome letters of the
16th ult on the 27th That was very soon for me to get them,
they were posted on the 17th and therefore came in 10 days I
was agreeably surprised to receive Samuel's little Epistle I
either did not know, or have forgotten, that he could print so
well It was a curious thing that when I received the letter in
Mr. McC's, there were other people present, and when I was
reading them, rather quickly of course, I omitted to read the
part written by Mother on the separate sheet and across
George's letter, just the place where she told about what G
had said to A.G. and about Wm Graham, &c Perhaps it
was just as well that I did not read those parts till the second
"going over," (which was the next evening in my own room),
as I might have shown by my countenance that I was reading
something at which I was indignant, and on the other sheet
surprised It makes me "hope for better things" when I hear
of a certain person being for once a little candid, and revealing
the way in which he worked his plots on a certain occasion not
very long past At the other individual I am of course very
much annoyed that he should attempt to speak of Mother in
such a way—but better could not be expected of him I have
been thinking that as S knew that Wm Graham was acquainted with us that he would now try and take him into
favor, and by making himself very agreeable and pleasant to
W G so prepossess him in his (S's) favor, as to make him
believe a lot of things he might fabricate against me With
regard to the following I just mention it because I think it my
duty, and it may be of some service to A. G I am not sure that
all in the Office would like him to be there, that is, if he goes
with the prospect of becoming a Traveller I know that Mathey
has his heart set on that job He was at it in my time and liked

nothing better He could take his time on the "road," and was always full of great accounts of the jolly time he had of it when he returned I would not like anyone I cared about to get into a disagreeable position there, as I know too well how he runs the chance of being treated You will say this is very bad writing, but there is no table in my room—they are going to give me one though—and I write sometimes on my knee and sometimes on the window sill The ink is bad, therefore I use my pencil You will observe that I have changed my boarding house to the above address The landlady's name is Mrs Eliza Swinsen She is a member of the 4th Street M. E Church The McCormacks thought Dr Richardson's rather high, and Mrs McC kindly procured this place for me The proper address is simply 303 W. 12th Street, though the house is situated on Abingdon Square Quite near there are the "Eagle Mills," they are flour mills The name however brings my mind to dwell on certain events, which I would fain forget

I am now getting $6 in the office (per week) which pays for me here I expect to get an advance shortly, or perhaps I will get another place before I receive any advance I called on Mr Lavery who received me very kindly and promised to try and procure me a better place than McKillop's. Friday 7th December—I received your paper, which was lying at Mr McC's for a few days, when I went there last night So Wm Graham is gone to Grey's! Well, I wish him all kinds of success You did not tell me how he got clear of Mr Blain I would fain hope it was by quiet means, as if there was a lawsuit impending, you would hardly forget to tell me of it I think when sending me newspapers in future it would be better to address them to this place—for the McCormacks are so kind they will not hear of my paying anything on the papers Though what is to be paid is very trifling, still, of course, I would not like them to pay for me every time They are most considerate, kind people, and they always receive me so kindly that I feel quite at home with them Indeed I think if I had not them to go to sometimes, I should feel very lonely, for nearly everyone else whom I have met here, has that cool, calculating, hard, *all for self* manner which does not suit me at all I never have any hesitation however in going to the McCormacks to ask advice or guidance on any subject, for they appear to make all my concerns theirs also

Yesterday week—Thur 29th. Nov was Thanksgiving Day Each Governor of the several States appoints a day for Thanksgiving once a year, and the day for this state is the last Thursday in November On that day the office was closed and I went with the McCormacks to Brooklyn—which is on the other side of the river, to hear the celebrated Henry Ward Beecher preach in his own church He preached a very fine sermon—full of thanksgiving—and made it his principal subject to show that justice and right appears to have the upper hand all over the world, by giving a running commentary on the various episodes in the history of nations during the past year He spoke in very high terms of *Irishmen*—said they were of "brilliant imagination, had unbounded powers of mind, exceedingly well-adapted for almost any kind of work they may make up their minds to labor at " (What people do not, I want to know) but to proceed "They prosper and thrive in a wonderful degree in this country, and the only place they do not appear to do well in is at home. England is harassed and troubled by them and says it does not want them, but we want them here, and they are always welcome in this country " He said a great deal more also in praise of them. He also likened France to "a ship that has lost the wind or one tack, *and has not got it on the other!*" He is a very eloquent man, but like all the ministers here, he reads his sermons His church is a very fine one, and capable of holding a great many people. There are two galleries, but the top one is smaller than the other. There is a back as well as a front entrance to his church There is a splendid organ and a choir to match I think his church may on the whole be considered as a model I am happy to say that Henry's right in supposing Mr. Ezray to be "an exception to the rule." All the other ministers here

are very good preachers, that is as many as I have heard I
am told that he is the oddity of the Conference I believe there
are oddities to be found everywhere, but certainly he goes to
great extremes. I do not think that dearest Mother could forget to ask about any one of my little concerns, I really wonder
how she can think of asking after so many matters both while
here and on the voyage But I think I ought not to have
written this, as I ought to remember that it has been always
the same, and that she has ever made all my joys and sorrows
hers also In my letter written on the 15th ult. (which I suppose you received about the same time as I did yours here) I
told you that I had a little neuralgia I am now wearing
and my drawers There has been some frost here, but the last
few days it has rained some, but to-day it is just like a beautiful, sunshiny Irish Spring day The skies are far more cloudless
here in fine weather than in Ireland, and when the sun begins
to shine it does so without intermission I see that you are
ahead of us in Ireland in snow, but when we get it here, we
need not expect to see much solid earth for a good while You
will be surprised to hear that I have for office companions
some veritable Fenians—one of these a very lanky Irishman
named Maguire—went up to Canada the time of the raid but
was late for the battle I have discovered that I have with me
in the office two Fermoy men and one Ballynakill (Sammy
ought to know the latter place very well) I would like to see
my likeness in which I look astonished, for I really don't
know what I had to be astonished at when it was being taken.
Perhaps you could send it in a newspaper and I can return it
in the same way. There is a very cheap kind of likenessess
taken here in which the bust only is given—they are called
"ferrotypes," and are done for 25 cents for 4 copies or 12
copies for 50 cents, at the latter rate they cost something less
than *2d* each! These are first rate likenesses at the price too
Contrast these prices in this *very dear* country (for so it is in
reality, on account of the very high taxes) with the prices in
the old country (as England, Ireland & Scotland are in-

discriminately termed here). The principal way they have here of taxing is by issuing revenue stamps They are compelled to put a 1 ct. stamp on a matchbox and cancel it! I am very glad we did not follow Mr Graham's advice about not buying my clothes in Ireland for they would cost more than double here, and there is very little of the so-called fashion here (especially among males) which has so many votaries in Ireland. Everyone wears what he or she thinks proper, and there is no "keeping up appearances." The day I was at Brooklyn, when returning on the ferry boat there were two girls dressed in the "Bloomer Costume"—that is wearing trousers and having the hair cut rather shorter than Anna's. What do you think of that? The trousers were rather loose, and made of the same material as a man's would be They had petticoats made of some kind of cloth coming just a little down below the knees, a dress of the same length, and a kind of coat over all This dress is very much worn here in the winter time by the ladies as a skating dress, but some wear it all the year round It was invented by a Mr Bloomer, who thought that women had not their rights (*rights* is an everlasting Yankee word) and that they ought to be allowed to vote and take part in public assemblies like men! There was a meeting held by ladies who advocated these views, in the Cooper Institute last night, some of the ladies spoke most eloquently

The way the houses are numbered here is rather curious, they have all the odd numbers on one side of the street and all the even on the other, for instance the number of our house is 42, Mrs. Harrison's would be 43, and Donaldson's 44, then the police Barracks 45 and Lupton's 46, but there are very few such gaps as between Harrison's and the Barracks to be found here

The diet on board the steamer was extremely good we had good vegetables every day, also fresh milk in our tea. They have some way of preserving the vegetables, I know not of, and they "condense" the milk. There was meat morning, noon & night, this was certainly rather much of it for my taste, but some appeared to like it. At dinner after soup, there was a choice of about 6 or 8 dishes (there was a French Cook) after this cheese and nuts, or pies or puddings of a great many descriptions, and afterwards fruit and nuts I can assure you the sea an agreed well with me, and I never enjoyed a better appetite I think I hope George will soon begin to paint pictures from the mind, and that his genius, guided by the celebrated Mr Leonard, will be led to paint the picture of the porpoises &c which I hinted to him about in one of my letters. I hope when he draws it he will send it to me, and I shall hang it up in my room

The American ladies, at least the N Y ones, are a great deal more dressy than the Newry ladies Mother remembers the pictures of ridiculous bonnets, which we saw at Miss Kinnear's, well I think that all those shapes, and a great many far more foolish looking are the fashion here Nearly every lady uses false hair in getting up those big lumps of hair at the back of their heads called "waterfalls," which are almost universally worn

There are countless telegraph wires traversing the streets, they have a great many in connection with the police offices all through the city and now and then you meet an office called the "Burglar Alarm" or some such name On one telegraph post I counted 23 wires. On Saturday the 24th ult I saw Barnum's giant. Major Hansen, a Norwegian, 8 feet high, reeling on the street, quite drunk! That was a curious sight. I would not like him to follow me Sunday the 25th was the anniversary of the evacuation of New York by the British, but the holiday was kept on Monday There were a great many flags displayed, and among them was the *Fenian*, but they are always wily enough to have the stars and stripes above it!

> 11 Ninth Street,
> New York, Thursday Evening,
> 13th December, 1866

My own beloved Mother,

I received your welcome letters of the 28th & 29th ult.

today I think before I commence answering it at all I will explain how it is I am writing from Mr. McCormacks I have
been a little indisposed—only a little, and on my visiting the
McCormack's while so, they advised me (that is, it was Mrs
McC) to leave McKillop's, as they thought it was not agreeing
with my health, and at the same time, she said that though
they had not room on my arrival to receive me, that they had
a spare room which was only occupied with old furniture &c
which she was about having cleaned up for me Of course I
was very much surprised and said that though I felt exceedingly obliged by the kind invitation, yet I could not think of
accepting it, and would therefore continue where I then was
(303 W 12th Street) and that if I left McK's as she advised
as hoped I would not be long without employment. She however put it so kindly and assured me that they would like me to
stay with them for a while, until there was a really suitable
place found for me, and that when I was not well she felt that
I would be very lonely, and that nobody but strangers could
do anything for me, and that perhaps I would feel more comfortable and at home with them. (the McC's) I do not think
that any one could have spoken more kindly to me unless a
relation, in fact, I could not (I think) have refused them with
anything like a "good grace" for though I repeatedly said I
could not think of doing such a thing, she over-ruled all my
objections, and I finally had to consent to live with them for a
while I do not think that there could be kinder people found
anywhere short of old Newry and of course of my relations
They have a very fine little son, who is exceedingly smart,
named Randolph Foster, after Dr Foster, a very good minister
here,—I think he is one of the most earnest men ever I met
Just now little Randolph asked me if I was writing to "Cousin
Charlie" (a relation of his) I said I was not, and his Mamma
told him I was writing to my little brothers and sisters. Miss
Jass, a young lady who works with Miss Martin, and boards
and lodges here, said—"Be sure you write what the Irishman
did, who, when sending his love to all his brothers and sisters

said—"But be sure that among them all you do not forget the
Asses," (of course, insinuating that he belonged to the same
noble family) So you see they will not allow me to forget that
I am an Irishman, though living in the land of Yankees Mrs
McCormack told me to put this witticism in my letter I
cannot say I have regularly joined a class yet. I went a couple
of weeks ago, (For some time after I came there were no class-
meetings on account of the Centenary Meetings) to Mr.
Gedney's Class, where Mrs McC attends He is a very good
old man But the reason of my not attending regularly was
that they expected me to speak I was some time before I
could make up my mind to do this, but both Mr & Mrs McC
spoke to me and said it was my duty to do so, and I felt myself
that it was wrong of me thus to absent myself from a place
where I might receive good Mrs McC. told me the first
evening of my going there, when returning from it, that she
was really astonished that I was not a Christian She thought
it was an awful thing for people to live without Christ, but
the idea of my resisting all the influences that I had round me
since my very birth was terrible She earnestly and faithfully
urged me to give up everything that would hinder me from
pursuing the right path I have often since thought that it was
remarkable that I never before so fully realised the extent of
my wickedness in sinning against light and knowledge I made
up my mind to go last Tuesday evening again and speak. It
cost me a severe struggle to make up my mind to speak, for I
felt a great many difficulties in my way, but when I went to
the class-room I was tempted in an awful manner. All the old
objections which I had previously (as I thought) overcome,
now returned with more than doubled force and in such a
confusing mixture that I was so much harassed I could not
collect my thoughts When it came round to be my turn to
speak, I did my best to shake off this evil influence but was
unable I stood up, but it really appeared as if I was attended
even then, and all kinds of wicked thoughts, and conflicting
opinions were so mixed up in my mind (more especially at

that moment than at any other) that I could not utter a word and had to sit down I felt this to be a great mortification—not to be able even to let my thoughts and desires be known, and I am sure the people present must have thought it very queer too It appears to be very curious to me that nearly everyone says that when he or she comes into the class-room or place of worship they always feel a calm and holy influence, which supports and strengthens them It was just the very opposite feeling which I experienced on that evening, and it was (I think) the fiercest temptation that ever I encountered Mr McC kindly spoke to me the following day and gave me good advice, I think. I believe, I feel more than ever determined to live aright

I went on Tuesday evening last to take leave of McKillop, Sprague & Co I believe I had made myself useful there, for shortly before I left they had given three new books into my charge to keep exclusively. The old manager, Mr Jordan, said he was very sorry I was leaving, and when I asked to see Mr Killop, who was in his private office, to thank him for giving me a place in the office, and explain why I was leaving, he sent out word he was very busy, but that he was sorry I was going and that he appreciated the motives which prompt me to leave his employ I am happy to say that your dream was false, for I found him a very considerate, agreeable man, and a very good one also. He feels his wife's death very much

I am very sorry to hear that Henry got his foot scalded so,—it must have been very bad, and I am also sorry to see by his letter that he fretted over the disappointment also. Of course it was a loss, and it is hard to keep an even, contented mind when one is disappointed, but the time could be made very useful at home Though the climate of India may do very well for people who are delicate, I would not like the idea of Henry getting "acclimatised" and then when we would see him next to be a yellow, shivering, dyspeptic, for though good habits may partly obviate these evils, yet I believe it is hard to keep entirely free from them I am not sure that it would be

much good my going immediately to Australia or whatever
place may be decided on Though of course I would rather be
with you all than here, yet I do not think it would be the best,
and I do not think that changing to Australia &c would make
the circumstances much better for me Before next July or
whatever time you may start I cannot hope that I would be
worth very much, for it takes a few months to get rightly used
to the customs of the country, and few men like to engage
any one who has not been in the country for a while—that is
at a good paying salary I think I might be of more service in
stopping here for a while, and soon be enabled to help you

You asked in your letter how I liked Waldo and May, well
my answer is that they were altogether too cute for my taste
They were by far the most old-fashioned children ever I met,
and even young as they were, they had the nasal "twang" to
a very great degree It is a curious thing that every child here
calls their Mamma—Mam-ma, and then papa—pap-pa, laying
the emphasis entirely on the first syllable How do you like
their fashion?

I am glad to hear that any expressions I may have used
in writing gave you pleasure, for my part, the way I feel is
that I cannot get words to express half of the love I feel for
any of you

Friday, 14th.—I hardly think you will have this letter
on Xmas Day, unless the steamer makes a very quick passage,
but it will be in time for New Year's I am sorry that it did not
occur to me before to write in time for that day I wrote last
week from Abingdon Square, and the week before I sent
Henry a German newspaper I received your two newspapers
There is a matter which I forgot to mention in my last letter —
A short time before leaving Grey's I was throwing some stones
in the yard in the evening with some others, and unfortunately
broke a back-window in the dwelling-house I put off telling
you about it until I might have a favorable opportunity of
getting it in without Mr Grey's knowledge, and by so doing
let the matter entirely escape my recollection, I am sorry that

I did forget it so long, and am sorry that I should put you to any expense on my account I hope Grey will not think I wanted to act dishonorably in the matter

There has been frost here for about a week, and in a short time I expect the skating ponds will be sufficiently frozen to allow people in them There are some people beginning to skate already in a rink on the 5th Avenue, the water there is of a uniform depth of 18 inches Sleighs are exposed for sale everywhere, and they are certainly most elegant looking vehicles In a short time we expect to have snow and then they will be in requisition

I forgot to answer your enquiry in my last letter about how I liked the food here It is not very different from the sort in Ireland except in the vegetables, of which they use a great deal larger quantity than folks generally in Ireland They have sweet potatoes, which are very nice, but I prefer the common "pratie" They use the Indian Corn ground and made into "homily," which somewhat resembles stirabout, but is a great deal nicer They also use it whole with butter They have tomatoes also which I do not care much about. They are far fonder of pastry and puddings &c than the "Oirish." and use them far more

The McCormack's have luncheon about 1 o'clock and dinner at 6 p m There is no tea They drink tea at luncheon. I have made the acquaintance of Mr Ridgway, the "pastor"— he is a nice quiet, clever, cold man There is no twilight in this country hardly The sun goes down quickly now at 4 30 p m and it is then quite dark I prefer the twilight.

Little Randolph is going to have a Xmas tree and they are buying things for it He is a very nice little boy I must now conclude, and wish a "Merry Xmas and Happy New Year to you all " Do not fear for me that I will not feel very happy this Xmas for the McC's are so very kind that they make me feel quite at home Do not either be afraid for my health, for I feel quite strong, & the little sickness I had is quite over now. Indeed it is not worth mentioning, but that I promised to let

you know when I was not well Please send my fond love with
the customary greetings of the season to Cousins Anna, Mary,
George &c. &c Remember me kindly & convey my greetings
to the Kinnears, Davidsons, Andersons, Lytles, Glennys,
Langstons, Murrays, Wm Graham, the Elliotts, Haddens,
Alston, Mr Hamilton, Mr Nicol, James Swan, Geo White,
Shaw, & ask one of these last to do the same for me to Geo.
Morton, Mrs. Hansby, Gilliard, Dan Curran & all the rest of
the men Lastly I send my fondest love & kisses to each & all
of you (not forgetting little Bill What is his other name?) &
please accept the same my dearest Mother from

> Your ever fondly attached
> Son James

Rev J Higgins,
    42 Queen St Newry
        Ireland

> 11 Ninth Street,
> New York
> 29th. Dec 1866

My beloved Father,

    I received yours and Mother's letters (No 5) written
on the 12th inst on Thursday the 27th, so you see I did not
get it on Xmas day as we both expected, I would have been
very glad to hear from Henry, especially as you said he had
lots of news, but it appears that Mother was hurried and he
was likely at School

    I have still been thinking for a second name for little
Bill What do you think of Emmanuel? I think William
Emmanuel sounds very well I would like to have something
like an "Official bulletin" about him in every letter for I
suppose you treat him like a little prince and I don't suppose
very many people would care to have it in the papers every

morning how he slept through the night &c as is the custom
with other princes. However, if I receive the said bulletin, I
venture to say that I will feel a little more interest in its
contents than most people do in ordinary bulletins What
makes me say this is that I received no news of him in your
last, which I venture to say was on account of Mother being
hurried, and I also remember that "no news is good news."
I sent Johnny the Xmas number of Harper's Weekly on the
27th I suppose you will wonder what all those pictures in the
centre are about "Santa Claus " Well, I did not know of such a
distinguished person till last Sunday, when Mr Ridgaway
gave out that the annual Sunday School festival would be
held on Xmas day—that the children were first all to meet in
the church and after singing &c go to the lecture room down
stairs to receive Santa Claus On making enquiry I found out
that this individual is a renowned friend of children, and
makes them a visit on Xmas Day, and gives them all manner
of presents On Xmas morning after singing some of those
beautiful songs which they learn in the Sunday School here,
we all adjourned to the lecture room, which was very nicely
decorated, but with no profusion of evergreens as there always
is in Ireland, for they are very scarce here There were two
Xmas Trees lit up with little coloured candles, and decorated
very nicely

There was a very nice feast of sweet cake, sweetmeats &c
laid out on a table, which was afterwards divided among the
children After a short time the Superintendent Mr. Cornell
asked the children when "Santa Claus" was coming. This
aroused their curiosity, and they straight way shouted out
"tell him to come " He then gave the bell three taps, and
there was then a tremendous noise in one of the adjoining
rooms, and shortly after "Santa Claus" himself appeared. He
was dressed in the most outlandish style with a false face and
long flowing white hair After making a short speech to the
children and wishing them a merry Christmas, he said that he
had not forgotten to bring presents for the little ones, and

went back to the room returning with a basket (just like Margaret's clothes basket) filled with beautifully dressed dolls and all sorts of boys and girls toys He went up stairs to the church, and the children belonging to the primary class were told to follow him, which they did with alacrity I believe this was originally a German custom It is something more than the Irish custom of leaving out the stocking to be filled by some good fairy He is altogether a mythical personage and has the wonderful power of appearing in many thousand places at the same time In the evening there was a kind of homely party here and they had a Xmas tree beautifully decked out with little wax candles and many nice presents There were present there besides all belonging to the house, Mrs McCormack's brother (Mr. Andrew Martin) and his wife and four children, Mr Joseph E McCormack, brother of Mr W G and a Miss Scholes There were a great many nice presents on the tree, principally for the young ones Mrs McC had on it for me a very pretty little pocket edition of the M.E Hymn Book. Their hymns here are very different from those in the Wesleyan Book Most of the Wes Hymns are in this Hymn Book, but they are nearly all minus a few verses, either at the beginning or end of the hymn, and there are a good many others added Of course I had on a few presents as well as the rest of them

I have written all after the line this evening, Friday Jan 4th We had a Watch night service on New Years Eve I could not help thinking how little I thought this time twelve months ago that I would commence the year 1867 in America It seems a *very* long year to me, I suppose partly on account of so many changes and events happening in it You will please excuse my writing in pencil as the ink is bad

I was greatly delighted to receive the Telegraph last night and to read Henry's name so often among the 1st places I hope and certainly think he got a premium. He must certainly have worked very hard to be able to beat those who were there all the half Who is that boy—King—whose name appears so often, and so close to Henry's? I suppose he must be in the same class I hope Henry liked the German newspaper I sent him The letter which I received on the 27th was in mistake given to a Mr. M. T. Higgins, who lives near this, on the 6th Avenue He thought it was for his son James who is in Europe, but he sent it to me with a note saying that he had discovered it was not for him as soon as he read the heading of the letter

New Years Day is even a greater holiday than Xmas here All the gentlemen go out visiting their acquaintances and friends on that day and the following is the "ladies day" when they do the same There was very good sleighing on New Years Day and the New Yorkers made the most of it It is delightful to hear the beautiful little bells ringing which are fastened round the horses I think the sound is very invigorating. I have not had a sleigh ride yet The weather is rather cold now, but it was *awful* the week before Xmas People went about walking with their hands to their ears and often rubbing them, to try to keep the least feeling in them I never felt anything like it

I was at a splendid concert in the Steinway Hall on Wed evening last Mrs McC had two tickets, and was disappointed in going, so she gave them to Miss Whittaker and myself, I never was so pleased in my life with any musical performance Everything was perfect. There were more than a hundred singers in the Cecilian Choir. and about fifty in the Orchestra I could not help wishing that you were all enjoying it as well as I You would have been especially pleased to hear the violins—of which there was a great number of every size, and Signor Strini, an Italian, and Masters Coker and Toedt (pronounced Tate) I send you the Programme. I think Mr & Mrs McC are gone to hear Mr D Kennedey, who is mentioned on the programme for to-night I am still stopping here (Ninth Street), but I do not intend to do so much longer The McCs are exceedingly kind

Mr McC. has given me employment in his store to keep accounts for him, and I have also a good deal of out door exercise Though I said I would not like to receive anything from him at present, while stopping with him &c he insisted upon giving me $7 per week I have not been able yet to ascertain enough about carpenters' prospects here, but will report fully in my next It is now pretty late, so I think I will close I forgot to mention lest you might be uneasy that I am quite healthy and well, and I want no additional clothing Please give my love to Cousins Anna and Mary, George and Thomas, &c &c and my kind remembrance to the Kinnears, Davidsons, Lytles, Andersons, Glennys, Murrays, Elliotts, Langstons, Mrs Hamilton, Rolston, James Swan, White, and all the men at Grey's &c I hope you all enjoyed Xmas and New Years Day as well as I did Perhaps we will all be together on this time next year Fondest Love and kisses for each and all. Be sure and do not forget little Bill, he ought to get double quantity.

> Believe me to be
> As ever, Your very affectionate
> Son James

Rev J. Higgins,
    42 Queen Street,
        Newry Ireland.

P S I return you my likeness, I think it is very good, and greatly superior to the first one

> James

> 11 Ninth Street,
>   N Y 15th Jan 1867
>   (Tues. Evening)

My ever beloved Father,

I received your six welcome letters on this evening week (the 8th) also the copy of cousin—Mary's I am delighted that all were in good health when you wrote, I think that is something more than ordinary George says you have not had snow Well, I surely saw, in one of the "Telegraphs" you sent me, a notice about the weather, saying that there was a slight fall of snow Perhaps it was so slight that it required the smart people connected with the "Telegraph" to see it I use the vinegar with my chest as Mother advised I feel very thankful to Sam for writing a letter of four pages to me It must have cost him a good deal of trouble, and I hope he will often send me all the news Nobody told me how Xmas day was passed I am sorry to say that poor little Randolph has had the Scarlet Fever since Saturday, but in a very mild form Miss Whittaker, who came out with the McC's also has it It commenced with her in a sore throat They are both in the house, and are attended by a Dr Andrews, a Hom. Physician (The McC's are all in favor of the Hom treatment) They (the patients) are progressing very favorably It is nearly the same disease as Scarlatina, therefore I am not liable to take it Mr McC went yesterday evening to Lafayette, Ind it is more than a thousand miles from here, and if there is no delay on the road (they travel in the same train day and night) they will be there about to-morrow morning There are very nice carriages on nearly all the railways here. They have direct communication between them all. Have them well warmed by stoves, and have sleeping apartments, where there are regular bed-rooms and comfortable beds Mr McC was very sorry to have to go, while Randolph was so ill, but the business was very urgent It is about Mr. W H Martin, the invalid in France He was accompanied by Mr Andrew Martin, brother of the above

I have heard something curious which may perhaps surprise you. Mrs McC has been married twice—her former husband was Mr McC's brother This is not according to English Law, but it is permitted in the U S, and is very common I think Mr Geo Kinnear is mistaken about the Mercantile Agency business (That is—in thinking that it can be carried on with a small capital) But I perceive that you call it the Common Agency business There is a great difference

between the two The Mercantile Agency is established on a
very large capital, and it requires a person to be a good many
years in the business to get much to do (That is if there are
any "opposition shops," which were established before him).
McKillop has upwards of a thousand agents all over the
States, to whom he pays a yearly salary for reporting the business worth standing and credit of every man in business in the
town or district for which he is agent There are reports in the
books since 1840. Then it requires a very large staff of clerks
to keep all the books of reports written up, &c These are
paid very low salaries, however, as they do not require any
very great smartness If a man can write a hand as good as
George's, that is all they want They are a queer lot of men in
McKillop's, as they do not require a man to have any kind of a
character to get in, so you may guess they are a motley crew
The way in which the business is paid is 1st, by the regular
subscribers who pay from 100 to 2 or 3000$ p ann and by
those who require to know the worth &c of any man who pay
so much for each question asked

I heard from Dr Scott the day before Xmas, if I have
time before I conclude I will send you a duplicate of it I have
not seen Mr. North since the day I called with Mr McC I
must have forgotten to tell you that Dr McClintock is now
in the country, and he has been for a good while, so that I had
no opportunity of seeing him It was very kind of Mrs Johnston to call down to see you in that way The last accounts
from Mr. Wm H. Martin were very favorable, he appeared
to be improving and sent his Carte-de-Visite It would, I
think be very proper to call Bill "Baker"—as one of his
names. And would not Emmanuel (GOD with us) be an
appropriate name. How does William Emmanuel Baker Higgins sound? I think very well. In order to let you have my
opinion early I sent a paper last week to "W E B Higgins,
Esq." I am sure you laughed at the little rogue to see what a
great man he had got, when you received the paper (There
was no writing inside it).

I received a letter from Rolston on Saturday the 22nd
Dec Please thank him for it and tell him I will answer as soon
as I have time and opportunity He tells of an ugly trick that
Stewart played the first day that Swain came to the office.
He sent Swain down to Carvill's to buy sizes of plank, which
they were short of, and Swain not being known by Carvill,
pretended to be buying for himself and of course bought a
good deal lower than Grey could have bought it I received
two "Liverpool Mercurys" from Mr. Langston Please thank
him for me I sent you a Xmas number of "Harper's Weekly,"
which, though there was a little writing in it, I hope you
received safely.

I am sorry Henry did not get the German newspaper, it
was as well as I could read it —"Frank Leslie's *Illustrate
Zeitung*"—I am just as well pleased you did not get the paper
before that, as it contained a little bit of foolish poetry about
the great little Bill, which I was ignoramus enough to try to
compose Does not that same little Bill get a great deal of
petting? I am afraid he does Father says "he is a very sweet
pet," and Johnny says "he is a very nice, fat little fellow "
Johnny's description is like that of a well-conditioned little
rabbit or squirrel But I would like to know from Mother if
the Higgins family were not all thought the same of when they
were babies I am pretty confident they were, so you see I have
somewhat of an opinion of myself. I am very much astonished
to hear of William Graham's conduct I never thought very
highly of him, but I did imagine he would keep his distance
with Stewart, especially on account of knowing his character
so well His cringing obsequiousness in the presence of Grey
or Stewart is remarked by Rolston, and he begins about
him—"I am sorry" &c &c (speaking about "your friend,
Mr Graham") How did he get clear of McBlain Rolston tells
me that they are doing very little business at Grey's I received Plinch's Almanac from George, which is very entertain-
ing I am very glad to hear of Henry's usual success at the
Exams in Potterton's That must be a very interesting book
he got

I would have been more glad to hear that Johnny was getting firsts in French, German or Arithmetic than in Latin I think that we all have a learning towards languages, especially the dead ones I know Henry and I always preferred them to anything else, but I thought that Johnny was fond of Arithmetic &c , and I can assure him that studies in that branch are of far more service in business than any language

17th. January, I suppose you are not aware of the fact that New York is the third German city in the world Vienna and Brussels alone exceed it in numbers It appears to me that it is also a grand receptacle for countless people of every nation. It is quite a common thing to see Chinamen At nearly all the principal restaurants there are black waiters, which I think makes everything look very foreign

There are a very great number of Germans very extensively connected with the Dry Goods business. Some of the largest wholesale houses in Church Street are occupied by Germans and some French At all these stores they have clerks of their own nation (and some Americans) who are all able to speak English fluently Modern languages are far more cultivated here than in the U K Church Street is fast becoming one of the principal business streets in New York Ground and house property is exceedingly high in it. Just opposite Mr McC's is an old wooden shanty, falling to pieces and occupied by negroes and some poor white folks The ground which it and its rear occupies is just a little larger than our yard in Newry. For this small portion of ground the owner asks twenty thousand dollars—and he will get it before long too

I have been shown a plot of ground in Broadway about the size of the grass plot before the door in Abbeyleix and the little side garden taken together The *narrow* side faces the street For this, *has* been paid the sum of two hundred and fifty thousand dollars! To finish up this business digression, which I suppose you will consider dull, I say that for this house (11-9th) Mr McC pays $1750 per year This is about £350! !

One could nearly *buy* the house for this money in Ireland You
will be glad to hear that I have seen a veritable snow-storm
Last night, about 11 o'clock it began to snow, continued all
night, and the greater part of to-day.

This morning (Thursday) when getting up I thought it
looked very dark, and saw what I thought smoke out in the
street When I looked well, however, I found it was very fine
snow, which was being driven so fast by a very strong wind
that it appeared to be going along quite horizontally, and
that it would hardly ever touch the ground The road and
paths were so covered that it was impossible to distinguish
them. The ground was so hard with the frost, which has been
pretty hard for the last few days, that it did not melt at all
It is so very fine that when a strong gust of wind comes, it
lifts up the snow and whirls it along like the dust on a summer's day The snow on the top of the houses was just the
same way This is what they call the snow "drifting" and it
forms sometimes against a large object the dangerous heap
called the "snow-drift" The poor horses had very hard work
the whole day, though the railway tracks in the streets were
swept by a machine for the purpose There were more sleighs
than cars out, though the snow was rather deep for them

I am happy to say the patients are progressing very
favorably Dr Andrews says that Randolph is "getting along
shamefully" Miss Whittaker had an attack of the same sort
before, so that it was very light this time I have found out a
few facts which may likely be interesting to James Swan and
Geo White The errand boy who is in Mr. McC's Store furnished me with the following —His father is a carpenter They
rent four rooms at the top of a house for which they pay $11 50
per month (I ought to have written this plainer for you It is
11 dollars & 50 cents The period separates the cents from
dollars) Meat averages from 20 to 30 cents per lb Butter is
about 40¢ per lb. Coal is about $7.00 per ton. His father does
not work many machines and is in a small shop, all the ma-
chinery of which is driven by horse power He gets $3 per

diem For £1 in gold here you get about $7. Some days it is
worth less or more as the case may be There is nothing
fluctuates so much as the American money market This
leaves the dollar worth abot 2/10 3/6 is however nearer its
true value I am sure if James Swan or George White were to
get into one of the monster box manufacturing or Joinery
Mills here, where there are a great many machines worked,
they would after some short time get from $4 to $4.50 per
diem They always however begin with light pay, and then
as the real worth of a man makes itself known, they increase
his wages I have heard that they find it hard to get men who
fully understand the working of machines, and they therefore
would be willing to pay them good wages. This boy's father
is a Belfast man, and was a cabinet maker by trade His
name is Edgar All these particulars were furnished me by this
boy, and I have reason to believe that they are pretty correct
If either J S. and G W continue to think seriously of coming
out, I will gladly make all possible inquiries and do what I
can for them It is certainly a serious thing to meditate, and I
would not take upon myself to positively advise emigration
for them, but certainly as far as I have seen hitherto, there is
among *all* classes of society something of the appearance of
independence, comfort, and *"well-off-ness,"* which I suppose
some of the old country "purse-proud folks" would hardly
like to see I like it very much however

Henry certainly is a splendid imitator of writing, he
signed Cousin Mary's name exactly the way she does She
wrote very kindly indeed, and I was glad to receive the copy
of her letter Please send her, Cousins Anna, Thomas, George,
Elizabeth &c. my best love when writing

I was sorry to hear of the two deaths in the Connexional
Was that Walker, brother of one they used to call "the Jarvey"
long ago? I think that was the only Walker except those of
Rev J Walker's family, I was with at school I think I have
written the longest letter ever I did, and I have found pleasure
in the task When at school I used not to like much letter-

writing, but my feelings in this respect have undergone a change over since placing such a distance between us as now exists I shall anxiously expect some tidings every letter of how matters are progressing with relation to your seeking another land I hope all will be made plain and easy for you

I suppose you have great consultations about what to christen little Bill Somehow I have got to like the name Emmanuel (God with us) I think it is a very pretty name, and beautifully expresses the thankful feelings which Mother wanted to find a word for. Please remember me to all whom I mentioned in former letters, (I do not want to have much of the paper crossed) Give my fondest love and kisses as ever for each and all of the loved circle, and accept the same from

Your ever devoted and loving
Son James

Rev. J. Higgins,
42 Queen Street,
Newry Ireland

P.S. I send George by this mail a book called "The Singing Pilgrim" which contains a great many of the beautiful Sunday School Hymns, I hope he will be able to play them well and like them I have marked one in particular which they are very fond of singing in the Sunday School Stephens has been deposed from his seat as Head Centre He pretends to have gone to France, but was discovered to be living secretly in a house in 13th St & paying $ 45 per week for board &c.

James

Sat morning, the 19th. Jan The patients are rapidly improving I was there last night You will ere this reaches have heard that I am getting 7 dollars a week, so that I am not at all badly off. I had occasion to borrow five at one time, but was very soon able to repay it Of course I would not think of asking you to send me any though I know the feelings that prompt you & Mother to offer to do so I know how hard it is at home to live comfortably on the pay of a Methodist Preacher, and I hope before long to be able to do something for those who have done all for me hitherto. A third time Adieu with fondest love and kisses

James

11-9th Street,
New York
1st Feby 1867

My beloved Mother,

I have not received any letter from you since the 8th of January,—I wrote in reply to it on the 12th I received the "Telegraph" in which you wrote about George and Anna having the whooping cough, and promised to write next week I cannot but think that there has been a delay in the mail when I have not received a letter yet I got letters from Cousins George and Mary on last Wednesday week (the 23rd) They both write as kindly as ever They tell me that you have sent them all my letters since leaving home. Now, I am sure there are very few of my letters that are fit to be seen by any person but those at home I write down everything as it occurs to me, as I wish you to know all about me, and I trust that on that account you pass over my numerous blunders, but I would suggest that when writing to them in future you would select those particular which are of any interest, of course at the same time improving on my unfinished sentences Please tell them when writing next, that I will reply soon. I trust both George and Anna have got over the whooping cough safely Just as I write their forms appear to rise up before my mind's eye, and I think it is funny they are together in sickness, as they greatly resemble one another I sent George last Saturday the "Singing Pilgrim." I had to take the cover off and put it up like a pamphlet as they charge 48¢ per oz (the rate for letters) when they are put up as bound books, even though the ends are open I am sorry the cover could not be sent as it was very pretty I am sure you will find some beautiful tunes in it (I hope George will be able to play them all) I marked one tune—"Shall we gather at the river?" which I heard (I think the first Sunday) in the Sunday School I was delighted with it as soon as I heard it. It is such a beautiful tune for the Sunday School, that is, if justice is done it by the Scholars.

I do not think I ever heard a lot of people who were not a trained choir, who sang so sweetly and in such perfect time and tune as the children of that Sunday School The singing is managed by a young man called Mr John D Slaybach, who sings beautifully, and a Miss Thompson plays the harmonium which is a splendid instrument

Would Father think of introducing that, or other tunes in that book into the Newry S. School? I would be happy to be the means of getting nice new tunes into it. Ask Father to please remember me to my class How is Johnny Massey? When writing last I said that I sent the book that same day, but when the boy in the store brought it and letter over to the Post Office, and asked the postage on the book, they told him upwards of five dollars, but then I found out that by taking the cover off, it would go for less, and therefore sent it last Saturday This boy's name is Samuel Edgar—came originally from Belfast—and says he has a grandfather of the same in Newcastle—a Methodist Does Father happen to know him? There are a great many Irishmen—both North & South— who are in the Dry Goods business here, and deal with Mr McC

Did you know any people of the name of Dickson of Ballykelly, near Banbridge? Mr Dickson—Mr McC's partner—comes from there I am told that every person here has to get very light clothes for the summer, in fact that no person could wear the same clothes that he wears in Winter. Clothing of all sorts is so very dear here that I have been thinking that perhaps you could send me some, at very little expense for the carriage, and thereby save a larger outlay The steward of the "Iowa" would I think take charge of such a parcel for a small consideration I could ask him the next time she is in port. She is in now and sails early to-morrow morning Perhaps this outlay would inconvenience you, if so, of course I will manage the best way I can, as I would not think of any of you wanting on my account, but I hope to be able to do, that which was my motive in coming out here—be able to do something for those I love so dearly How I should like to have all your likenesses! I bought a cheap little frame for a photograph, and have Father's likeness in it on my dressing table I send you a photograph of all the Presidents of the U S I think it is very well finished I may now and then be able to pick up a good likeness, but good likenesses are scarce

I went on last Wednesday evening to hear a lecture by the Hon Horace Greeley, the celebrated Statesman, on "Self-made Men " It was a pretty good lecture, though I fully expected to have heard a better one He has a very slow and accurate delivery but lacks expression

Mr McC has not returned yet, but Mrs McC had a telegram this evening, saying he would be here at 7 A M. to-morrow Miss Whittaker & Randolph have both entirely recovered. Theirs was the lightest attack of Scarlet Fever I ever heard of It only lasted a week, and Randolph did not remain in bed. but got up every day as usual We have had some of the very coldest weather this winter, yet. during this week—that is on Monday, Tuesday & Wednesday Thursday was mild, and to-day was very much so, and a thaw has set it in People here say that it has been the heaviest fall of snow, & the longest frost there has been for several years There has been 36 days of uninterruped sleighing, and the ice in the river was so thick & firmly wedged in, that the passage of the ferry boats was interrupted & a great many people crossed over to Brooklyn on foot I send Henry the German paper promised I hope he will like it I would not wonder if I received a letter to-morrow after I have this posted, If so I can

let you know by sending a paper addressed in back-hand
Please remember me to the Kinnear's, Davidsons, Glenney's,
Lytle's, & Andersons, Langston's, Elliott's, Murray's, Men
at Grey's & Swan & White as usual, Mr Hamilton, Mi
Nichol, Rolston, Gilliard &c &c When writing next please
give my love to Cousins Anna, Mary, George, Thomas &c &c
and accept the same for each and all of you, with numberless
kisses, and hoping soon to hear from you

I remain,
Your ever attached & loving
Son James

Rev J Higgins,
　　42 Queen Street,
　　　　Newry
　　　　　　Ireland.

11 Ninth Street,
New York
1st March, 1867 (Friday)

My Beloved Mother,

I received the nine welcome letters last Monday week
(18th. Feby.) containing the tidings of the sudden death of
poor, darling little Willie, our lovely flower, which bloomed
awhile through the bleak Winter, but GOD thought fit to
transplant him to the beautiful gardens above I say "sudden," for it was altogether so to me, though you knew before-
hand that he would not live. I feel very lonely after him, and
thought it so queer to have a little brother born and dead,
and never to have seen him, though I suppose if I had seen
him, I would have felt far more sorry for him As you told me
that he was Henry's charge, I was sure that he missed him
very much, so I sent him a very pretty picture of a little
child-angel in a newspaper last Saturday When I bought the

picture it was on a large piece of pasteboard, but I had to
separate it in order to be able to send it It would be well worth
putting on a nice piece of thick paste-board and getting framed.
I bought one exactly the same for little Randolph at Xmas,
they got it framed, and it looks very pretty Would it not be
nice to have it up in the parlor? (I have been a long time writing this much of my letter, as there is no table in my room
but the bureau and wash-stand, and as there are drawers in
these, I cannot sit at them properly, there being no place for
my legs, and have to come down to the parlour, where there
are several people already talking and sometimes shaking the
table) You will observe that I am still stopping with the
McC's, though I have been looking out for a suitable boarding house for some time I do not like to go back to Mis
Swinsen, as it was a very small room at the top of the house
with a low ceiling, and there was no regular sitting room for
the boarders, so they had either the alternative of stooping
all the leisure time in their own room, or going out I can
assure you these things are not very pleasant in the winter
time, unless there be a fire in the bedroom

You will observe by a slight change in the writing that I
have commenced again the task of finishing this epistle It is
now Monday evening, the 4th March I was very sorry I
could not finish it for Saturday's mail, but I think that even
if I was in perfect retirement on Friday evening last, I would
either have finished a very unsatisfactory letter, or have left
it over till now, as I was not then very well. On Wednesday
night or rather on Thursday morning early—I got rather sick
and threw up a good deal It was a bilious attack, and I did
not get up until the evening Next morning I got up and went
to business as usual, but felt very weak, and (I will use that
slang word, for it is so expressive) squeamish. On Saturday I
was about the same, but to-day I feel a good deal better
However, I think this letter will not be much behind time, as
it will leave Boston by a swift steamer (which generally ar-
rives as soon as the New York one) With reference to your

thoughts of emigration to America (by the way, I forgot to mention that I have received this evening your always-welcome fortnightly letter of the 15th. Feby) I think if it is that a warmer, and more equable climate than that of Ireland is recommended for the invalids, *America would not suit* You can have no idea of the severity of the winter here I really think that if it was nothing else but the exposure for one half hour (while playing out of doors) to the blast that sometimes sweeps through the streets here, it would be pretty certain that—at least the small children—would get chilled to such an extent that they could not recover I have often seen people—and I nearly always do it myself—running along the streets and turning down some by-street (if their way lies in that direction) to get out of the way of this terribly chilling blast And, though in winter the air is very little changed, the weather changes a good deal though not so much as in Ireland On last Thursday week there was the heaviest fall of snow by far since I came here, and I heard Mr. McC saying that he thought it was the heaviest that had fallen for 10 or 12 winters It melted away pretty soon however, as the ground was not hard Yesterday was very dry, and a sharp wind blowing—it snowed last night—thawed to-day—and it is raining this evening. I can bear this well enough, because I am quite strong and healthy, (though for this winter I am getting acclimatised, and feel it rather more than most of those residing for some years in the country) but I very much doubt if it would suit any of those for whose sake you are thinking of emigration I have met no person who appears to feel the weather so little as Mr. McC. I never saw him cold to my knowledge, or with anything like a cough or cold I have seen him on very cold days—not the very worst though—coming to the store without a top-coat, when I could not attempt to go even a short distance without mine His hands especially are very hot, just as hot, perhaps more so, than mine would be after holding them to the fire for a long while The summers here are exceedingly hot, and there is very little change of

weather during the months over which the summer extends.
The water becomes so hot that all people have to use ice in it
Mr McCormack has been out this evening since tea time, but
I do not think there would be any use in speaking to him as
you say, for I feel convinced that America would not suit

I cannot tell you how grateful I feel to Mr Geo Kinnear
for the very delicately kind service he rendered to the memory
of our departed darling, Sweet-William (I always loved that
flower, but I shall now prize it above all others) It is truly
some of that real friendship and sympathy which is so seldom
found in this world, but when found, it is a priceless treasure,
and should be hidden away in the innermost recesses of the
heart for a whole lifetime I am sure none of us will ever forget
it. Please excuse me for not writing to him before now, I am
sure I have ample grounds for excuses, also to Cousins Mary
and George, and Rolston

I learn with little surprise of the advancement of Stewart
to the position of partner, though I thought the firm would
be "Grey, Stewart Bros & Co' I observe the "Brothers" is
not in it More than a year and a half ago (I think) when I
was one day alone in the inside office with Stewart, he wrote a
short note of a few lines (on business) and signed it "Grey,
Stewart Bros. & Co " then laughed, and asked me "Would not
that be a nice-sounding firm?" told me not to tell anybody
that he wrote or said anything of the sort

Really I feel lowered that we ever thought anything of
W G at any rate, I am not sorry that he keeps away from our
house, now that his real character is showing itself I have
begun to think could he have been in communication with
Stewart at the time that I was uncertain whether to leave in
the way I did or not You remember the evening he met Geo
Kinnear in the sitting room, and when we determined to set
aside his counsel in the matter you at once observed that he
looked disappointed Could it be possible that he was playing
that game for Stewart, and wanted me to remain, while there
was every prospect of you moving this year? I do not at all

like to be uncharitable but the thought did come across my mind very forcibly

You mentioned in your former letter about the Fosters, and thought that Dr. Foster might be one of them I shortly after asked the McC's if he was an Irishman, but they told me that he was a genuine Yankee, born and bred in the far Western States Besides this he is quite an old man, with very gray hair, and not at all like either of the likenesses you sent in your last. You say for me to write to both of the Fosters, but I think this would be queer, at any rate I need not write till I have your reply saying if I shall do so

Mr Dickson's name is William The name of the place he comes from is Ballykelly I have not had an opportunity of asking him anything about his family He has a brother Isaac in Rathfriland, and another a doctor in Ballynahinch, who was lately married I think the letter you got on the day of Willie's funeral was the one which was very long (I think 16 pages) in fact the longest one every I wrote I am glad it came on that day and was of any comfort to you

I have not got any hat yet, nor will I (I think) till near Summer The style of hats they wear here are different from the sort they have in Ireland, but though the tall hat (called here the "stove pipe") is very common, I could not think of wearing one yet a long while. When next getting boots I will most certainly get a pair of long ones, as in some seasons of the year here they are almost indispensable They are worn outside the trousers in duty weather With reference to the other clothes, I would like them made just the same as my last suit got in Savages, only let the coat be looser, and the trousers not so long by an inch A plain light material that will not fade in the sun would be the best If you do not know of a more convenient way of sending the parcel, you might write first to the Second Cabin Steward on board the "Iowa' at Glasgow, or, as they sometimes change the Stewards, it would be safer to try some other way of sending it As it might be a bad fitting pair of boots you would send (the last I got at

Koruahan's were too tight in the left foot) I will get them here in the store where that McNeice (whom I know at Richardsons) is. I would get my letters a little sooner in the day by addressing them to Care of Dickson & Co, 202 Church Street, and I could pay for the news-papers here (I am now writing on the premises) I am not regularly boarding with Mr McC in payment for services rendered, and though they have asked me to stay longer, I feel I have stayed far too
- long and will leave as soon as suitable place offers.

I received a good many papers from you of late, and some from Geo Kinnear. (Please thank him for me). I send you two more pictures in this letter (I have just two more besides these) and when you receive the last of them (in my next) you will please give one or two of them to Miss Kinnear from me, and if you think them worth while, you might send some to Cousins Anna and Mary. I think they are the most beautiful lot ever I saw. I wish James Swan & Geo White were safely away from the spying eyes and meanness of W G &c I would like to hear the same of Mr. Hansby, I wondered to hear when he discovered W G spying, that he did not give him a good beating, he is just the man who is able, and if roused, would do it It is troublesome crossing lines, so I will only say remember me to all acquaintances as usual, with love to Cousins Anna, Mary, George &c &c, and with the very fondest love and kisses to all of the loved circle

Believe me always,
Your attached and loving
Son James.

11 Ninth Street
New York, Mon. 8th April 1867

My dearest Mother,

I received you welcome letters on Thursday, April 4th, and was glad to learn that all were in good health when you wrote 20th March You appear to be rather uneasy about my health, and I now remember that when I last wrote I was in rather low spirits, only wrote a short letter and mentioned about my having rheumatism and chilblains. Though these ailments were very insignificant, and have since passed away, I am afraid you might be frightened about me I have not however been well for the last few days On Friday last while at the store I felt a sudden weakness coming over me, and had to sit down They brought me a glass of water and a little brandy and after a little while I felt rather better, but soon after, not feeling very well, I determined to return to the house. In the evening I saw Dr Andrews (the Homeo) who gave me some pilules to take, and said that I should soon be better The fact of the matter is—and it is only about a week since I or the McCs discovered it that the winter has gone rather hard with me, and as the saying is has "pulled me down" a good deal I have, almost unconscious to myself been getting thin, and I have had a cough for a week or so, which is especially troublesome at night Mr McC first and Mrs McC afterwards, said that a trip to the "Old Country" and a stay there of a couple of months would do me a great deal of good; and if I was not better by the time the hot weather came, this would become absolutely necessary I asked the Doctor if the trip would be good for me and he said it would, but he also said that before I went I ought to see him, for I might be entirely recovered before the warm weather came on, and then he would *not* deem the voyage necessary at all (I hope this may be the case) I also asked him particularly if he thought the country suited by constitution He said in reply that though the country had rather a severe climate, he had great faith in it, and believed it would suit my constitution If it should so turn out that I had to go home for a time, the McCs would lend me enough to go home, and I could repay then on my return But I know that while at home I should be an expense to you, and it might be a long time before I could be able to return the money for the return trip I hope I may recover soon and not need any trip You need not feel at all uneasy about me, for I am taking very good care of myself. I have not been at business since Friday, and on Saturday I went to the Central Park Today I have been out for a long walk, and I am going out again this evening I take before breakfast and tea about a tablespoonful out of a bottle Dr Richardson gave me It is composed principally of quinine but there are several other things mixed with it. It is *very* bitter, but he says it will strengthen me

You may imagine the kindness of the McCs when Mr. McC said this to me this morning when I was commencing this letter "Miss Martin was just saying this morning that she would gladly pay the expenses of your returning home, and then we could send you money to come out again " Of course I was very much surprised at their kindness in speaking to me in such a manner, and I said that I was very much obliged indeed, and that if I required money I might thankfully receive it as a loan from them but of course, I could not think of receiving money in any other way. Then she said she could not think of my father being at the expense of the journey, but of course I do not intend dear Father shall be at any expense that I can help, and I think I could earn enough on my return here to pay for them (the trips) both But I hope that all this is groundless, and that I will be all right in a short time You and a good many others will think me very lax for some time past, for instance not writing quite regularly, not replying to a good many letters lying over, especially G Kinnear must think very badly of me for not attending to his cheese, dried fruits &c out of which he intended me to make money and not calling on Mr. Lavey nor Mr North. Well, I will have to explain all these in this way. Since about a month after my arrival I have not been a week free from some kind of ailment or other proceeding from cold, I did not mind them much but they hindered me in a good many ways (Of course I was always careful and tried to avoid them, and get rid of them as soon as possible) If I wanted to visit either

Laveny or North, the best time would be during the day, and then I would have to get leave out I can assure you I always found it a hardship in the very cold weather to go on any message, much less to go feeling and looking wretched to see either of these parties, though I should like to have seen them very much Mr Laveny was an exceedingly gentlemanly and pleasant man. Though I did write my letters out of time, and did not write very long ones either, I can assure you it was very often a "hard job" to write at all I am sorry for G Kinnear but, at least for the present, I could not transact any business for him Please excuse me to all to whom you know I should write I am glad to hear that George has gone to the Connexional, and appears to like it so well, I have no doubt but that he will get on well from the very first, if he thinks fit to act under sage Johnny's directions—But I am afraid that is an open question

Though I did not weigh the letter I sent you with the photographs, on which you say you paid 2/—in mistake, I knew perfectly well by the weight in my hand that it was not overweight. Though I had not time the morning I sent you the "Singing Pilgrim" to ask the postage on it, and only stuck on as many stamps as I thought were right, and I think there was one at least too many on, I believe you were charged in error there too You perfectly comprehended my feelings about staying here, which I had till about a few days ago I did feel unhappy, and there was no prospect of getting a boarding house for some time, but now I feel that I would do wrong to risk making any move, and I know, the McCs would not allow me to do such a thing

I must say that when (as I may call it—"commencing life") in coming over here—I little thought that the first persons I should come in contact with should be far more really kind and considerate, than I ever expected to meet in the world (of course outside the pale of my own immediate relatives and friends) Nothing could exceed the kindness and consideration I have received since I came here I am sure I shall never forget it.

I sent Henry a French paper by the same mail as my last letter. If German and French papers would be of any use to him, I could often send him one The New York Conferences are having their sessions now. You will be surprised to hear there are two separate Conferences for New York City and surrounding districts One of the Conferences—the one in which our church is—is in Bedford Church—not very far off. Mr. Ridgaway our Pastor, is leaving this year, it being his third, and Dr Foster is coming in his place This is the second time for Dr Foster to be in that church. He cannot be any of the Fosters you wrote about, as he is a born American-born and bred far away west, and his name is Randolph Foster. There was a great teaparty at the Church (under it) this evening week, and Mr Ridgaway was presented with $900, which was collected by the ladies, and presented to him in their name by Mr Cornell, who is Supt. of the S. School, and one of the principal men of the Church He said the ladies did not like an even-looking number, else they would have made it $500 or $1000

Please give my kind remembrance to all Newry friends, my love to Cousins Anna, Mary, George, &c when writing, and my fondest love and kisses as ever for each and all of the loved circle, as if named. Do not be at all anxious about me, as I am in good hands, and taking care of myself, but believe me,

> As ever, your devoted loving son,
> James

Appendix C

Nanny Bournes Wallace's[1] petition to Queen Victoria, dated 30 August 1853,[2] was accompanied by a long list of signatures. The names affixed to her petition number in the thousands but only those from the Ballina, Co Mayo area are given below Thus we are able to have a kind of quasi 1853 "census" of this community.

The identification of some of these signatures is doubtful Reverend Terence P. Cunningham of St. Patrick's College, Maynooth, Co Kildare, students at the college, John P. Bournes of Stonefield, Co Mayo and the author have made an effort to be as accurate as possible in deciphering the penmanship However, it is suggested that those who may question our efforts, or wish to see the entire list of signatures, should study the original documents held by the State Paper Office, Dublin Castle, Dublin

TEXT OF PETITION

To Her Most Gracious Majesty Queen Victoria, Queen of Great Britain and Ireland.

[1] Nanny was the daughter of Dr Matthew Bournes See Stonefield family
[2] W 10/1853 Copyright State Paper Office, Dublin Castle

283

May it please your Most Gracious Majesty, I venture in the humblest and most respectful manner to prefer my petition to your Majesty upon the occasion of your Majesty's auspicious visit to your Irish subjects I humbly yet most earnestly implore that your Majesty will be graciously pleased to pardon and liberate my husband Zachariah Wallace, who is now incarcerated in Cavan gaol, and who is the only political prisoner in any of your Majesty's gaols in Ireland I am told

My husband was arrested in August last and from that until he received sentence of the 21st of April his entire time and attention were given up to the ruinous prosecution instituted against him by your Majesty's late Irish Law Officers The prosecution for a libel published in the *Anglo-Celt* of which journal my husband is proprietor during the excitement of the general election upon your Majesty's 31st Regiment, and the moment my husband discovered his error he hastened to apologize in the frankest manner for the injury he had done, although previously told by the then Law Adviser to the Castle, Mr William Hayes, Q C , that his doing so would be of no avail, and it was of no avail for my husband was tried, convicted and on the 21st of April last sentenced to six months imprisonment and a fine of £50

May it please your Majesty, I would be most reluctant to trespass on your Majesty's precious time when favoring our land with your Royal Presence were not the case most urgent My husband's health was impaired for months previous to his confinement and since that event it has become much worse He is not allowed to see any of his workmen and the gentleman whom he had engaged to conduct his business while in prison has died, and owing to his own absence and other causes his affairs are in much confusion Therefore I implore your Majesty to have him liberated and the fine remitted, and the more particularly as I have already had (owing to the anxiety and care caused by his prosecution) a premature confinement of a still born baby

With every good wish and sincere prayer for your Majesty's health and long life

> Your devoted subject and humble petitioner,
>
> (signed)   Nanny Wallace

Cavan, August 30th, 1853

BALLINA AREA SIGNATORIES

Richard J Cowan Green, Rosserk, Mayo
Robert Rollos, Mayfort
M H Devlin, M R C S L Med Officer Ballina Workhouse and Fever Hospital
William Hackney Halliday, Inspector Ballina and Galway
James Meehan, Clerk, Ballisakeery, Glebe
William Guer, Bank, Ballina
John Little, Ballina
Joshua Bartlett, Ballina
Thomas C G Bournes, Rosserk, Mayo
John Halliday, Dooneen, Co Sligo
Robert and George Scott, Ballina
Peter Nolan, Coroner, Moyne, Mayo
John P Nolan, Moyne, Mayo
John Nolan, Boaghadoon, Mayo
Geo S Malley, Ballina
Peter Kelly, Ballina
M Handly, Ballina
John Scott, Ballina
Robt G Baxter, Ironmonger, Ballina
Michael Foley, Ballina
John McAndrew, Ballina
John McGrath, Ballina
Stephen Loftus, Ballina
William Wilson, Ballina
George Shields Ballina
George Noble, Ballina
David W Fare (Fan), Ballina
Charles Mulheany (Mulhany), Ballina
Christopher Dunlevy, Ballina
Thomas W Nealon, Woolen Draper, Ballina
Michael Blake, Ballina
Nicholas Murphy, Ballina
Peter Clarke, Ballina
G W Shields, Ballina
Thomas McAndrew, Solicitor, Ballina
Patt Egan, Shopkeeper, Ballina
Patt McDonough, Clifton
Martin Sweeney, Ballina
Henry Lochran, Merchant, Ballina
Michael Sweeney, Ballina
Robin Goodwin, Co Sligo
Patrick Crean, Ballina
James Jordan, Ballina
Simon Dixon

Theady Brown
Irving Newcomb (Newcombe)
William Robinson
James Timlin
Robert McNamara
John Moran
William Moran
Arthur Patterson
Patt Carden
Wm Shenick, Ballina
John Dowling, Ballina
David Bahey (Cahey), Ballina
Michael Flemming
Edward McArthur, Ballina
Thomas Timlin, P P, Ballisakeery
William Reynolds
John Brown
Patt Fox
Edward Breenan
Edward Flemming
James (his mark) Flanagan
James (his mark) Kincaid
Michael Nery
Patt Mullery
Thomas Holmes
Thomas Kelly V G
John (his mark) McAndrew
Thomas Lynch
Christy Taylor
Morgan Sweeney
Daniel Devany
Francis Farrell
Thomas (his mark) Brown
Hugh (his mark) Kelly
Pat McAndrew
Michael Munnelly
Edward Sweeney
Michael Heneghan
Pat Mully (Nally)
Pat Holmes
Martin (his mark) Walsh
Terence Mulherin
Thomas Lyons
Patrick Mulhern
Michael Kearney
Charles McDonagh

Pat McDonagh
James Dempsey
Arthur Jones
Peter Mangan
Thomas Hughes
Edward Lynch
Samuel Durkain (Durkan)
John Roach
Hugh Gallagher
James Genly
Henry Lochian
Joseph Robinson
John Timlin
Edward Devers
Patt Egan
John Patterson
Thomas Reddington
James Walsh
William Walsh
William Patterson
John Brenane
Michael Langan
Michael Barrett
Edward McLaughlin
Thomas Barrett
Joseph Bourke
Michael Bourke
James Canden (Carden)
John Barret
Michael Hopkins
Patt Kelly
John Carden
John Ryan
Thomas Humber
Pat Morrison
Jas Matthew, Ballina
James Bournes Jr, Castleconnor
William Ham C E, Ardnaree, Ballina
Atkinson and Baird
William Gallagher
John Prescott, Merchant Tailor, Ballina
James Perkins, Farmer, Killala
Edward Bourke, Grocer, Killala
Charles Wood, Farmer, Co Mayo
Henry Rogers, Esq, Foxborough, Co Mayo
Henry Rogers Jr, Foxborough, Co Mayo
James Robinson, Ballibrooney, Co Mayo
John Robinson, Ballibrooney, Co Mayo
Malcolm MacGregor, Presbyterian Minister
Hugh Magauran C C
Patrick Gilroy C C, Drumlane
Francis O'Reilly C C, Drumlane
John Reilly
Patt McCall (McColl)
James McCormick
Patt Mundy
Michael Fitzpatrick
Patrick McCaffrey
Hugh Sheridan
James Keeinan
Thomas Burns
John Blessing

Michael Cassidy
Mick McGragh
John Murphy
Edward Murphy
James Farley
James Fitzsimmon
Thomas Sherman
James Reilly
James McGrath
Hugh Fitzsimmon
Pat Tully
James Sheridan
James Fairrelly
James Bolyal (Royal)
Thomas McDonough, Ballina
John Wood, Skreen, Co Sligo
Robert Johnstone, Mullifarry
Patt Royan, Newtown Crummer
Henry Royan, Newtown Crummer
John Royan, Newtown Crummer
James Royan, Newtown Crummer
William Gardiner
Charles Gardiner
Arthur Foster
Richard Fausett
John Wills, Rosserk
Charles Gardiner
Mathew Bourns
John Gardiner
Thomas Bourns
William Carson
James Bournes Sr, Knockroe, Castleconnor
John Dillon, Ballina
Robertson & Dunlop, Merchants, Ballina
Thomas Perkins, Killala
Alick Boyd, Rosserk
Thomas Wood, Farmer, Co Mayo
James McEntire, Ballaghadalla
Thomas Lush, Foxborough, Co Mayo
Francis Carroll, Mullifary, Mayo
Hamilton Magee, Clerk, Killala
Martin Carney
Hugh Keeinam
Dan M_____
John Magauhiam
James M Carmen
Mark Leddy
John Smith
Francis Fitzpatrick
Andrew Magaghran
Phil Sheridan
Owen Fallon
Thomas Cormce
John Connell
Thos McAvay
William Sheridan
John McQuire
James Mulligan
John Liddy
David McCoffy
Thomas Sheridan
James McDonald

James Magaghran
Thomas Flood
Michael Liddy
Owen Carnely (Connely)
Andrew Leddy
Phil Reilly
P Gilroy, C.C , Bellmullet
John Latowndle, Esq.
Patt Farrelly
John Farrelly
Andrew Farrelly
Bernard Carney
Phil Fitzpatrick

Garrett O'Reilly
Edmund L Winslow
Owen Calvin (Galvin)
John Reilly
Thomas Leddy
Owen Carney
John Carnev
Phil Carney
Daniel Colgan
John Fitzpatrick
James McQuire
John Donnelly
Peter Donnelly

Appendix D

Erris Poems

William Samuel Bournes, son of William Bournes of Porta-cloy, was widely known as a poet in the Erris community. According to accounts, related in the Corduff Manuscript, William Samuel was a gentle, articulate man who transferred to paper impressions of his home and the people in the western Mayo barony of Erris

Although his writings were extensive, covering all phases of Irish life during the late nineteenth and early twentieth century, few examples of his work have survived

The four poems, or songs as they are known in Ireland, are presented here in order that his contributions to the Irish scene may not be forgotten. The first two poems are in the Corduff manuscript (Vol I, pp 72-74; Vol III, p 455) The last two were sent to the author by Mr Bournes' daughter, Mary Anne Bournes Collins, Los Angeles, California

Lament for the Porturlin Tragedy

I

It was on the 4th of April, in the year of '78
This sad and sorrowful occurence
In Porturlin did take place

The crew was five in number, went out at the dawn of day
But shortly they were drowned and lost,
All on Porturlin Bay

II

When the news it came to hand, their parents and dear friends,
Their loving brothers and sisters, and neighbors did attend.
For to describe that scene of woe,
It is sorrowful to relate,
That such a noble and generous crew,
Should meet so sad a fate

III

Such melancholy weeping, and clapping of all hands
The likes never was witnessed upon this Irish land.
Loving brothers and sisters and neighbors in despair,
By the wringing of their hands and the tearing of their hair

IV

And now their leading seaman, Pat Cox it was his name,
He was a man of talent and of a noble fame
He was skillful and courageous upon the ocean wide,
But now he's lying low with his body in the tide

V

Pretty Michael Cox, he was the flower of them all
At the age of sixteen, he met his sad downfall,
He was a lad of intellect, being both brave and young,
But went to his doom that morning, by the rising of the sun.

(Several verses follow but are presumably lost Mr Corduff
writes that the last lines were)

It was everyone's opinion, that when hauling in the plank,
The curragh capsized over them, and to the bottom sank.

Adieu to Youth

I

Farewell, dear youth I now must leave you
And travel through old age alone,
For it often grieves me, likewise deceived me,
To see it stamped on the face of man.

II

Youth is lovely when it is in season;
When health and beauty are both in bloom.
But they soon decay and fade forever,
Like the fragrant flowers of early June

III

But when I ponder on life's rugged station,
And think how soon we must pass away,
On our guileless childhood, and its amusements,
We seldom think of our near decay

IV

When youth is gone, and passed forever,
And all our innocence is no more;
We fondly think of our early treasures,
And heap them all in a golden store

V

I've seen fair ladies wearing silks and satins,
In their vain glory they dress so grand
Overspangled with jewels and laces,
And costly bracelets around their hands.

VI

It's little they think of their end approaching,
Of the fleeting time that is on the run.
Sunday service—they might oft renounce it,
Or seldom think of their "Kingdom come"

VII

Time is fleeing, it is never stopping,
Its always in motion, like the tide so strong
But I am compelled by the laws of nature,
Never more to be young again.

(Title Unknown)

I

I traveled West through lonely Erris,
    o'er mountain ranges and heath clad hills,
A barren region, uncultivated. where the
    fox and hares do roam at will
The mode of labour is rather ancient, the
    spade and creel is their plough and cart,
Their plains and valleys are undecorated,
    no shrub or tree for to cheer the heart

II

It's bounded coast-wise by the broad Atlantic,
    and lofty walls of majestic height,
That have stood the rages of storms frantic,
    tremendous breakers that heave their might.
The cliffs abound them with caves of splendour,
    Stalactic brilliance illuminates their dome.
Here the seal and otter are free from plunder,
    and rest secure in their regal home

III

I sailed its harbours of tranquil waters,
    from Portacloy to Elly Bay,
The seal and porpoise along the borders,
    were shooting fountains of ocean spray
The gulls and gannets in thousands hovering,
    o'er countless shoals of the "finny tribe,"
This mine of wealth around the coast aroaming,
    their vast dimensions I can't describe

IV

The curing station is standing vacant,
　　no sound of labour attracts the ear,
To reap the harvest, here adjacent,
　　they go uncaught for the lack of gear
We miss the "Gráinne" since she quit those waters,
　　and her gallant members whom her deck did throng,
With hearts unfettered they'd improve the harbours
　　that are now neglected and things go wrong.

Do You Remember?

Do you remember dear Mary
　　The stream that flows down by our home?
Where we picked the cow slips and daisies
　　When together we did rome.

And do you remember dear Mary
　　The day we were down by the shore,
We picked the Cockels and Bornocks
　　To put in your little pinafore?

Claimants For Compensation 1798

At the time of the French invasion of Co Mayo in August
of 1798, some inhabitants of that area did not support the
local uprising These inhabitants, following the defeat of the
French forces, applied for, and received, compensation for the
losses they incurred They also received the title of the "Suffering Loyalists." Those persons who were members of the

Bourns (Burns, Byrne) families and were so named are listed below.[1]

Claimants for compensation from Co Mayo.

> Matthew Bourns of Rosserk
> Thomas Bourns of Lybourn
> Thomas Bourns of Newtownwhite
> Matthew Bourns of Mullafarry
> Robert Bourns of Rosserk
> George Burns of Killala
> William Burns of Knockaskeane
> Matthew Burns of Ballina
> John Byrne of Ballybeg
> William Byrne of Ballybeg

Claimants for compensation from Co. Sligo

> Margaret Bourn of Dooneen
> Sarah Bourns of Scormore
> William Burnes of Park
> Andrew Bourns of Scormore
> Matthew Bourns of Scormore

× × × × × ×

Some Early References to the Bourne name

1299   William de Bourne, Chief Clerk of Court of Common Pleas, Dublin (Registry Judge) Many references to him in Judiciary Rolls

30 April 1570   Sir John Bourne of the Holte, Worcestershire, England and his daughter, Elizabeth Elizabeth Bourne was the great-niece of Anne Butler, widow of Dublin Fiants, Elizabeth I, no 1524

15 Jan. 1575   Grant to Nicholas White Esq of the Manor of Lexlippe, Co Kildare, lately held by Richard Bourne, of Esker, Co Kildare Fiants, Elizabeth I, no 2690

---

[1] Chichester House, London Loyalist Claimants T O'Rorke, *History of Sligo, Town and Country*, Vol II, Appendix I, Richard Hayes, *The Last Invasion of Ireland When Connacht Rose* (Dublin, 1939), Appendix

18 Oct. 1579   William Bourne of Cloghran, Swords, Co Dublin, yeoman, pardon for accidental killing of Robert Mey(?) of Cloghran Fiants, Elizabeth I, no 3608.

c.1620-1641   Andrew Bourne, Rental of Coleraine, Co Londonderry P R O , Belfast, #T 724, p 7

1625-1627   George Bourne, Armagh Primatial Manor Rolls P R O , Belfast, #T 475, p 55

1649   Letter from Commander of the Garrison of Ballysonan to Parliament in England, containing a reference to "Estates wrongly enjoyed by Dillon, Bourne and Taafe." Journal, R S A I , Vol IV, p 114

1664   Hugh Bourne in Campbell's Regiment Ormond MS, 162

1686   Garret Bourne discharged from Army Ormond MS, 418

22 Feb. 1694   Indenture between Elizabeth Hamilton and Martha Bourne of Dublin, widows Both daughters of Margaret Smart, late deceased of the first part and Arthur St George of Athlone, Co Roscommon Esq of the other part Lands at Athlone, Co Roscommon, enrolled 25 Feb 1694 Lodge's Record of the Rolls, Vol IX, p 59

1707   John Bourne, Chief Chamberlain Exchequer List of Patentee Officers

1714   Anthony Bourne, Shankill Parish district, Co Armagh, or Clonduff Parish district, Co Down Quaker Marriage Certificate, P.R O., Belfast, #T 1062/37/54.

Bournes

(This pedigree is designed to clarify the Connaught Bournes family and contains some conjectural material indicated by dotted lines.)

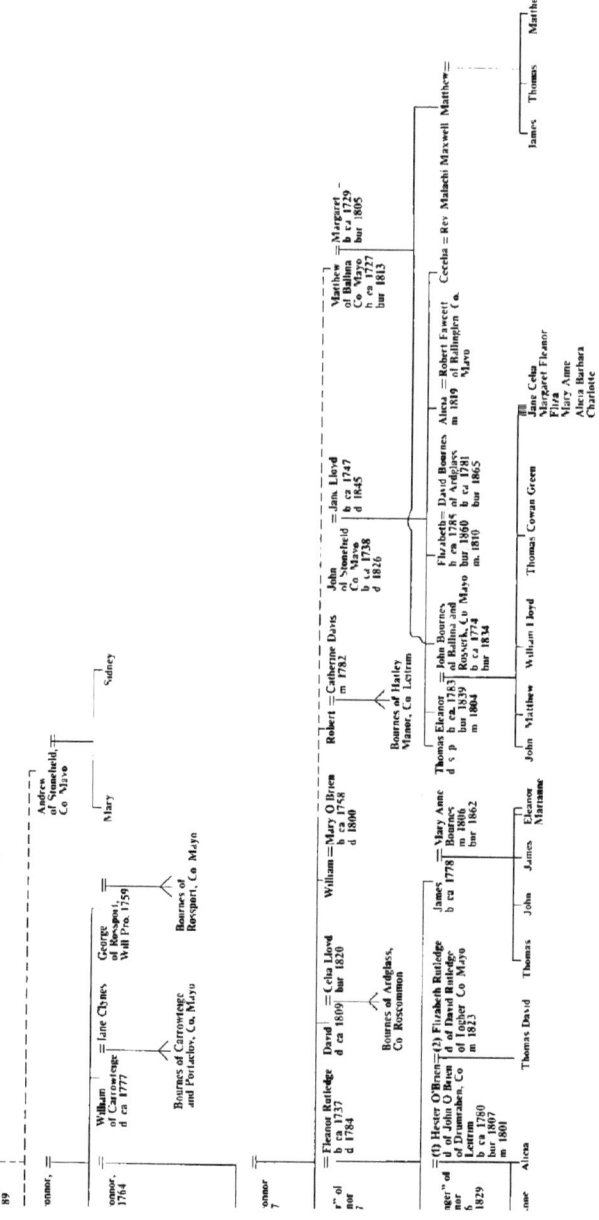

Index to Persons

(Pages 11 to 178 inclusively)

297

Lightning Source UK Ltd.
Milton Keynes UK
UKHW022041280219
338227UK00005B/305/P